# THE AFRICAN AMERICAN
# EXPERIENCE IN CYBERSPACE

# THE AFRICAN AMERICAN EXPERIENCE IN CYBERSPACE

## A Resource Guide to the Best Websites on Black Culture and History

Abdul Alkalimat

Pluto Press

LONDON • STERLING, VIRGINIA

First published 2004 by Pluto Press
345 Archway Road, London N6 5AA
and 22883 Quicksilver Drive, Sterling, VA 20166–2012, USA

www.plutobooks.com

British Library Cataloguing in Publication Data
A catalogue record for this book is available from the British Library

ISBN    0 7453 2223 9 hardback
ISBN    0 7453 2222 0 paperback

Library of Congress Cataloging-in-Publication Data applied for

10   9   8   7   6   5   4   3   2   1

Designed and produced for Pluto Press by
Chase Publishing Services, Fortescue, Sidmouth, EX10 9QG, England
Typeset from disk by Stanford DTP Services, Northampton, England
Printed and bound in Canada by
Transcontinental Printing

# **Contents**

# Foreword

## Cyberblack: African American history and culture on the web

At the beginning of the 20th century, public, university and research libraries were virtually bereft of books documenting the history and heritage of people of African descent. Indeed, the reigning 19th century myth that Black people had no history or culture was so strong that the vast majority of people worldwide did not expect to find the Black experience as a part of the written record of human historical and cultural development. Black people were widely believed to be a species outside of the human family, a strange position for the progenitors of humankind. The myth of Black historical and cultural invisibility was so strong that even Black people had started believing it.

Arthur Alfonso Schomburg was not among those who shared this belief. Convinced as he was that Blacks had been centrally involved in the making of human history and human civilization, Schomburg aggressively collected books and other resources documenting Black life. By the 1920s, even though mainstream libraries had few books on the Black experience, he had amassed a collection of over 10,000 items – books, manuscripts, photographs, artwork, etc. – a compelling body of evidence to refute the myth of Black historical and cultural insignificance. In the subsequent decades, frequently based on the Schomburg Center's catalog, American libraries have developed substantial collections on the global Black experience, especially since the 1960s.

By the 1990s, the Internet had begun to emerge as the prospective 21st century surrogate for libraries. Recognizing its ability to capture and transmit vast amounts of information on all aspects of the human experience across the globe, colleges and universities, libraries and research centers, corporations and enterprising individuals began to post significant quantities of information on their respective websites.

Regretfully, at the beginning of the 1990s, relatively little of this related to African American, African Diasporan or African history and culture. The Africana content of this emerging virtual library of the 21st century was looking far too much like that of traditional libraries of the late 19th and early 20th centuries.

Recognizing the potential implications of this fact, the Schomburg Center convened a national conference entitled "Africana Libraries in the Information Age." The conference was held on January 28–29, 1995. Representatives from libraries, museums and other repositories as well as scholars in African American, African Diasporan and African Studies gathered at the Schomburg Center to assess the current state of information on the Internet on the Black experience and to explore strategies for ensuring that there would be a robust presence of Africana resources there in the 21st century. The major findings were that there was relatively little material on the Black experience on the web and relatively few institutions were planning to create such content. A decade or so later, the Internet is literally brimming full of Africana-related resources. Abdul Alkalimat has gathered together in a single volume, the most comprehensive inventory of Africana-related websites and resources available on the Internet to date.

In an era when the advances of the Internet and web technologies have threatened the very existence and relevance of printed books, Alkalimat, a cyberspace maven if there ever was one, has written an indispensable book for students, teachers and scholars of the Africana experience who want to know what the Internet can do for them. Other writers and webliographers have prepared both online and print guides to Internet resources on the Africana experience. Alkalimat's *The African American Experience in Cyberspace* is unique in that as a sociologist and pioneer in the development of Black Studies, he has brought an informing paradigm and interpretive framework to the study of the Black experience that structures and grounds his and the readers' approach to the Internet resources for the study of the Black experience. His book is organized by the major periods and themes in Black historical development and social and cultural life. Of equal significance, Alkalimat has evaluated most of the sites, providing critical assessments of their usefulness vis-à-vis the study of the period or theme. This printed book will certainly make it easier for students of the Africana experience to more efficiently reap the benefits of the virtual library on African American and African Diasporan history and culture that millions of individuals, organizations and institutions have created on the World Wide Web over the last decade and a half. Whether it will drive the stake into the heart of traditional printed books or inspire others remains to be seen. With the publication of *The African American Experience in Cyberspace*, Alkalimat, pioneer in the development of Black Studies, has made an outstanding contribution to research, teaching and scholarship in both fields.

Howard Dodson
Director
Schomburg Center for Research in Black Culture

# **B**lack**STUDIES**

RESOURCES:
JOURNALS
ORGANIZATIONS

DEGREE
PROGRAMS:
UNDERGRADUATE
GRADUATE
GLOBAL

FEEDBACK

eBlack Studies is a project in cyberspace.
Its purpose is to provide information for
students and scholars in all academic fields
that focus primarily on Africa and the African
Diaspora. Our mission is one stop shopping
for everyone in the field of Africana Studies,
especially graduate students, faculty,
librarians, departmental webmasters, and
interested search engines.

**THE E BOOK** Introduction to Afro-American Studies. A Peoples College Primer

This site established February 21, 2000 / Edited by abdul.alkalimat@utoledo.edu

# Introduction:
# The Black Experience
# in Cyberspace

This book will introduce you to the African American experience in cyberspace, a guide to the very best sites on the World Wide Web.

The African American experience is global. It begins in Africa and extends to all parts of the world as African peoples have gone everywhere based on many forms of migration including the slavery trade. The common experience of African Americans, African peoples located in the Americas but in this case particularly the United States of America, is based on three main aspects of their history: the retention of traditional African culture, the racism by Europeans and others against them based on skin color and cultural practices, and the universal struggle for democracy and social justice.

The information revolution has transformed the development, design, and dissemination of knowledge in all forms. Everything is subject to the universal digital code of 0's and 1's. There has been an explosion, moving knowledge about the Black experience into digital code and making it accessible to everyone on the World Wide Web. The best example of this is the number of full-text books that are available on the web, for free, all the time, for everybody. All forms of information about the Black experience are being moved into cyberspace, including all kinds of collections of primary documents found in hard to access archives. Indeed, as most of us know, increasingly our way of communicating everyday is online via email.

The purpose of this book is to guide you to the very best websites. This kind of directory is important because it connects the producers of Blackness in Cyberspace with the consumers of information about Black people. This is the fastest and most democratic method for gathering and sharing information, to place all knowledge on the World Wide Web with open access. Our suggestions are basic solid sources of information, and should be thought of as being at the top of the list, first with the very best ones and then followed by additional sources. There are many more. The serious student will start with what we suggest here and go way beyond. Have you ever thought what it would be like to try and look at the 30,000 or 300,000 sites a search engine might come up with? The more serious you are the closer you will get to exhausting all search engine selections. What we are saying, however, is that you can't go wrong by starting with our highly selective list.

We used four criteria to develop this collection of websites: content, scope, aesthetics, and navigation. Virtually all of the sites we have in this collection rank near the top of our scale on these criteria. This is important because we have aimed this book at the following:

- teachers and students who use the web for course work and research;
- librarians who are increasingly integrating the web into their everyday reference work and for research;
- other information specialists like journalists, writers, and human relations experts; and
- the general reader interested in using the web for information and study, especially parents and tutors helping younger people.

The use of information technologies like the Internet and the World Wide Web are becoming as universal as libraries, i.e., physical places where people go to get information are being supplemented with online sources. This book can be as important to you as the card catalogue in a library. You can't count on most search engines as they operate on the basis of popularity and market position based on commercial criteria. This text is based on careful selection of sites based on professional criteria from the academic field of African American Studies.

This book should be in the home of every African American because it is the best guide to what's on the World Wide Web about African Americans. But it will be valuable for many more people than that. Every educational institution and library will find this a useful tool for all forms of multi-cultural study and any general inquiry into the American experience. The main point is that many of these sites give basic information, primary data, and documents. This is the material that will help people think for themselves about the African American experience and not be limited to choosing between the views of a few.

Our goal is to guide you to sites that have as much primary documentation as possible on the subject. This includes letters, diaries, government reports, photographs, sound files, census statistics, chronologies, biographies, maps, newspapers, laws and court decisions, full texts of books and articles, and institutional and individual archives. This is a major opportunity to speed up the information flow based on using the World Wide Web.

This kind of collection is also important because like any dictionary it represents an organizational design for knowledge, a basic architecture. We have divided this book into two parts: history for Part One, and society and culture for Part Two.

## History web resources

Our historical approach is structured around a logic of change: modes of cohesion versus modes of disruption, at one time sustainable with continuity and then revolutionary conflict and change. This has been spelled out in our online text "An Introduction to Afro-American Studies" at **www.eblackstudies.org/intro**.

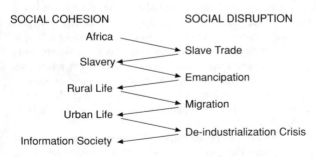

*Figure 1*  Historical change and the Black experience

This is not a chronology because history does not march in lock step according to any nice neat diagram. Each of these categories is a modal experience in an environment of conflicting modes of existence. Free Black people lived in cities in the 1820s, but at that time plantation slavery was the modal experience. Of course this is reversed by the 1960s. These categories are critical structures that define main tendencies in history. There is an alignment between political economy, social institutions, culture and consciousness. We take a holistic approach, a Black experientialism.

We have selected websites that will take you inside of these historical experiences. You will see and hear and read what each successive generation saw, and heard, and read. Each moment is real. So much of popular culture is a bit of reality and a great deal of fantasy in the service of ideology. What TV and Hollywood portray as reality is market driven fantasy. These websites for the most part replace edutainment (the convergence of entertainment and education) with a guided tour of the most important historical documentation of each experience. The wealth of the archives of the world are being liberated as they are being reborn as interactive databases. This is a guide to the best.

## Society and culture web resources

The second part of this book is focused on society and culture, a guide to the life of African American people today. Cyberspace is not like a closet where you put things and then go away. Everything gets hyperlinked and easily accessed with one or two clicks of a mouse. People live with cyberspace as a vital part of their everyday lives. We are using the Internet to communicate, to even compete with the telephone, although increasingly these are but options on the same all-purpose communication device. Information on the web is included in our everyday life, giving people the opportunity to rapidly include a large amount of details.

We use cyberspace to access information, to communicate, to act, and to structure the future. Everything we do in real life we seek to do in our virtual lives as well. The actual and the virtual go together. Everything we need is not yet available on the web, but enough is so we can begin to transform our lifestyles even more toward a better integration of the actual and the virtual. This book will convince you that the virtual Black community is alive and well, although just in infancy barely taking baby steps.

The topics we include are a general list that covers most social and cultural issues. It is not inclusive of what is on the web as that changes every day. What we have done is provide lists of links to sites we believe will be active for the foreseeable future, but one must be cautioned to use these links along with a good search engine and other reliable web directories. We have tried to use the domains of edu (educational institutions), gov (government), and the ones used by community organizations, org and net. However, these domains are now being used more widely than their initial designation would suggest, so every site must be looked at critically just as you would a book or an article.

## eBlack Studies

There are basically four approaches to the use of cyberspace in Black Studies. One is digital history, the digitization of historical information that brings a topic back to life in a digital format. This is a major task, to empty out the archives and turn them into digital computer files. Experiments are being explored with various kinds of storage strategies and designs for database management and data mining. The main center for this is the Virginia Center for Digital History, especially their collaboration with the Woodson Institute, also at the University of Virginia. A second approach is called AfroFuturism. This is a school of cultural criticism taking on the notion of a race-less cyberspace by demonstrating that the social production of racisms and "cyber-typing" will continue into the age of information. The third approach is virtual community, the use of information technology to digitize the social life of a community. The fourth approach is cyberorganizing to produce cyber power for the empowerment of a new movement for social justice in the information society.

The Black experience in cyberspace takes on three tasks. The above four schools of thought/practice are part of the digitization of experience. There are also the digitization of scholarship and the digitization of discourse. Each of these three is vital to being able to communicate and advance in the 21st century. One skill is being able to use what others have done. This is basic literacy. But one has to go beyond this to become a creator of information in cyberspace. In the first instance one is a downloader, taking information one finds on the web. In the second instance one is an uploader, creating new information on the web.

We have examples of uploaders in this collection from university professionals to undergraduates, from the campus and the community. This is important as the Internet and the World Wide Web are bringing an end to the elitism and hierarchy that has stifled the global production of knowledge. People have been demobilized and increasingly taught to rely on experts. We hope this volume encourages people to become active again in creating their own knowledge about the lives they live and the world as they see it. The great task of the first part of the 21st century is to get people more active as activist scholars, as both the objects and subjects of study. We hope this brief introduction to the best on the web about the Black experience is not only useful, but a stimulus for people to get busy and start a new renaissance of knowledge based on uploading, based on bringing the diversity of Blackness to cyberspace for all of humanity.

# PART ONE
# Guide to the Best History Sites

Introduction
Index
Chronology
Family
Speeches
Photographs
Bibliography
Webliography
Study Guide
Conferences
Words
Radical Black Tradition
Legacy of Malcolm X
Search
What's New
Research Organizations

**MALCOLM**

Malcolm X: Radical Tradition and a Legacy of Struggle
1991 Conference

**Critique of the**
MIDDLE CLASS

ENTER

*2003 Update Calendar*
July: 1991 Conference - Sexism

August: 1991 Conference - Poetry

September: 1991 Conference - Global
Struggle

Our greatest challenge is to follow Malcolm X's method of critical independent

# Overview

This part deals with sites that contain information of a historical nature. We have organized this material in stages of history and processes of historical change. The stages of history are Africa, slavery, rural tenancy, urban industry, and the information society. The processes of change include the slave trade, the emancipation, the migration, and the de-industrialization crisis. Each of the websites listed has a great deal of information so it is important to understand the logic of a site's structure so you don't overlook information that may well be there but not easy to find.

We are trying to immerse you into Blackness, to see the historical experiences of Black people as they lived it and discussed it within their community. These are the voices seldom heard today, especially by a majority of Black youth. This book attempts to give deference to the masses of poor and silenced Black people. History is better told by our experiences aggregated into all of the trends and dynamics of community life, and not the lone voices of academic or middle class elites. Everyone has a role to play.

Three key values make the use of information technology essential for the study of Black history.

1. Cyberdemocracy: everyone being literate and having access to the tools for state of the art knowledge production, distribution, and consumption.
2. Collective intelligence: everyone being able to upload and have their experiences considered and their voices heard.
3. Information freedom: everyone being able to access information without having to buy it, using the public library model and not the marketplace.

These three values can guide us all as we use this new way to study Black history.

# 1
# General

The fullness of the African American experience is the content of Black history, with every aspect of what has happened to the African American people included, from the very visible elites to the day-to-day life of the majority of people. This point is critical as much historical writing, and certainly popular summations in the media, often tends to stress the activities of the elites and ignore the day-to-day routines of the masses. The fact is that the day-to-day activities of the overall community can often reveal more about the historical moment than speeches by leaders.

The main point about the Black experience online is whether the content takes you inside the Black experience so that one gets access to the activities of the masses of people and whether one can "share" the Black experience from within its own subjectivity. When this can be accomplished, based on the documentation of the Black voice, then online content is authentic. The key is to take actual experience into cyberspace rather than create a virtual reality that makes no attempt to represent our actual historical experience.

Online content is usually text based, but necessarily augmented by cultural information in all forms of multi-media presentation. This is the magic of cyberspace, to be inclusive of all forms of information that encodes the actual experiences – the sights, sounds, texts, and motion (but not yet the smells and tastes). Some institutions are digitizing Black history and making it available in cyberspace as a project inclusive of the experiences of a town, or a period of history, or the life of a person or institution. They have a holistic conception of what they are doing.

In this chapter you will find two kinds of general sites about Black history, the annotated webliography and the online archive. The webliography is a listing of URLs, links to pages with content. This is the new version of a card catalogue, a guide to specific collections of material based on choices made by the organizers. But rather than having to go to another physical place to see the material it can be accessed by navigation using a keyboard or a mouse, all connecting to cyberspace. The online archive is actual content placed on the web based on original primary documents being digitized and placed in cyberspace. In this sense the webliography is a guide to online content, and an online archive contains content.

## H-Net
Humanities and Social Sciences Online
Michigan State University
www2.h-net.msu.edu
The Internet has created a new way to study history – the virtual seminar. The use of email communications enables people to maintain an asynchronous dialogue, much like a seminar. H-Net leads the way in the humanities and social sciences.

There are many lists that directly and indirectly involve African Americans. The main one is H-Afro-Am, a list edited by Abdul Alkalimat with about 1,500 subscribers (11/2002). There are discussion lists that focus on Africa, with a general site H-Africa, and also ten specific sites that focus on arts, research, literature and film, politics, Hausa, Lusophone, South Africa, and West Africa.

Overall there are more than 100 lists, including 100,000 subscribers in over 90 countries. There are many useful features that H-Net offers you: book reviews and online discussions with authors, announcements of events and conferences, jobs in research and teaching about Black history, and a series of essays on teaching and technology. Their general site is lively and easy to navigate. H-Net is one click away, so it is easy to ask questions and get free subscriptions to their information networks and discussion lists.

They define their identity and their goals:

An international consortium of scholars and teachers, H-Net creates and coordinates Internet networks with the common objective of advancing teaching and research in the arts, humanities, and social sciences. H-Net is committed to pioneering the use of new communication technology to facilitate the free exchange of academic ideas and scholarly resources ...

The goals of H-Net lists are to enable scholars to easily communicate current research and teaching interests; to discuss new approaches, methods and tools of analysis; to share information on electronic databases; and to test new ideas and share comments on the literature in their fields.

**Virginia Center for Digital History**
University of Virginia
www.vcdh.virginia.edu
This center is the leading research facility for the digitization of historical materials about the Black experience. It is based at the University of Virginia, and is connected to other units on that campus that are also engaged in such work, including the Carter G. Woodson Institute for Afro-American Studies. The Woodson Institute is led by Dr. Reginald Butler and assisted by Dr. Scott French. Dr. William Thomas directs the VCDH, and is also the co-author of *The Civil War on the Web: A Guide to the Very Best Sites*.

There are six nationally important research projects and websites from this center that deserve close study by all serious students of the Afro-American Experience. What is particularly interesting is the institutional focus on the self-organization of the Black community and the freedom struggle.

*Valley of the Shadow*: This project has digitized material from two communities on opposite sides of the Civil War – Augusta County, Virginia and Franklin County, Pennsylvania. This is the most complete research site on the Civil War, including easy navigation and detailed site mapping throughout. They include the role of Blacks and provide wonderful curriculum support. This is a model for all future work to bring history back to life.

*Virginia Runaways Project*: This project is digitizing all newspaper ads from the 18th century about runaway slaves in Virginia. The ads are displayed plus the full text and related information.

*Proffit Historical District*: This is a website to document a small all-Black community established near Charlottesville, Virginia after the Civil War. There are five sections: oral history, census data, primary documents including personal papers and letters, a photo gallery, and a community contact page.

*Race and Place*: An African American Community in the Jim Crow South. This site contains information about Charlottesville, Virginia from the 1880s to the 1950s. There are six sections: personal papers, newspapers, images, maps, political materials, and oral histories. This site is well laid out with a search function on each page.

*J. F. Bell Funeral Home Record 1917–1969 (Charlottesville, Va.)*: This project was co-sponsored with the local Afro-American Genealogy Group. This site includes everyone buried by this funeral home, including last name, place of birth, place of death, and burial place.

*Investigating Massive Resistance in Charlottesville (1954–1964)*: This site was developed for the Center for Technology and Teacher Education at the University of Virginia.

**African American World**
Public Broadcasting System
www.pbs.org/wnet/aaworld
This is a wonderfully comprehensive site that serves as a companion to the programming of the Public Broadcasting System and National Public Radio. This site is user friendly and accessible for the general public, all ages. They have joined forces with Encyclopaedia Britannica and included over 300 articles about individuals and topics relevant to the Black experience.

PBS/NPR have the customary practice of building a web page to accompany all major programming. They have consistently developed Black programs that cover historical subjects through the fields of art, culture, social issues, politics, and education. They use excellent primary source material in all forms: text, images, sound, and video. This site is excellent for educational purposes at all grade levels. There is a curriculum section with course plans for grades from 3 to 12.

There are six basic sections to this site: timeline, reference room, kids, classroom, community, and resources.

**General**       

1. Timeline: there are four sections within which items are listed chronologically, with links to relevant material (1400s–1865, 1866–1953, 1954–71, 1972–present).
2. Reference room: this space includes links to a selection of the best programs that have been aired on PBS and NPR, as well as individual profiles and articles on a wide range of topics.
3. Kids: this space provides online activity for children in elementary and secondary schools.
4. Classroom: this site contains curriculum materials for grades from 3 to 12.
5. Community: this page provides an opportunity for dialogue in four general categories (history, arts in action, newsmakers, and roots), and everyone can join the online discussion.
6. Resources: this page contains a webliography to continue your search with the recommendations.

This website is a virtual museum of popular culture and historical documentation.

**The African American Mosaic: A Library of Congress Resource Guide for the Study of Black History and Culture**
www.loc.gov/exhibits/african/intro.html
This is a site based on a publication by the same name. Its contents have been drawn from the permanent collection of the Library of Congress. There are four basic topics covered by the site: colonization, abolition, migration, and the WPA.

The colonization section is focused on Liberia, the American Colonization Society, and portraits of individuals including Joseph Jenkins Roberts (1809–1876), a Black man who became the first president of Liberia and fought against slavery. The abolition section focuses on key individuals and documents of key abolitionist activities. Some of the people include William Lloyd Garrison, John Brown, Frederick Douglass, Wendell Phillips, and Susan B. Anthony. The migration section is outstanding as it presents the fullest account of Nicodemus, Kansas to be found anywhere. This was one of the main destination points for the out-migration from the South after the end of the Reconstruction in the 19th century. There are many documents about Chicago as well, the main destination of migration in the 20th century. The WPA section is about the writers of the Works Progress Administration, a wonderful publication about Black history (*Cavalcade of the American Negro*), and the narratives of ex-slaves collected as part of the research carried out by the WPA.

## United States Historical Census Data Browser
University of Virginia/University of Michigan
fisher.lib.virginia.edu/census
In this digital age every study of the Black experience should be accompanied with relevant statistics so that what is being focused on can be viewed in relation to the entire population and not simply one part of it. The census statistics about Black people are available on the web and therefore everyone can have access to the relevant statistics to discuss the Black experience.

Current statistical information is available from the Bureau of the Census, **www.census.gov**. This site is user friendly and has news releases, topical fact sheets, as well as the full details of the general reports on population down to the census tract level. When some information is reported about the census in the press, you can get more details at this site including all Census Bureau press releases.

Now we have a site that will enable you to compile statistical data from all of the census reports from 1790 to 1960. It clearly states what it offers: "This site allows you to browse the data files for each decade and choose from the lists of variables. You can produce lists of data by state or county that can be sorted, calculate proportions, or graph any of the variables."

This site is excellent for high school and college students.

## Schomburg Center for Research in Black Culture
New York City Public Library
www.nypl.org/research/sc/sc.html
The Schomburg Center is located in Harlem, New York. Howard Dodson is the Director and its most active researcher. This is the preeminent public library research institution specializing in the Black experience, covering the entire globe. It is named after Arturo Schomburg, an Afro-Puerto Rican,

bibliophile and activist, who sold his collection to the New York Public Library System. Its website contains the usual information about what services are offered in its capacity as a public library facility, and general comments on its holdings. One important feature is its listing of programs and exhibitions. The Harlem Renaissance lives in the spirit and vitality of their program. The website contains a lot of valuable digital content.

## Digital Schomburg

*African American Women Writers of the 19th Century*: African American Women Writers of the 19th Century is a digital collection of some 52 published works by 19th century black women writers. A part of the Digital Schomburg, this collection provides access to the thought, perspectives and creative abilities of black women as captured in books and pamphlets published prior to 1920. A full text database of these 19th and early 20th century titles, this digital library is keyword-searchable. Each individual title as well as the entire database can be searched to determine what these women had to say about "family," "religion," "slavery," or any other subject of interest to the researcher or casual reader. The Schomburg Center is pleased to make this historic resource available to the public.

*Images of African Americans from the 19th Century*: This is a collection of images selected to accompany the African American Women Writers of the 19th Century website. The photographs and drawings are organized in the following categories: civil war, culture, education, family, labor, politics, portraits, reconstruction, religion, slavery, and social life.

*Finding Aids*: This is unique material for the serious student of African American History. This site contains 96 finding aids to collections held at the Schomburg Center. These collections cover 278 years from 1724 to 2002. Finding Aids is an inventory of an archival collection of personal or organizational papers.

## Online exhibitions

*The African Presence in the Americas*: This is basically an online general survey course from 1492 to 1992. There are images and text. This material is useful for grades 6–12.

*Harlem 1900–1940 An African American Community*: This is a series of short essays with graphics on several topics concerning Harlem: activism, arts, business, community, sports, writers, and intellectuals.

*The Schomburg Legacy. Documenting the Global Black Experience for the 21st Century*: These materials reflect the archival holdings of the Center, including text and graphics.

## Library of Congress
www.loc.gov/exhibits
The African American Mosaic: A Library of Congress Resource Guide for the Study of Black History and Culture
The African American Odyssey: A Quest for Full Citizenship
The Library of Congress is the national library of the United States. In this role it has built two web portals of information about Black people by digitizing primary documentation from its collection about the experience of the African American people.

The African American Mosaic is a digital presentation of a publication that focused on four historical moments of the African American experience. Colonization is the first section and it contains material on Liberia and the American Colonization Society. The second section is about the abolitionist, and the third is about the great migration with a focus on Nicodemus, Kansas and Chicago, Illinois. The final section is about the WPA experience.

The African American Odyssey is a set of five digital libraries in addition to a general introduction that surveys the entire African American experience. The collections cover the following: Frederick Douglass, Jackie Robinson, slave narratives, African American pamphlet collection (1824–1909), and slavery and the courts (1740–1860).

These are wonderful sites that contain very good reproductions of primary research material, including maps, letters, articles, photographs, legal documents, and published material in book and pamphlet form. The slave narrative page is particularly important in African American Odyssey. It contains the full texts of 2300 slave narratives including 500 pictures and full documentation. The material is presented in multiple formats including higher resolution images. These materials were collected as part of the WPA Writers Project, 1936–38.

**General**                                                     **17**

Clear guidelines are provided for using the site. However, not many sites yield the full depth that they promise so it is easy to get used to not probing deep. This is a site that is for serious students of slavery. Use it and you will be rewarded.

## Portals

### The Encyclopaedia Britannica Guide to Black History
search.eb.com/blackhistory
Well designed, easy to navigate site based on a timeline, from 1517 to the present. Plenty of graphics and photographs. Good for elementary and secondary school reports.

### Black History Pages
www.blackhistorypages.com/
A general portal to a large number of links, easy to navigate, lots of topics. Good for general interest.

### The African American Registry
www.aaregistry.com
Comprehensive site organized around a chronological listing of Black historical facts.

### The African American Almanac
www.toptags.com/aama/index.htm
Easy to use collection of material including full texts of key historical documents, biographical sketches, and short articles on historical events.

### Afrocentric Scholars (NBUF)
www.nbufront.org/html/MastersMuseums/MastersMuseums.html
This website has a biography and full text writings of five major Afrocentric scholars: Yosef ben Jochannan, John Henrik Clarke, John Jackson, Leonard Jeffries, and Runoko Rashidi.

### Afro-American History and Culture
www.si.edu/resource/faq/nmah/afroam.htm

Extensive list of links to Afro-American resources of the Smithsonian Institution.

**African American History**
afroamhistory.about.com
Easy to use site with over 30 topics, including original articles and links to other websites.

**Our Shared History: African American Heritage**
www.cr.nps.gov/aahistory
General site by the National Park Service. Topics include underground railroad, historical sites, and sites for historical study.

**The History Channel**
www.historychannel.com/index2.html
This site provides a search function to all the History Channel's Black programs as well as a special page dealing with resources for Black History Month (February).

**In Those Days: African American Life Near the Savannah River**
www.cr.nps.gov/seac/ITD/longversion/itd-lg1.htm
Assemblage based on oral histories covering slavery through migration, as experienced in one locale.

**Information Please: Black History Month**
www.infoplease.com/spot/bhm1.html
Oriented to families and teachers, an Internet compendium from a 60 year publisher of print almanacs and reference guides.

**Gale Black History Month**
www.gale.com/free_resources/bhm/index.htm
Classroom oriented materials ranging from activity ideas and plot summaries and contexts for key books to a Black History Month quiz.

**Librarian's Index to the Internet: Black History Month**
www.lii.org/bhmonth

A large, organized collection of relevant websites, with comments on each from the LII project volunteer librarians. Useful for many audiences.

**Kaboose: Black History Month**
www.kidsdomain.com/kids/links/Black_History.html
Appealing to children. List of links to related games, stories, and activities.

**Art McGee's Guide to the Web**
www.sas.upenn.edu/African_Studies/Home_Page/mcgee.html
This is the main webliography by a pioneer on the web. Good set of links.

**Black Websites**
www.blackwebsites.com/Black
Good general portal to Black oriented websites.

**Floyd Ingram's Resources Center: African American Resources**
www.coatopa.com/fi-afram.html
This site contains a massive set of links to Black oriented websites.

## Curriculum

**Black History Past to Present: An Interactive Treasure Hunt**
www.kn.pacbell.com/wired/BHM/bh_hunt_quiz.html
Twelve question exam with immediate feedback feature.

**The African American Internet History Challenge**
www.brightmoments.com/blackhistory
Short quizzes with immediate feedback scores on three levels of difficulty. They give you material to study, and multiple opportunities to repeat the quiz and make a better score.

**Black Facts Online**
www.blackfacts.com

Useful source of facts, searchable by date or topic for every day of the year.

**Lesson Plans on African American History**
edsitement.neh.gov/tab_lesson.asp?subjectArea=3&subcategory=18
This site is maintained by the National Endowment for the Humanities as an annotated listing of lesson plans dealing with African American historical topics.

## Good books

Adams, Russell L. (1976) *Great Negroes, past and present*, 3rd rev. ed. Chicago: Afro-Am. Pub. Co.

Alkalimat, Abdul. (1986) *Introduction to Afro-American studies: a peoples college primer*. 6th ed. Chicago: Twenty-first Century Books and Publications.

Aptheker, Herbert. (1990) *A documentary history of the Negro people in the United States*. New York: Carol Publishing Group.

Asante, Molefi K. and Abarry, Abu Shardow, eds. (1996) *African intellectual heritage: a book of sources*. Philadelphia: Temple University Press.

Franklin, John Hope, and Moss, Alfred A. (2000). *From slavery to freedom: a history of African Americans*, 8th ed. Boston: McGraw-Hill.

Frazier, Edward Franklin. (1957) *The Negro in the United States*. New York: Macmillan.

Gates, Henry Louis, and McKay, Nellie Y. (1997) *The Norton anthology of African American literature*. New York: W. W. Norton & Co.

Karenga, Maulana. (2002) *Introduction to Black Studies*. 3rd ed. Los Angeles: University of Sankore Press.

Kelley, Robin D. G. and Lewis, Earl, eds. (2000) *To make our world anew: a history of African Americans*. Oxford: Oxford University Press.

Marable, Manning, and Mullings, Leith, eds. (1999) *Let nobody turn us around: voices of resistance, reform, and renewal: an African American anthology*. Lanham, Md.: Rowman & Littlefield.

# 2
# Africa

Almost 50 years ago Ghana won its independence from British colonialism (1957), and so began a new era of African history. In this sense the figure of Kwame Nkrumah and his peer leaders of the African independence movements are a necessary starting point for the understanding of African history. One of the main reasons is that the most significant step toward the continental unity of Africans came after independence from European colonialism from their efforts in the last half of the 20th century. The Organization of African Unity was formed in 1963 as an organizational expression of this historical motion, a feat never before accomplished. Nkrumah is joined in this regard by such important figures as Amilcar Cabral (Guinea-Bissau), Agostino Neto (Angola), Eduardo Mondlane (Mozambique), and Nelson Mandela, Chris Hane, and Steve Biko (South Africa).

The historical relevance of Africa in the context of this book is twofold: its role as the source of labor to facilitate the European settlement of the Americas, and its role in shaping culture in the African American community as well as the mainstream. Slave labor simultaneously represented the depopulation of Africa and the rapid increase in the colonial production of wealth for Europe. From the western shores of Africa, from Ghana down to Angola African peoples were subjected to enslavement, what many have called the African holocaust. As a cover-up, Africa was removed from world history by racist views that Africans were sub-human and had made no contribution to world history. This has been proven false and exposed as an evil ideological offensive against Africa and the African Diaspora.

Now we are becoming aware more than ever before of the great accomplishments of ancient African civilizations which were at least on par with the other ancient world civilizations. This includes Nubia and Egypt, as well as the kingdoms of Mali, Songhay, and Ghana. But the direct link between Africa and the New World necessitates a focus on traditional African society, and that also reveals wonders of great cultural significance. The music, art, and language use represent a wonderful diversity of aesthetic achievement. These forms of cultural production have been absorbed by every generation of people throughout the world who have had any contact with Africa. The healing of the world from the racist legacy of Eurocentrism is necessary if humanity is to survive the storms of the 21st century.

## H-Africa

H-Net: Humanities and Social Sciences Online
Michigan State University
www2.h-net.msu.edu/~africa
This website is the most comprehensive website for serious information about Africa. This is state of the art scholarship for the 21st century, a tool that provides global access to everyone for free.

H-Africa is composed of a network of people with a serious interest in Africa: academics, journalists, and others. The advisory board and editors come from seven countries, and subscribers come from every country in the world with Internet access. The main activity is a discussion list for the daily discussion and sharing of information. All of the exchanges are archived and maintained as a searchable database on the website. You can access these archives (called "logs") by month, and then sort by date, thread, or author. The wide variety of topics and current information contained in these logs makes it the most up to date resource of contemporary research on Africa. In addition, dialogue is encouraged via a forum for position papers and debate.

The H-Africa website is a bountiful oasis of information on Africa. This is your best bet for one stop shopping for information on the World Wide Web about Africa. It has a comprehensive database of the tables of contents of the major academic journals in the world, of academic programs to study Africa all over the world, and a comprehensive listing of other websites containing information on Africa.

H-Africa includes the most comprehensive set of book reviews available in any context. What is especially unique is that on many occasions the reviews come out very quickly and the author is invited to discuss the issues on the discussion list. The major writers make up an online resource available to the participants in H-Africa. Moreover, the list is international and therefore the discussion is often more representative of global scholarship than is usually found in any one given location.

Another feature of this website is a wide-ranging list of links to digital collections, libraries, and exhibits. One can find posters, photographs, art, music, languages, population statistics, and global economic data.

In addition to H-Africa, there are nine other Africa related lists: African arts (H-AfrArts); African literature and cinema (H-AfrLitCine); African political history (H-AfrPol) Teaching about Africa (H-AfrTeach); African archival research (H-AfResearch); Hausa language, literature, and culture (H-Hausa) Lusophone African Studies (H-Luso-Africa); Southern Africa (H-Safrica); and West Africa (H-West-Africa).

## CODESRIA: Council for the Development of Social Science Research in Africa
Senegal
www.codesria.org
CODESRIA is an umbrella organization that covers the social sciences and history in Africa. It is the "non-governmental center of social knowledge production" linking together scholars and researchers in every African country. The official activities are bilingual, in both English and French. The organization sponsors a General Assembly every three years that often meets for over two weeks during which African scholars present papers and have discussions about the state of the university in Africa, publishing for scholars and the general public, policy research and the state of democracy, gender relations, and modes of social transformation.

This website is a key place to find out what scholarship in Africa is all about. CODESRIA publishes five journals, and one quarterly newsletter which is also available online. The newsletter is especially important for teachers, students, and librarians. There are detailed accounts of major crises facing African scholars, e.g., there are accounts

**BEST HISTORY SITES**

of crises at the University of Cape Town, from the Mafeje affair (1968) when an African scholar was prevented from joining the faculty, to the Mandani affair (1998) when an eminent scholar appointed to head the UCT Center for African Studies had his syllabus rejected because he relied on African scholars rather than white American and European scholars. There is a great deal of silence in the western press about these matters, so this website provides a vehicle to hear the voice of Africa regarding its internal affairs.

There are four basic areas of activity: direct support for research (grants for field work, seminars in methodology for quantitative analysis, and awards for outstanding doctoral theses), coordination of research efforts (national, multinational, transnational, and comparative networks are organized and supported), publication, and policy advocacy by bringing scholars and government officials together to discuss issues of importance, especially relative to matters of democracy and social justice concerning gender relations.

### Internet African History Sourcebook
Fordham University
www.fordham.edu/halsall/africa/africasbook.html
This site is a listing of websites within an outline that generally fits a general education program that covers Africa, from ancient societies to the contemporary situation. It is maintained at Fordham University. This site can be easily used with survey courses on Africa or for a systematic self-study of all or part of Africa. But one of the problems with this site is its reliance on material hosted by others that is not always maintained. However, it's so easy to use and provides such a diverse set of resources that the odd broken link should not deter you. This is after all the problem of a democratic World Wide Web, working collaboratively with others to maintain a secure set of resources available to everyone.

The organization of the website is much like a course syllabus, and therefore easy for students to use, high school and college. One can find detailed accounts of the role of specific European countries in the slave trade and colonialism. For example, there is an abolitionist article from 1774 titled "Thoughts on Slavery" by John Wesley, the founder of

Methodism. There are also documents that discuss the role of European imperialism from John Hobson (1902), V. I. Lenin (1916), and Joseph Schumpeter (1918). There is also the 1871 account by Henry Stanley of his finding Dr. David Livingstone while on assignment from the *New York Herald* newspaper.

Also, there is material on specific African countries, including full text documents. There are contemporary African constitutions and other official documents that are good for understanding the process of African liberation and decolonization.

The main weakness, other than the odd broken link, is the need for the content to be updated to reflect the last 25 years of developments, especially the changing ideological foci of policy in the age of globalization. As a model, and for the content it does have, this site is highly recommended.

### African National Congress

South Africa

www.anc.org.za

The website of the ANC is a portal into the most important information about the liberation struggle against European colonial domination. The ANC was founded in South Africa in 1912 and has been among the leading forces of change in that country since then. This website is also linked to the ANC organizations, the ANC Women's League and the ANC Youth League. In addition there are links to the other two members of the Alliance (the three organizations who together make up the overall leadership), the COSATU and the South African Communist Party (SACP).

One of the important aspects of this website is the online ANC archives and a wealth of full text historical documents that chronicles the struggle in great detail. One example of this is the full text archive of all ANC Constitutions (1919, 1958, 1991, 1994, and 1997). The official ANC Archives is at the historically Black institution, the University of Fort Hare, and fully accessible through this website. Also, there is an archive of ANC press releases that go back to the 1950s, including leaflets distributed from the ANC underground through "leaflet bombs." This website enables you to relive the struggle from the experience of an underground ANC cadre.

There are several ways that this ANC website provides access to current events. There is a solid list of news sources, and a free weekly newsletter one can subscribe to via the site. As the leading national economy in Africa, and because of the moral and political leadership status of Nelson Mandela, South Africa is a key source of information about the future of Africa from an African point of view. So while this is only one country at the southern-most tip of the African continent, it is the most important country through which one can understand more about all of Africa.

The websites of the SACP and COSATU are also full of information about the history and current situation in South Africa. Particularly useful are the documents that enable you to have access to the ongoing debate about public policy and international affairs. This includes the documents for national legislation (green papers for discussion and white papers for policy), and policy debates like over the collectiviza-tion of land and the danger of either the "neo-liberal right" or the "ultra-left," polar opposites on the political spectrum. Again, this presents you with the opportunity to see the world as the African sees it. Given the global monopoly of news by a few multinationals it is important that these web resources be used so that a more inclusive picture can be discussed in our classrooms and general discussions.

### African South of the Sahara: Selected Internet Resources
Stanford University
www-sul.stanford.edu/depts/ssrg/africa/guide.html
This is the best of the broad, university-based guides to information on the web about Africa. Karen Fung has organized and updates this website for the Information and Communication Technology Group of the African Studies Association.

It is an attractive, easy to navigate website with useful annotations for each website listed in its directory. You can access the information by topic, by country, or by keyword searching the entire database. This website has very practical information for the user. You can click a link for breaking news, for translation of text, for turning off the graphics to a text-only format for slower connections, and instructions on how to access web pages if all you have is email. This website is constructed for people to use at all levels of education and in all parts of the world.

## Directories

**University of Pennsylvania Africa Links**
www.sas.upenn.edu/African_Studies/Home_Page/WWW_Links.html
This is the state of the art webliography about all aspects of Africa maintained by Dr. Ali Ali-Dinar at the University of Pennsylvania.

**A–Z of African Studies on the Internet**
www.lib.msu.edu/limb/a-z/az.html
Excellent and comprehensive list of annotated links on Africa maintained by Peter Limb at Michigan State University.

**African Studies Resource Links**
www.isp.msu.edu/AfricanStudies/asc_side.htm
In addition to a comprehensive listing of relevant websites, this site reports on many of the African Studies Center's innovative programs, including: the African Internet Connectivity Project (1997–2002) including web pages being hosted for groups in Africa; the African Diaspora Program directed by Ruth Sims Hamilton; and the African eJournals Project to use the web to promote the circulation of journals published in Africa.

**African Studies Internet Resources**
www.columbia.edu/cu/lweb/indiv/africa/cuvl
A very comprehensive and easily accessible listing of websites on African topics edited by Joe Caruso.

**Africa Online**
www.africaonline.com/site
This website bills itself as Africa's largest pan-African Internet service. It is modeled on the US based America Online, and has national affiliates in several countries. There is a downside due to the commercial aspects of the list, but as a general information portal it provides access to

websites based in Africa. These websites include hard to find organizations and institutions at the grass roots level. The material is organized by topics as well as in a searchable database. The database organizes the website by country so it is possible to find information very quickly.

## General

**The History of Africa** (World History Archives)
www.hartford-hwp.com/archives/30/index.html
Easy to use set of full text primary and secondary sources for the serious student

**Kwame Nkrumah**
www.nkrumah.net
Project to make Nkrumah's work – images, sound files, video, and text – widely available.

**Lesson Plans on Africa**
edsitement.neh.gov/tab_lesson.asp?subjectArea=3&subcategory=31
A site maintained by the National Endowment for the Humanities with excellent lesson plans for grade K through 12.

**Women's Net**
South Africa
womensnet.org.za
"Women's Net is a vibrant and innovative networking support program designed to enable South African women to use the Internet to find the people, issues, resources and tools needed for women's social activism."

**African Photo**
www.africa-photo.com
Very large commercial database of photographs, but a great deal of the material can be viewed for free.

**Afrique francophone** (French Speaking Africa)
www.lehman.cuny.edu/depts/langlit/french/afrique.html

This very important site includes a comprehensive listing of websites about Francophone Africa, mainly in French.

## African Philosophy Resources
www.augustana.ca/~janzb/afphil
This is a comprehensive listing of websites organized around activity (e.g., discussion lists, conferences, journals, etc.) and substantive issues (e.g., gender, panafricanism, politics, literature, etc.).

# Ancient

## Ancient Nubia
www.us.sis.gov.eg/nubia/html/nubia00.htm
A general overview of Nubia with mainly text, but also including photographs, sound, and video files of cultural activities.

## NubiaNet
www.nubianet.org
Professor Ron Bailey of Northeastern University has created this curriculum resource about Ancient Nubia.

## Ancient Manuscripts from the Desert Libraries of Timbuktu
www.loc.gov/exhibits/mali
Over 50 pages are exhibited online, covering the 16th to the 18th centuries. This is the best proof of a literary tradition in pre-colonial Africa.

## Association for the Study of Classical African Civilizations
www.ascac.org
This web page is a major portal for Afrocentric historians, containing full text articles and information on conferences and travel-study tours to Egypt.

## Institute of Egyptian Art and Archeology
www.memphis.edu/egypt

This website is about an institute based at the University of Memphis. It has a comprehensive exhibit of the Institute's artifacts and a photo tour of over a dozen sites along the Nile River.

### The Afrocentric Debate Resource Homepage
members.tripod.com/kekaitiare/afro1.htm
Very important documentation of the debate concerning the Egyptian origin of knowledge previously attributed to Ancient Greece and Rome. Much of this is taken from a website set up by a publisher to facilitate a debate between the white scholars Martin Bernal and Mary Leftkowitz.

### The Oriental Institute
www-oi.uchicago.edu/OI/default.html
This website has a great deal of content based on the leading research of this institution. This will be of great use to the serious student who wants original documents and detailed documentation.

## Culture

### National Museum of African Art
www.nmafa.si.edu
General overview of this Smithsonian museum including online documents from their collection, overviews of exhibits, and educational materials. Visuals are very good.

### Ghanaian Kente and African American Identity
www.nmafa.si.edu/exhibits/kente/top.htm
This site is maintained by the Smithsonian Institution and is great for elementary and secondary school students, with clear directions on how and when to wear Kente cloth, as well as audio files for help with the correct pronunciation of key terms.

### African Indigenous Science and Knowledge Systems
www.africahistory.net

A wide-ranging list of websites organized by Gloria Emeagwali at the Central Connecticut State University, especially good on how modern science views traditional African healing and food cultivation practices.

### The African Music Encyclopedia
www.africanmusic.org
A comprehensive site organized by artist, country, and also containing a glossary and links to other sites. Very useful for photographs and biographies.

### Art and Life in Africa Project
www.uiowa.edu/~africart
This project is based on a commercial CD but contains a great deal of information on the free website. Good documentary photos and country by country data.

### Yoruba and Akan Art in Wood and Metal
www.fa.indiana.edu/~conner/africart/home.html
This site is maintained at Indiana University and includes detailed narrative and many clear and useful photographs.

### African Writers Series (40th anniversary)
www.africanwriters.com/Writers/Default.asp
Biographical sketches of over 70 contemporary African writers associated with the African Writers Series published by Heinemann, including information about their countries.

### African Writing Systems
www.library.cornell.edu/africana/Writing_Systems/Welcome.html
Using a map of Africa, a set of symbols, or categories, you can navigate to impressive and fascinating images and short explanations of various writing systems and other symbols used across Africa.

## Good books
Babu, Abdul Rahman Mohamed. (1981) *African socialism or socialist Africa?* London: Zed Press.

Cabral, Amilcar. (1980) *Unity and struggle: speeches and writings*. London: Heinemann.

Davidson, Basil. (1994) *Modern Africa: a social and political history*. 3rd ed. London: Longman.

Jeyifo, Biodun, ed. (2002) *Modern African drama: backgrounds and criticism*. New York: W. W. Norton.

Magubane, Bernard. (2000) *African sociology – towards a critical perspective: the selected essays of Bernard Makhosezwe Magubane*. Trenton, N.J.: Africa World Press.

Mamdani, Mahmood. (1996) *Citizen and subject: contemporary Africa and the legacy of late colonialism*. Princeton, N.J.: Princeton University Press.

Mandela, Nelson. (1995) *Long walk to freedom: the autobiography of Nelson Mandela*. Boston: Back Bay Books.

Nkrumah, Kwame. (1973) *Revolutionary path*. New York: International Publishers.

Rodney, Walter. (1981) *How Europe underdeveloped Africa*. Washington, D.C.: Howard University Press.

Thompson, Robert Farris. (1983) *Flash of the spirit: African and Afro-American art and philosophy*. New York: Random House.

# 3
# Slave Trade

The European slave trade of captured Africans was a devastating blow to the African continent. It was a historical process that stunted the growth and development of African societies and left a legacy of conflict and terror that continues to haunt African peoples till recent times. It lasted over 400 years, an unprecedented and systematic process of dehumanization. The evil of this holocaust was redefined and legitimated. By political ideology, religious theology, and the brute force of guns and economic power Europe rationalized this process over all these centuries. Almost every major European power had a role in this process, and every part of Africa has felt its impact.

Debates continue about the slave trade. One of the great historical debates is over the role of the slave trade in the rise of industrial capitalism. Eric Williams in his PhD thesis/book *Capitalism and Slavery* made the classic statement that the profits of the slave trade provided the critical capital to finance the industrial revolution. He argued that the cumulative impact of the triangle trade that linked Europe to Africa to the New World multiplied profits at each step ending up with super profits for England and the rest. This is second only to the debate over how many people were captured and transported in this terrible trade, raging from the 100 million reported by W. E. B. DuBois in his Harvard doctoral thesis/book *The Suppression of the African Slave Trade* down to estimates of 10 million. The third debate is over the thesis that the economic stagnation of Africa today is linked to its devastating destruction during the slave trade. This thesis is associated with Walter Rodney in his book *How Europe Underdeveloped Africa*.

The debate has been created by the false argument that the slave trade was a mission of great benefit in that it saved Africans from the barbarism of their past and introduced them to the culture and social life of Europe, even though as slaves. The main reason this has been rejected is that the discourse now includes the voices of the descendants of the slaves who have a voice and can repudiate the rationalizing lies of the defenders of the slave masters.

On the other side of the Atlantic it is clear that the slave trade made a dramatic impact on most countries in the Americas. Africans far outnumbered Europeans on many Caribbean islands, and certainly African culture became the basis for culture in far deeper ways than can be discounted, even if their expression is housed within European cultural forms – the Catholic church covering African gods, European languages being used to convey African linguistic patterns, or African rhythms being played with musical instruments from other parts of the world.

### Virtual Visit to Goree Island: The House of Slaves
webworld.unesco.org/goree/en/screens/0.shtml
This is an important website because it places you into the actual environment of the slaves as they waited to board the ships to cross the Atlantic Ocean and enter New World slavery. "This House of Slaves" is located on the Island of Goree, Senegal (West Africa). It is a historical restoration project recognized and supported through this website by UNESCO, as part of its mission to preserve World Heritage. The world will never forget the horrors of slavery and therefore will be encouraged to avoid repeating this history. Boubacar Ndianye, the chief conservationist, wrote the text and narrates the site.

Europeans invaded the Island of Goree in 1444, and the Portuguese built the first slave fort there in 1536. This House of Slaves is the last one built there in 1776, the year of the American Revolution. The House of Slaves held 150 to 200 people who waited up to three months before being shipped to the New World.

The material is presented in two basic formats on this website. You can click through slides and you can watch a ten minute video. The site is beautiful, with photography that captures the historical significance of each aspect of this historical horror.

If you can't make a trip to Goree Island this website will give you a virtual experience you will not easily forget.

## The Atlantic Slave Trade and Slave Life in the Americas: A Visual Record
University of Virginia
gropius.lib.virginia.edu/Slavery
This is a web based archive of images concerning the slave trade and slavery. This website is based at the University of Virginia, a continuation of a project that started at Southern Illinois University (Carbondale). Jerome Handler and Michael Tuite are listed as authors of this website. This site is available freely to everyone, but people are cautioned not to use any of the material for commercial purposes.

The material is organized in 18 categories, and includes hundreds of images. This is an amazing archive that will inform, challenge, and transform. It is documentary evidence of the slavery experience, compelling even for those who do not believe that slavery was all that horrible. You see people being captured, branded, shipped, sold, and at work in the fields. In addition there are images of all aspects of everyday life – housing, religion, food, family life, cultural life, and resistance of all kinds. This database is also searchable by keywords, and therefore can be used to supplement a course of study, to help with a particular research interest, and reading any other material about these matters without sufficient visual documentation.

## Liverpool and the British Transatlantic Slave Trade
Merseyside Maritime Museum
www.liverpoolmuseums.org.uk/maritime/slavery/slavery.asp
This museum has a website that provides two important online exhibits of relevance to the slave trade: Transatlantic Slavery, and the Slave History Trail. It is presented as a series of web pages that include graphics and text.

Transatlantic Slavery has six pages: the trade triangle, Africa, Europe, middle passage, Americas, and further information. Each of these pages includes a clear and lucid overview of the topic, images, and primary documents. The primary documents are presented as text and audio files. The main source is the slave narrative by Olaudah Equiano, but there are also selections from the journal of a slave trader, and the log of a ship detailing the constant rebellions on the ship by the captured Africans.

The Slave History Trail is an interactive map showing relevant locations in Liverpool and their connection to the slave trade. This information is also presented as text without the map.

The site also gives information on the International Day for Remembering the Abolition of the Slave Trade. Successful revolutionary struggle against slavery in the New World began in Haiti on August 23, 1791. In commemoration of this event, UNESCO chose August 23rd for this annual observance.

### Sankofa's Slave Genealogy

www.rootsweb.com/~afamerpl

This website is important for what information it has and for the method that it uses. There are two key databases on this site, slave plantations and slave markets. The method it uses to build these is based on volunteers joining the process. The incentive is clear: if everyone who uses such a database can each contribute a little to it, then we as a whole will benefit all the more.

This website is structured to present information on every plantation and every market site where slaves were bought and sold. Organized by US states the data is presented along with links of other resources relevant to the topic and the area.

The idea of having people in the community join in building a database has been the main method for most Black social science scholarship in the 20th century. W. E. B. DuBois held annual conferences at Atlanta University to deliberate on problems or key issues based on surveys a network of people completed (1898–1914). Charles Johnson founded a Peoples College at Fisk University and used students and community residents to collect data for reports in articles, books, and monographs (1927–56), and Carter G. Woodson built the popular movement to preserve and study Black History from 1915 to 1950. Monroe Work built databases on topics such as lynching based on newspaper articles and letters of first-hand accounts sent to him by his contacts throughout the

South. In this case the website is interactive, to solicit participation by people prepared to contribute what information they have and to do research for more.

### The Atlantic Slave Trade: A Demographic Simulation
Northeastern University
www.whc.neu.edu/afrintro.htm
One of the great debates in world history is over how many people were taken from Africa during the Atlantic slave trade. W. E. B. DuBois said 100 million, while contemporary historians often follow a more modest estimate.

This site is based at the World History Center of Northeastern University. It was developed by the demographic historian Patrick Manning. It is not a site for beginners but it offers the serious student of history an opportunity to visualize and hence think deeper about the assumptions we make about history. This site compares the relative growth of three populations: the source for slaves, the African population involved in the slave trade, and the population where the slaves were taken. Obviously the source population declined through capture, but also through the resultant fall in birth rates and an increasingly unbalanced sex ratio. On the other hand the other two kinds of populations increased, but each in a specific way.

The slave trade was a holocaust for African people. There are no clear records for much of what happened. Historical interpretations are often based on what kinds of assumptions one makes, so caution often requires one to make high and low assumptions on empirical measures and then to make reasoned statements based on the full range of possibilities.

### Breaking the Silence: Learning about the Transatlantic Slave Trade
www.antislavery.org/breakingthesilence/index.shtml
This is an international experiment in education. When you go to the page you are invited to watch a 17 minute video of Black British and Afro-Caribbean youth taking a tour of places related to the slave trade in London, and then participating in a teleconference with a group of white British youth in Liverpool. This is an extremely useful tool because it is short enough to be used in all kinds of settings, including being

screened in a class before a general discussion. It is informative, and sensitive to all points of view without compromising on the essential features of slavery and the historical legacy of racism that still faces us in the USA as well as in the UK and other parts of the world.

A group of cooperating institutions organized this site, including UNESCO, the British Council, and Anti-Slavery International. It is run under the banner of the Associated Schools Project Network and seeks to organize people all over the world in coming to grips with the African Holocaust. There is little general knowledge of the issues involved in this historical global process of enslavement for the benefit of Europe and the USA, and therefore the title is its mission, to break the silence.

The main content of this website is organized in nine categories covering the main aspects of the slave trade. Within each category there are PDF files of packaged lesson plans to teach the topic, as well as specific resources that can be used to "pick and mix" for instructional purposes. These are useful for both primary and secondary school levels.

In addition, there are maps and descriptive essays that enable the students to find out how various regions and countries of the world were involved in the slave trade. Finally there is a newsletter that gives current information about the project, and ways that schools and educational groups can get involved with this global experiment to break the silence.

## General

### Slave Movement During the 18th and 19th Centuries
dpls.dacc.wisc.edu/slavedata/index.html
This is the most serious free source of empirical data on the slave trade. There are eleven data sets that can be used. This is for the serious researcher at the college level.

### The Slave Trade Archive Project (UNESCO)
webworld.unesco.org/slave_quest/en/index.html
This is a wonderful global project to preserve information about the slave trade.

**Captive Passage: The Transatlantic Slave Trade and the Making of the Americas**
www.mariner.org/captivepassage/index.html
Overview of the slave trade in six categories: introduction, departure, middle passage, arrival, abolition, and legacy. Good design, easy to read text.

**African Slave Trade and European Imperialism**
www.cocc.edu/cagatucci/classes/hum211/timelines/htimeline3.htm
This is an excellent compilation of web links, including full text of historical documents.

**The Slave Trade** (The Spartacus Internet Encyclopedia)
www.spartacus.schoolnet.co.uk/slavery.htm
A very useful directory of information and links to original documents in five categories: slave accounts, slave system, slave life, events and issues, and anti-slavery actions.

**H-West Africa**
www2.h-net.msu.edu/~wafrica
This is an online discussion list about the history and current situation of West Africa.

## England

**Bristol and Slavery**
www.headleypark.bristol.sch.uk/slavery
A lively and easy to use discussion of the slave trade with special focus on Bristol, the leading slave trading port before the rise of Liverpool. Good for high school.

**Britain's Slave Trade** (Channel 4, London, UK)
www.channel4.com/history/microsites/S/slavetrade/main.html
This is a website that accompanied a TV program. It is useful because of the links it provides to information about Bristol and Liverpool.

# New England

## The Rhode Island Black Heritage Society

www.providenceri.com/RI_BlackHeritage

Good local history site with short essay about slave trade and Rhode Island.

## Slave Trade and Portsmouth

www.seacoastnh.com/blackhistory/slaves.html

Documentation of the slave trade and slavery in Portsmouth, New Hampshire.

# Amistad

## The Amistad Case: The Digital Classroom National Archives and Records Administration

www.archives.gov/digital_classroom/lessons/amistad_case/amistad_case. html

This site contains curriculum guides and full text of primary documents concerning the 1839–41 Supreme Court case to free Africans from slavery.

## Primary Sources Concerning the Amistad Case

www.arts.adelaide.edu.au/personal/DHart/ETexts/Armistad/Amistad-Docs/1807.act.barsslavetrade.html

Excellent collection of government documents and newspapers articles.

# West Africa

## Olaudah Equiano, The Interesting Narrative of the Life of Olaudah Equiano, or Gustavus Vassa, the African

history.hanover.edu/texts/equiano/equiano_contents.html

This is the full text of the 1789 book that is regarded along with the auto-biographies of Frederick Douglass as the best slave narrative. A must read.

**Elmina and the Cape Coast** (Slave Castles)

www.theviproom.com/visions/slave.htm

A good essay and photo documentation of the role of the Ghana coast in the slave trade.

## Good books

Curtin, Philip D. (1997) *Africa remembered: narratives by West Africans from the era of the slave trade*. Prospect Heights, Ill.: Waveland Press.

DuBois, W. E. B. (1999) *The suppression of the African slave-trade to the United States of America, 1638–1870*. Mineola, N.Y.: Dover Publications.

James, C. L. R. (1989) *The black Jacobins*. 2nd ed. New York: Vintage Books.

Johnson, Charles Richard. (1990) *Middle passage*. New York: Atheneum.

Klein, Herbert S. (1999) *The Atlantic slave trade*. Cambridge: Cambridge University Press.

Lovejoy, Paul E. (2000) *Transformations in slavery: a history of slavery in Africa*. 2nd ed. Cambridge: Cambridge University Press

Manning, Patrick. (1990) *Slavery and African life: occidental, oriental, and African slave trades*. Cambridge: Cambridge University Press.

Northrup, David, ed. (2002) *The Atlantic slave trade*. 2nd ed. Boston: Houghton Mifflin Co.

Thornton, John Kelly. (1998) *Africa and Africans in the making of the Atlantic world, 1400–1800*. 2nd ed. Cambridge: Cambridge University Press.

Williams, Eric Eustace. (1994) *Capitalism & slavery*. Chapel Hill: University of North Carolina Press.

# 4
# Slavery

The geographical origin of the USA was in the South. Most of the early presidents and all important figures in the government were slave owners beginning with George Washington and Thomas Jefferson. The US economy was based on slavery until well after the supposed abolition, some 150 years ago. The national economy was based on slavery in that more wealth was invested in the slave system than all the rest of the economy combined – the banks, industry, railroads, and agriculture. The slaves produced the cotton that dominated all US exports. This was the majority of cotton traded on the world market. It is impossible to discuss the history of the USA without giving center stage to slavery.

Slavery was the evil twin of the industrial system, as the slaves produced cotton while the industrial working class was formed in the textile mills that took the cotton and made cloth. But it was more than a system of political economy. The slave system gave rise to a society and culture. The privileges for slave owners within this society are kept in the consciousness of people today as the drama of the movie *Gone with the Wind* rehearses, but also the superiority of the industrial system of the Northern states. But the voices of slaves are usually not heard.

Black scholars have done pioneering work, especially since the Black Studies explosion in the 1960s, to change this picture dramatically by finding the voice of the slaves. One of the major bodies of work to do this was the collection of personal narratives by slaves themselves. This constitutes the first new genre of literature in the African American intellectual history, the narratives of slave autobiography. In addition there are letters, petitions, oral histories, quilts, folklore, graveyards and even archeological sites that tell more complex tales of the slave experience. Every Southern state archive, and every library, undoubtedly still has stories to tell that have yet to be gathered and used to shed more light on this "peculiar institution."

### Slavery Petitions
University of North Carolina at Greensboro
history.uncg.edu/slaverypetitions

One of the great advances resulting from the new information technology is about archives, once hidden away but now being brought out into the open and transformed into actively used research and curriculum materials. In 1991 Professor Loren Schweninger began actively traveling throughout the South to county court houses and state archives. He was on a mission to collect all of the petitions he could find that dealt with slavery. He found over 3,000 documents, and this website opens his research materials to everyone. The site in maintained by the Department of History at the University of North Carolina at Greensboro.

From 1777 to 1867, according to this database, people petitioned the government for various reasons concerning slavery. There are petitions from Black and white, free and slave. The site presents the petitions as a searchable database. It is possible to choose from 300 subjects, seven states, and the petitioner's name, gender, and color. A search will get you to a description of the petition and a summation of its content. There is also a page giving over 30 of the full text documents, both a photo reproduction of the original handwritten petition and a typed transcription.

Also on the website is a link to a collection of petitions published by Prof. Schweninger with the University of Illinois Press. They have the full text of 160 petitions (click on Books and Publications, then click on the book *The Southern Debate Over Slavery* and you will get to this additional set of petitions).

These petitions are a primary source for direct information about slavery. If you choose to search only for Black petitions, for example, you would be able to get a range of opinions from Black people able to write or get someone to write a petition for them. This is a necessary supplement to the slave narratives.

### The Levi Jordan Plantation
www.publicarchaeology.org/webarchaeology/html/Default.htm

**BEST HISTORY SITES**

This website is a major example of campus community collaboration in public history. This is a website of the Levi Jordan Plantation Historical Society documenting the plantation from 1848 to 1890, from slaves to sharecroppers. It is the best case we have of creating a virtual living museum of a plantation society and the descendants of everyone, Black and white, slave and free, who ever lived or worked there.

Levi Jordan (1793–1873) started this plantation that was operated with slave labor. One of his descendants, Carol McDavid, owns the land and leased it to the Society for 99 years to carry out historical restoration and this virtual museum. Click on her name and you will find out that she has studied for a PhD in Anthropology and has posted many of her papers on the site. This project has been carried out with the help of the Anthropology Department of the University of Houston, especially Prof. Kenneth Brown. There is an interview of Prof. Brown, and a set of several papers from a session he organized on the Levi Jordan Plantation for the Society for Historical Archeology.

You have to read the site carefully to get all that it has to offer, but there is a table of contents that is a very helpful guide. This site is full of primary documents from the 19th century, and genealogical information on specific families Black and white, archeological findings from excavations of the plantation, census records, etc. This is the most comprehensive virtual plantation available.

**Documents on Slavery**
Avalon Project
Yale University
www.yale.edu/lawweb/avalon/slavery.htm
This is a documentary collection of material regarding slavery in the USA. There is no introductory material, so this is not a site for casual readers. However, this is the best such site for the serious student of slavery. These documents cover federal statutes from 1794 to 1854, and many treaties and other historical documents.

The Avalon Project is one of the major digitization projects based on a university campus designed to preserve and make available significant texts that make up the national heritage. This site also has full text reproductions of work by Frederick Douglass, Sojourner Truth, W. E. B. DuBois, Booker T. Washington, and Martin Luther King. The nationalist tradition of Martin Delaney, Marcus Garvey, and Malcolm X is omitted, but this is an excellent site for what is covered.

## North American Slave Narratives

University of North Carolina

docsouth.unc.edu/neh/nehmain.html

Documenting the American South is a major project at the University of North Carolina at Chapel Hill. This site, North American Slave Narratives, is part of this project. It is the most comprehensive set of full text slave narratives on the World Wide Web. The organizers have digitized all known slave narratives written before 1920, including some biographies as well. This was started with a grant from the National Endowment for the Humanities.

These texts are organized by date, by author, and by title. This site has been constructed with the detailed scholarship befitting a state of the art project and provides a full discussion of the technical standards and practices used to create it. In addition there is a very informative essay introducing the site by the major scholar driving this project, Professor Williams Andrews.

## The Face of Slavery

The American Museum of Photography

www.photographymuseum.com/faceof.html

This website is a dramatic presentation of photographic images of slaves and their immediate descendents. The sight of 19th century captured Africans is dramatic because there is a sense in which they look very different and another in which they look as familiar as someone you might see on the bus or in an elevator today. Slavery is both distant history and a terrible legacy we live with in the present.

There is a historical necessity to keep the faces of slaves in front of people in this country. The American Museum of Photography is doing a wonderful, public service by making these photographs available online.

# General

**Slavery**
www.spartacus.schoolnet.co.uk/USAslavery.htm
This site is a mini-encyclopedia on slavery. It is great for one stop browsing.

**Slavery in the Western Hemisphere**
cghs.dade.k12.fl.us/slavery
This is a comprehensive curriculum aid for K–12 students created by high school students from Florida. Excellent.

**A Chronology of Slavery**
www.innercity.org/holt/slavechron.html
A comprehensive annotated chronology of the Black experience from 1619 to the 20th century. Excellent for providing context for any time period.

# US: General

**Aframerindian Slave Narratives**
www.people.virginia.edu/~pnm3r/afram
Presents almost 150 slave narratives by Africans mixed with Indians. This is a unique and very revealing source to reinterpret American history and demonstrate the unity of Africans and Indians.

**Slave Era Insurance Registry**
www.insurance.ca.gov/SEIR/main.htm
This website covers the role of the insurance industry in the slavery system based on a law passed in California in 2000. Lists specific companies and even the names of slaves being insured.

**Africans in America** (PBS)
www.pbs.org/wgbh/aia/home.html

This site provides historical material to accompany the PBS four-part series on the early history of Africans in America (1450–1865). Excellent supplementary material for high school and college.

## Eli Whitney Museum
www.eliwhitney.org/main.htm
This site covers the life of the great inventor Eli Whitney whose name is associated with the cotton gin, a machine that revolutionized cotton production and led to a great increase in the demand for slave labor.

## Slavery and Religion in America (A Timeline)
www.ipl.org/div/timeline
Very useful annotated chronology from 1440 to 1866.

# US: Specific locations

## Yale, Slavery and Abolitionism
www.yaleslavery.org
This website presents research that links Yale University to slavery and the slave trade. Produced by three graduate students at Yale.

## Slavery in New Hampshire
www.seacoastnh.com/blackhistory
Comprehensive survey of slavery in this small state in New England.

## George Washington and Slavery
www.mountvernon.org/education/slavery
This is the official version of history from the Mount Vernon Foundation, the home of George Washington that has been turned into a national monument.

## Slavery in Pennsylvania
www.afrolumens.org/slavery

A solid example of local history being shared via the web, covering slaves and slave owners' data, and articles about their experiences. Many layers of information so keep digging.

### A Historical Look at Slavery on the Lewis and Clark Expedition
www.artsci.wustl.edu/~sjboyd/lc
This site chronicles the experiences of slavery in the westward explorations by focusing on York, the Black servant of William Clark. Provides insight into the first contact between Blacks and Indians.

### German Americans and the Slavery Issue
www.serve.com/shea/germusa/antislve.htm
This site documents the abolitionism of German Quakers beginning in 1688, the first white anti-slavery protest in the USA.

### African Americans in Colonial America
www.history.org/Almanack/life/Af_Amer/aalife.cfm
This is a digital museum of the 19th century slave experience in colonial Williamsburg, Virginia.

### Slavery in Connecticut
www.yale.edu/ynhti/curriculum/units/1980/6/80.06.09.x.html
An excellent lesson plan prepared by David Parsons for the annual Yale–New Haven Teachers Institute, covering the period from 1640 to 1848.

### Stratford Hall Plantation (Home of Robert E. Lee)
www.stratfordhall.org
This is a virtual museum of the Lee plantation, including discussion and documentation of archeological findings and historical analysis.

### Getting Word: The Monticello African American Oral History
www.monticello.org/gettingword
Stories, photos, and historical documents concerning people held as slaves by Thomas Jefferson, and their descendants.

# US: Black perspective

**Depictions of Slavery in Confederate Money**
www.lib.lsu.edu/cwc/BeyondFaceValue/index.htm
This is a systematic presentation of how the Confederacy depicted Black people on their money. At that time different paper currency was issued by states or banks so many designs were used.

**The Frederick Douglass Papers at the Library of Congress**
memory.loc.gov/ammem/doughtml
This website contains the entire collection at the LOC. His major books are available via Project Gutenberg.

**Freedoms Journal**
www.wisconsinhistory.org/library/aanp/freedom/index.html
This site at the Wisconsin State Historical Society contains all 103 issues of *Freedom's Journal*, the first Black owned and operated newspaper in the USA from 1827 to 1829.

**Slavery** (Lest We Forget)
www.coax.net/people/lwf/slavery.htm
Wonderfully diverse body of material created and linked to by Bennie McCrae. He presents material from a Black point of view, based in the community and not on a campus.

**Solomon Northup**
docsouth.unc.edu/northup/menu.html
Digital reproduction of a complete slave narrative (336 pages) that was very popular. Originally published in 1853.

**Remembering Slavery**
www.uncg.edu/~jpbrewer/remember
At this site you can listen to the voices of ex-slaves telling about their experiences.

# Global

**The Liberian Letters**
etext.lib.virginia.edu/subjects/liberia
This website contains many letters written by former slaves from Liberia
(1834–35 and 1857–66) after resettlement by the American Colonization Society.

**Slavery and London**
www.fantompowa.net/Flame/slavery_in_london.html
Article with good supporting links, specifically useful for explaining
different historical moments, from the Romans through the slave trade.

# Courts

**The Dred Scott Case**
library.wustl.edu/vlib/dredscott
Comprehensive primary documents of the famous trial that denied any
slave equal rights under the law by the Supreme Court in 1857.

**Slavery and the Courts**
memory.loc.gov/ammem/sthtml
This contains over 100 documents arranged by subject, title and author.
Excellent project that is part of the American Memory Project of the
Library of Congress.

# Good books

Berlin, Ira. (2003) *Generations of captivity: a history of African American
slaves*. Cambridge: Belknap Harvard.

Blackburn, Robin. (1997) *The making of New World slavery: from the
Baroque to the modern, 1492–1800*. London: Verso.

Blassingame, John W. (1979) *The slave community: plantation life in
the antebellum South*. New York: Oxford University Press.

Davis, David Brion. (1984) *Slavery and human progress*. New York: Oxford University Press.

Douglass, Frederick (1993) *Narrative of the life of Frederick Douglass, an American slave, written by himself*. Boston: Bedford Books of St. Martin's Press.

Gutman, Herbert George. (1976) *The Black family in slavery and freedom, 1750–1925*. New York: Pantheon Books

Joyner, Charles W. (1985) *Down by the riverside: a South Carolina slave community*. Urbana: University of Illinois Press.

Linebaugh, Peter, and Rediker, Marcus. (2000) *The many-headed hydra: the hidden history of the revolutionary Atlantic*. Boston: Beacon Press.

Northup, Solomon. (2002) *Twelve years a slave*. Mineola, N.Y.: Dover Publications.

Winbush, Raymond A. (2003) *Should America pay?: slavery and the raging debate over reparations*. New York: Amistad.

# 5
# Emancipation

The end of slavery was a process and not an event. It involved the Abolitionist movement, the Civil War, and the Reconstruction. This was a process in which many forces converged against the slave system and paved the way for the total dominance of industrial capitalism and its form of liberal democracy. Ultimately slavery soiled the banner of high ideals championed in the American Revolution and the founding documents establishing its democratic system. Half slave and half free just didn't make sense in political terms nor in religious terms. The search for profits and power was the motivation to keep the slave system going, but not without intense opposition from the North as well as from within the slave system itself.

Black people had to fight to have their voices heard in the Abolitionist movement, though it needs to be said that this movement was the greatest example of courage and commitment to democratic ideals that the USA has ever seen. One example of this is Abby Kelley who insisted on having Black women with her on stage as she faced attacking mobs to advance the cause of Abolition along with the rights of women. The ex-slaves were well represented by the voices of Frederick Douglass, David Walker, and Martin Delany and others. The founding institutions of the Black community nearly all had their ideological baptism in the fight against slavery including the church and the newspaper. In every city and town Black people met in conference and convention to discuss how to end slavery. They petitioned the government and church, and they armed themselves to fight the slave catchers as they chased the runaways.

From within the slave system the spirit of resistance was alive. Slaves ran away from servitude via the underground railroad under the leadership of people such as Harriet Tubman and Sojourner Truth. Slaves rose up in rebellion to fight slavery under the leadership of courageous men and women like Nat Turner, Denmark Vesey, and Gabriel Prosser. Thousands of unnamed slaves practiced many forms of sabotage and ended up running away to join the victorious Union army.

In the end, the Reconstruction was ended by a deal between Northern and Southern interests called the Hayes-Tilden Betrayal. Northern industrial capitalists ended their alliance with Black people that had won the war in an agreement to solve an election crisis. Federal troops were pulled out of the South and political power was given back to the Southern ex-slave owners in exchange for Rutherford Hayes from Ohio getting the presidency. These troops that were pulled out of the South where they were protecting Black people who were trying to exercise their new rights of citizenship were then used to suppress the 1877 national railroad strike in which Black and white workers stood together.

In general, the emancipation process is one of the great periods in US history as it involves the high drama of a civil war, of a near Biblical story of ex-slaves fighting to be free, and of the hope for revolutionary land reform. Blacks were promised 40 acres and a mule by abolitionists but never got this nor any other kind of reparations. This emancipation process set the stage for the next 150 years of struggle that continues to go on today.

**American Abolitionism**
University of Indiana at Indianapolis
www.americanabolitionist.liberalarts.iupui.edu
The Abolitionist movement against the slave system was diverse and broad involving thousands of people, some as public figures and many as secret accomplices working for the end of slavery. This was morally righteous but illegal work. This site is a comprehensive resource on that movement from 1830 to the 1860s. It is based at the joint Indianapolis campus of Indiana University and Purdue University. Professor John McKivigan of the History Department is the main author of this site.

McKivigan provides a useful introductory essay. He classifies the movement into four types: the Garrisonians who were categorically opposed to slavery and took aggressive action for reform including the equality of women in the movement; the religious abolitionists who stressed prayer and appeals to religious-based moral arguments; the political abolitionists who worked against slavery within the political system; and the radicals who like John Brown were prepared to wage war to end slavery. The actual experiences of this movement are not generally well known, but should be as this was a high point of revolutionary idealism and vision against a historical terror. The abolitionists were heroes of democracy in the USA, a country that espoused democracy but did not practice it toward many, especially African Americans.

There are four other parts to the site: a biographical dictionary of about 200 key abolitionists, links to key documents, an extensive bibliography of print references, and a webliography of useful links on abolitionism. The biographical dictionary is very important as it can be used as a handy reference when looking at other material.

**Virginia Runaways**
University of Virginia
www.uvawise.edu/history/runaways
This is an important website for an understanding of the freedom impulse in African American history. The introduction to this site defines its purpose: "The Virginia Runaways Project is a digital database of runaway and captured slave and servant advertisements from 18th-century Virginia newspapers. When a slave or servant ran away, masters often placed remarkably detailed advertisements for their return. Sheriffs and other county officials also often advertised the capture of runaways or suspected runaways. This project offers full transcripts and images of all runaway and captured ads for slaves, servants, and deserters placed in Virginia newspapers from 1736 to 1790." Professor Thomas Costa is the author of this site, based at the Virginia Center for Digital History (University of Virginia).

The ads are available via browsing or searching the entire database or by decades. A reproduction of the original documents is provided, as well as transcripts of the text. Reading these ads will take you into the reality of the slave's flight to freedom, just as if you were reading the information in your daily newspaper. It's a "you are there" kind of experience to read some of this material. Reading these ads from the per-

**Emancipation**                                                          **55**

spective of the slave one feels the terrible emotions of the chase while facing the dogs, the vigilantes, the white man's "law."

The site contains lots of information that enables you to translate the language of the period and place these ads in their proper historical context. The ads refer to laws, currency, and clothing that no longer have any resemblance to contemporary speech. For example, the ads often state that people will be given the reward of one or more "pistoles." The site tells you what this means: "The pistole, a common coin in Virginia, at least until the 1760s, was a Spanish gold coin, sometimes called a doubloon. By the mid eighteenth century, a pistole was worth almost a pound (.83), or a little over 18 shillings." The supporting material gives some indication of what happened to the people who ran away.

## Freedmen's Bureau

www.iath.virginia.edu/vshadow2/HIUS403/freedmen/bureau.html

This website was built by four undergraduates at the University of Virginia for a course, titled Digital History and the Civil War. While it focuses on Virginia, the site is nevertheless a clear and accessible treatment of the Freedmen's Bureau as a whole.

The introduction gives an overview and describes the five main parts of this website: labor and contracts, social services, family services, violence and justice, and a newspaper archive. Each of the sections is a short essay with links leading to primary documents. Throughout the site there are reproductions of images from primary documents, both in each section and then also as a special image gallery as part of the introduction.

This site is a good example of how, using a very local instance, it is possible to find a way to generalize about a much bigger social and historical reality. The Virginia Center for Digital History is a pace setter for this kind of work. Students reading this should accept the challenge to replicate this kind of work in their local situation. This includes both high school and college students. In the 21st century information revolution all knowledge will be revisited using the new tools of information technology. The knowledge production game is wide open.

**Samuel May Anti-Slavery Collection**
Cornell University
www.library.cornell.edu/mayantislavery
This is a very important collection of material that covers all aspects of emancipation: the abolitionists, the Civil War, and the Reconstruction. Samuel May, an 1817 Harvard graduate, became an activist minister. He was an abolitionist, a fighter for women's rights, and for education reform. After a career as a pastor in Syracuse he donated his anti-slavery collection to Cornell University. In response to this a letter was sent out widely to assist in expanding the collection. The signers of the letter were William Lloyd Garrison, Wendell Phillips, and Gerrit Smith – all leading abolitionists and well-connected to help build this collection.

The collection was built as a national resource, and now all 300,000 pages of the 10,000 items have been digitized and are available on this website making it the single most accessible source of information on anti-slavery activities. The entire database is searchable based on keywords in the text as well as by author, title, and subject.

There is no way to merely browse the collection, hence you have to get used to pulling up pages and getting directly into the details of the material. It would be useful to have an A–Z index of the material by author, title, and subject.

The pioneering work of this website is supported by a page that explains in great detail how the material was digitized and stored in the Department of Rare and Manuscript Collections at Cornell University. This is a great teaching tool for librarians and archivists.

**Aboard the Underground Railroad**
A National Register Travel Itinerary
National Park Service
www.cr.nps.gov/nr/travel/underground
There are many underground railroad websites, but the best place to start is with this official website of the National Park Service. It features the 55 sites in 21 states that are officially registered as underground railroad sites. The largest number comes from the state of Ohio. For each site there is a photo and a brief essay explaining the experiences associated with the location.

There are four brief essays to place the general topic of the underground railroad in a historical context: slave trade, early anti-slavery, operating the underground railroad, and the Civil War.

An interactive map is privided that shows the escape routes from slave territories. One can find a route and then check the places where people may have stopped. There are very likely many more places yet to be identified as being stations on the underground railroad. Detailed instructions are given on how to apply to have a new place added.

One of the interesting aspects of this list is the Black abolitionists who were part of this freedom effort. They include one from Colorado (Barney Ford), and four from Ohio (James and Sophia Clemens, Wilson Bruce Evans, and John Parker).

## General

### *Uncle Tom's Cabin* and American Culture
jefferson.village.virginia.edu/utc
This site is a treasure trove of information about this book and its role in American history. Excellent!

### Juneteenth
www.juneteenth.com
This site presents information concerning the oldest celebration of the end of slavery. The name is based on the date when Emancipation is celebrated in Texas (June 19th).

### The Gilder Lehrman Center for the Study of Slavery, Resistance and Abolition
www.yale.edu/glc/index.html
This is the premier site for the academic study of slavery based at Yale. They provide a free email newsletter.

### Emancipation Proclamation
www.ourdocuments.gov/content.php?page=document&doc=34

This site describes the document, giving an image of the original and explanation of its historical context and significance.

**Freedmen's Bureau**
www.freedmensbureau.com
This site provides extensive documentation of records maintained by the Freedmen's Bureau. It is a good resource for genealogical research.

## Abolitionists

**John Brown of Kansas 1855–59**
www.territorialkansas.org/projects/index.shtml#johnBrown
This is a PDF file of a popular pamphlet on all aspects of John Brown in Kansas by the Territorial Kansas Heritage Alliance.

**John Brown Database**
wvmemory.wvculture.org/imlsintro.html
This is major collection on the great abolitionist John Brown, including over 20,000 pages of text and images, including over 100 letters from Brown to friends and family.

**The Abolitionist**
www.afgen.com/slave1.html
Full text archive of important writings by Black and white abolitionists.

## Underground railroad

**Williams Still**
www.undergroundrr.com/index2.html
Compilation of material on this famous Black conductor of the underground railroad, including biographies of over ten Black abolitionists.

**Flight to Freedom**
http://139.140.12.20:8080/flighttofreedom/live/intro.shtml

Very interesting website that combines interactive roleplay with factual events taken from slave naratives. The objective is to enable your chosen character to escape from slavery. Helps you experience what the escaping slave had to endure.

### Information on the Underground Railroad
scils.rutgers.edu/~kvander/clara13.html
This is a good set of links maintained at Rutgers University.

### The Underground Railroad in New York State
www.nyhistory.com/ugrr
This site provides detailed information about specific people, places, and events including newspaper articles and photos.

### The Underground Railroad in Rochester, New York
www.history.rochester.edu/class/ugrr/home.html
A brief set of short essays details the anti-slavery activities in this upstate New York city.

### Underground Railroad in Lancaster County (Pennsylvania)
muweb.millersville.edu/~ugrr
Excellent example of how a local history project has digitized primary materials to assist in research. Good explanations and navigational clues.

## Civil War

### Freedmen and Southern Society Project
www.history.umd.edu/Freedmen
This site is about a project at the University of Maryland under the direction of Ira Berlin to publish over 50,000 documents from the National Archives. Even though it is about a book project many documents are online.

### Buffalo Soldiers
www.imh.org/imh/buf/buftoc.html

This site documents the African American cavalry and infantry units created by an act of Congress in 1866 to fight Indians and Mexican revolutionaries.

### To Be More than Equal: The Many Lives of Martin Delany
www.libraries.wvu.edu/delany/home.htm
An extensive site on Martin Delany (1812–1885) that includes biographical information and full text of all his important writing.

### The Fight for Equal Rights: Black Soldiers in the Civil War
www.archives.gov/digital_classroom/lessons/blacks_in_civil_war/blacks_in_civil_war.html
This is a curriculum module that includes background documentation, exercises, and suggestions for student projects.

### African Americans in the Civil War Links
www.geocities.com/r_leddy/cw/cw-af.html
This is a good set of links to information on US Civil War colored troops.

### 5th Regiment Cavalry United States Colored Troops
mywebpages.comcast.net/5thuscc
This website is dedicated to the African American soldiers massacred by Confederate soldiers at Saltville, West Virginia in October 1864.

### 102nd Regiment of USCT
www.geocities.com/Athens/9425/102hp.html
This site is about the first Civil War African American infantry unit formed in Michigan.

### United States Colored Troops
www.coax.net/people/lwf/usct.htm
Best general site of links, by an African American independent researcher.

### Colored Troops in the American Civil War
www.homepages.dsu.edu/jankej/civilwar/colored.htm
This is a set of links maintained by Dakota State University.

### Camp William Penn Headquarters

www.awod.com/cwchas/1sc.html

This site documents the eleven regiments trained at this camp which was one of six established in 1863 to train African Americans to fight as Union troops in the Civil War.

### The First South Carolina Volunteer Infantry

www.awod.com/cwchas/1sc.html

This site has been developed and maintained by a Civil War reenactment organization.

### Black Dispatches: Black American Contributions to Union Intelligence During the Civil War

www.cia.gov/cia/publications/dispatches

Details the stories of African Americans who traveled North – and South – collecting intelligence that helped the North win the war. Most well-known among these individuals: Harriet Tubman. Site also provides sources for these stories.

## Canada

### Black Loyalists: Our History, Our People

collections.ic.gc.ca/blackloyalists/wireframe.htm

Excellent site on the Black experience in Canada resulting from escaped slaves settling there. There is plenty of content here.

### Buxton National Historic Site and Museum

www.ciaccess.com/~jdnewby

This site documents one of the few remaining Black settlements in Canada that dates back to the underground railroad.

### Ontario Black History Society Archive

collections.ic.gc.ca/obho

This website provides extensive historical information including biography, timelines, and other forms of historical documentation.

# Good books

Bennett, Lerone. (2000) *Forced into glory: Abraham Lincoln's white dream*. Chicago: Johnson Pub. Co.

DuBois, W. E. B. (1995) *Black reconstruction in America*. New York: Simon & Schuster.

Fast, Howard. (1995) *Freedom road*. Armonk, N.Y.: M. E. Sharpe.

Fields, Barbara Jeanne. (1985) *Slavery and freedom on the middle ground: Maryland during the nineteenth century*. New Haven: Yale University Press.

Foner, Eric. (2002) *Reconstruction: America's unfinished revolution, 1863–1877*. New York: Perennial Classics.

Painter, Nell Irvin. (1997) *Sojourner Truth: a life, a symbol*. New York: W. W. Norton.

Quarles, Benjamin. (1991) *Black abolitionists*. New York, N.Y.: Da Capo Press.

Tobin, Jacqueline, and Dobard, Raymond G. (2000) *Hidden in plain view: the secret story of quilts and the underground railroad*. New York, N.Y.: Anchor Books.

Turner, Nat. (1996) *The confessions of Nat Turner*. Boston: Bedford Books of St. Martin's Press.

Walker, Juliet E. K. (1983) *Free Frank: a Black pioneer on the antebellum frontier*. Lexington, Ky.: University Press of Kentucky.

# 6
# Rural Life

Black people thought the end of the slave system would bring freedom, but whilst they were no longer formally in slavery the 19th century freedom they got is not what they had hoped for. They ended slavery but got Jim Crow, not first-class but second-class citizenship. A good example of this concerns voting rights, as after the 15th Amendment giving the new citizens the right to vote many Southern states passed a grandfather clause which stated that only those people whose grandfather had voted prior to 1861 were eligible to vote. Black people were still forced to fight for democracy, as what they had was hardly democracy even on paper.

The Jim Crow system was a system to keep Black people as a source of labor without the democratic rights of liberal democracy. There were three basic features: peonage, lynching, and segregation. Before the Civil War slavery was based on a plantation form of agricultural production, gang labor in the cotton fields. After the war a system of tenancy evolved of much smaller land plots being used for production in which Black people were mainly working as sharecroppers. This meant that one worked the land based on being loaned the means for putting in and harvesting a crop while also taking care of oneself and family. In return one was bound to hand over a share of the crop as well as to pay off one's debts. The same owners controlled the land and the country stores so after trying to pay off one's share and debt for the year many found themselves still in arrears. The land owners had peonage laws passed which stated that if one was still in debt at the end of the year then by law one had to stay on the land and work until it was paid off. It is easy to see that this turned out to be slavery by another name.

This land tenancy was based on family labor, hence this form of political economy led to large families with strong ties. Economic survival demanded that this be so. In addition, the cultural life of the community was built around church life and the central role of the minister as spiritual and political leader. This gave the community a seven day rhythm, five days to work, one day for market and recreation, and one day for worship and community building at church.

Saturday became the day for play, and that's how Saturday night became associated with the Blues. This music was the secular alternative for cultural meaning. The blues songs about life became not only the national music of the African American people, and as such the foundation for all Black popular music from rhythm and blues to rap, but the framework and foundation for all popular culture.

## Black Families in the Alabama Black Belt

www.prairiebluff.com/blackbelt

This website is about six counties in central Alabama (Butler, Dallas, Lowndes, Marengo, Perry, and Wilcox). These are Black Belt counties that have had Black majorities and a high level of anti-Black sentiment and violence. This site provides an important background to the 1960s because the concept of Black Power and the image of the Black Panther emerged in an electoral struggle in Lowndes County in 1965 organized by SNCC, the Student Nonviolent Coordinating Committee. Further it is another example of building a website as an ongoing project, growing as people join in the process of contributing new information. It is a model for how every city and county or state might open a portal in cyberspace for broad community cooperation in compiling necessary and useful information for all to use.

There are several categories for information on a county by county basis, including: a county history, churches, cemeteries, online records, and a surname database. This site was established and is maintained by Brenda Smothers. She started this project to trace her family history, and has now expanded it to include the historical experiences of everyone in these six counties.

This site is one approach to reconstructing an unwritten history, as the people it concerns were without formal literacy. What they did have were their cultural practices and in those they were very literate, but it was an oral culture and not one based in writing. So it is important to gather information from the church, the cemetery, and from the formal documents (marriage licenses, wills, mortgages, etc.) that have survived. Of course there is also an oral history that could be added.

One of the best features of this site is a message board in which people can post their research and make requests of a growing research community. This bridging of campus and community, or professional and amateur researchers, is the wave of the future. The personal can become political when it is raised from the individual level to the community level. This site is an excellent example of how a genealogical project can become a tool for cyberorganizing.

## The Church in the Southern Black Community
Library of Congress
memory.loc.gov/ammem/award99/ncuhtml/csbchome.html
This website is a major collection of texts and images that document the African American church in the South. It is part of the larger program of research at the University of North Carolina that focuses on digitizing material to capture the Southern experience for access in cyberspace. They have focused this website "on how the Black community adapted evangelical Christianity, making it a metaphor for freedom, community, and personal survival."

This collection consists of two major databases. The first contains over 100 full text reproductions of major religious writings by African American clergy and church members. The second is a database of thousands of images of the leading people in the African American Southern church. It is possible to search the full collection by keyword, as well as to browse by subject. It is very instructive to read and look at the ideas and people who led the church in the 19th and early 20th centuries.

Included are the writings and images of some of the key activists in Black church history who fought for social justice, including Henry McNeil Turner, Anna J. Cooper, and Richard Allen. Also present are the three great works of historical scholarship that laid the foundation for the historical study of the Black church by W. E. B. DuBois (1903, 212 pages), Richard R. Wright (1916, 392 pages), and Carter G. Woodson (1921, 330 pages).

**Virtual Museum of Jim Crow Memorabilia**

Ferris State University

www.Ferris.edu/news/jimcrow/index.htm

This is an excellent site that documents all of the negative stereotypes and racist images of Black people. The purpose of this is to show the negative reality of racism as a basis for educating people to oppose all racist practices. This is an important site because many of these images get recycled and appear again and again in popular culture. People need to be knowledgeable about this history in order that such racist practices can be identified and opposed whenever and wherever they appear.

The main stereotypes that are documented are the following: the brute, the picaninny, Tom, Jezebel, Mammy, coon, the tragic mulatto, the golliwog. Each of these types is explained in clear and informative essays. There is a gallery of images to show the diversity of forms of making the same racist point.

David Pilgrim, Professor of Sociology at Ferris State University, is the author of this site. He states that five principles guided his work: racism is wrong, we have to fight against it, our understanding and action should be based on solid research, we are a community, and we must serve. The museum is really a teaching laboratory, but this website makes its message available to all of us.

**The Scottsboro Boys Trials 1931–37**

University of Missouri at Kansas City

www.law.umkc.edu/faculty/projects/FTrials/scottsboro/scottsb.htm

This website documents the famous trial of nine African American teenagers accused of rape on a train near Scottsboro, Alabama. From 1931 to 1937, and then all the way up to 1989, there were trials and other activities associated with this case. This is a comprehensive website covering all aspects of the case.

The main focus of this site is on the testimony of trials that took place in 1931, 1933, 1936, and 1937. Relevant Appellate Court decisions are also reproduced. This is high drama, reading the intensive questioning of poorly educated Black teenagers barely being kept out of reach of lynch mobs. Haywood Patterson was illiterate when arrested but in less than one year he was writing his own letters, some of which are included on this site. He was the most militant, and he escaped twice.

There is also information to place this trial in context. An introductory essay written by Douglas O. Linder gives a complete historical overview. Also included are a chronology, a map, biographies of all the key people, a gallery of images, and some letters. The site is maintained at the University of Missouri at Kansas City.

This case became a national campaign to save the youth from the death penalty. Mostly successful, the campaign also was a dramatic example of cooperation between Black leadership and the community party.

### Without Sanctuary

www.musarium.com/withoutsanctuary/index.html

This website is about a cultural ritual murder called lynching, a mob action practiced against people in the South, mainly African Americans. James Allen, an independent researcher/collector, is the author of this site. He describes his work as "proof, an unearthing of crimes, of collective mass murder, of mass memory graves excavated from the American conscience." This is a collection of commercially sold postcards with photographs of people being lynched. This barbaric practice will never again be forgotten.

The site provides a slide show with 81 images of different lynchings of men and women, some hung, some burned, some waiting to die and others being torn apart for souvenirs. There is also a ten minute film with narration by James Allen. He describes how his collection of these postcards got started and how it transformed his consciousness as a white Southerner having to face up to the legacy of racism.

When reading any fiction that mentions or deals with lynching in any way it would be useful to take a minute and get a visual reality check on what the real deal was like. The writer might use it as a metaphor linked with various meanings, but it exists as a social reality in the historical setting of sharecropping on cotton plantations. This website documents evil.

# General

**Booker T. Washington Papers Online**
www.historycooperative.org/btw/index.html
The University of Illinois Press is providing full text access to the collected works of Booker T. Washington. This is what should happen for every major Black thinker.

**Jump Jim Crow or What Difference did Emancipation Make?**
sunsite.berkeley.edu/calheritage/Jimcrow/
This site presents a full documentation of segregation including laws, images, songs, stories, curriculum guide, and a glossary of terms. It is maintained at the University of California at Berkeley.

**Remembering Jim Crow**
www.americanradioworks.org/features/remembering/index.html
This site has six basic sections, each with a set of documentary sound files and photographs that present segregation from Black and whites who lived through that period. Excellent material to make clear the evils of living under segregation.

**The Rise and Fall of Jim Crow**
www.pbs.org/wnet/jimcrow
Covering the years 1863–1954, this site is made up of small essays on people, events, and organizations representing both support for and opposition to the system of segregation.

**Uncle Remus**
xroads.virginia.edu/~UG97/remus/remus.html
Folklore animal tales that transformed African stories in New World contexts. Each tale has a critical guide to thinking about the moral and social lessons of this traditional knowledge.

## Violence against African Americans

**The African American Holocaust**
www.maafa.org/index.html
This site is a dramatic presentation of lynching photos with commentary in poetry and song.

**Internet Resources on the Tuskegee Syphilis Study**
www.dc.peachnet.edu/~shale/humanities/composition/assignments/exper
iment/tuskegee.html
A wide-ranging set of links on this government sponsored study in which African American males were denied treatment of penicillin and 100 people died. This rivals the Nazi experiments in the concentration camps.

**Scottsboro: An American Tragedy**
www.pbs.org/wgbh/amex/scottsboro
A detailed, navigable website that explains what happened and provides sources, background information, and a transcript from the film by the same name.

## Anti-racism struggle

**Radio Fights Jim Crow**
www.americanradioworks.org/features/jim_crow/index.html
This website presents excerpts from radio programs opposing segregation and advancing a positive image of Black people from 1938 to 1957. There are six programs and two slide shows on this site.

## Southern experience

**Through the Lens of Time: Images of the African American from the Cook Collection of Photographs**
www.library.vcu.edu/jbc/speccoll/cook
This collection contains nearly 300 photographs from all aspects of Black life in turn of the century central Virginia. One can search by keyword or browse by subject.

**Jackson Davis Collection of African American Educational Photographs**
www.lib.virginia.edu/speccol/collections/jdavis
This site provides the photographic archives of 6000 photographs by the State Agent for Negro Schools for the Virginia State Board of Education (1911–13).

**Nile of the New World (Mississippi Delta)**
www.cr.nps.gov/delta
This site details the political and cultural geography of the Mississippi River/Mississippi Delta with its legacy of cotton production through slavery and tenancy.

**The African American Experience, The Winedale Story (Texas)**
www.cah.utexas.edu/exhibits/WinedaleStory/green4.html
This site presents the experiences of African American ex-slaves in Texas. This site should be looked at with the sites on the Texas emancipation anniversary called Juneteenth (June 19th).

## Northern experience

**The African American Experience in Ohio: 1850–1920**
dbs.ohiohistory.org/africanam
This is a comprehensive digital database of manuscripts, newspapers, pamphlets, and photographs.

**Heroes in the Ships: Afro-Americans in the Whaling Industry**
www.whalingmuseum.org/kendall/heros/index_h.html
This site features Black mariners, including Paul Cuffe, from the 18th and 19th centuries.

**Art T. Burton's Western Frontier**
www.coax.net/people/LWF/ATB_WF.htm
The experience of the Black presence in the west has been ignored by popular culture, especially in movies. Burton is a good source to begin with to correct these omissions.

## Good Books

Daniel, Pete. (1990) *The shadow of slavery: peonage in the South, 1901–1969*. Urbana: University of Illinois Press.

Dray, Philip. (2002) *At the hands of persons unknown: the lynching of Black America*. New York: Random House.

Ginzburg, Ralph, ed. (1988) *100 years of lynchings*. Baltimore, Md.: Black Classic Press.

Haywood, Harry. (1976) *Negro liberation*. 2nd ed. Chicago: Liberator Press.

Johnson, Charles Spurgeon. (1996) *Shadow of the plantation*. New Brunswick, N.J.: Transaction Publishers.

Mandle, Jay R. (1978) *The roots of Black poverty: the Southern plantation economy after the Civil War*. Durham, N.C.: Duke University Press.

Shaw, Nate. (2000) *All God's dangers: the life of Nate Shaw*. Chicago: University of Chicago Press.

**BEST HISTORY SITES**

# 7
# Great Migrations

The Southern rural way of life was based on labor intensive agricultural production in the cotton fields – people picked and planted cotton with their bare hands. This was true during slavery and after. This did not end until the 1940s when a mechanical cotton-picking machine was invented which made it economically less profitable to harvest the cotton crop using Black field labor. At the same time there was a dramatic increase in the demand for labor in the Northern industries as both World Wars I and II took away white soldiers to fight. These two factors made up the push and pull factors that caused one of the great migrations of world history, the transformation of Black people from Black farmers to Black industrial workers.

As Black people migrated to the North to live in cities many things changed. In the complex, expanding cities literacy became increasingly necessary to live and to work. In the city there were various pressures to have some kinds of integration, at least in functional terms. One of the major features of this was the unionization of workers. When white workers tried to uphold segregation and keep Blacks out, management then used Blacks as scabs to cross picket lines and break the strike. Unions changed and brought Blacks in to protect their interests. Segregation in the military also proved to be awkward and cumbersome so Blacks were used in limited ways, but not excluded as this was deemed as important in subsequent wars as it had proven to be during the end of the Civil War.

Key patterns existed for the great migrations north. The journey from Mississippi to Chicago became the virtual aorta of the Black experience, along with paths that led from Alabama to Detroit, as well as up the coast from Florida and the Carolinas to Philadelphia and New York City. Not only families moved, but also entire communities. So many people from the same place relocated together that this meant transplanting community institutions as well. This is the background for familiar sayings to refer to the South as "down home," or the use of the region to create desire and appeal such as "Southern fried chicken" or "pit bar-b-q made like we used to do it down South."

### African American Mosaic

www.loc.gov/exhibits/african/afam008.html

This site is part of the African American Mosaic, a Library of Congress resource guide. It is a narrative with documents and photographs about the Great Migrations of African American people from the rural South to the industrial North. There are four pages, so take care when going through the site to proceed using the "next" button.

The first page gives a demographic overview of the population movement, presented as statistics and coded maps. The next page discusses the Western migration in general, while the third focuses in on Nicodemus, Kansas. The fourth page is about Chicago, one of the main destination points for living and working.

The Library of Congress is the official library of the United States and as such provides a wealth of information about all aspects of life and history of this country and around the world. This website is but one example of the great work being done there, and one would benefit from monitoring their efforts as new pages are surely to come soon that will be equally as good as this.

### North by South: A Kenyon College Humanities Project

For several years a humanities seminar at Kenyon College (Ohio), run by Professor Peter Rutkoff and William Scott, has worked on the issue of the migration of African Americans from the South to the North. Each year the seminar takes a Southern point of origin and links it to a Northern destination. They chose the following places: in 1998 Charleston and Harlem, in 1999 the Mississippi Delta and Chicago, in 2000 Birmingham and Pittsburgh, and in 2001 Charleston and the Mississippi Delta.

The websites for each of the above are a great example of the quality of work possible, even by undergraduates, in this period when all our knowledge is being reborn in a new medium. They use color and are quite playful in their presentation. They slide easily between text and image. The sights are engaging, and each hyperlink explodes with information in short, clear, easy to read essays. In this sense the sites are layered to meet the curiosity of young learners, answering lots of questions.

Each year the seminar participants were organized into five research teams. Each team had a specific theme for its research within the general framework of the same Southern and Northern places (see table).

*Table 1*

| 1998<br>Charleston to<br>Harlem | 1999<br>Mississippi Delta to<br>Chicago | 2000<br>Birmingham to<br>Pittsburgh | 2001<br>Charleston to<br>Mississippi Delta |
|---|---|---|---|
| Arts | Space | Style | Space |
| Music | Blues | Baseball | Music |
| Education | Family | Women | Education |
| Health care | Food | Newspapers | Food |
| Death rituals | Religion | Society | |

The following set of four sites is a wonderfully textured cornucopia of information on the dynamics of change and continuity in the African American migration from the South to the North.

### *1998*: Charleston to Harlem
northbysouth.kenyon.edu/1998
The first year was focused on the Charleston Low Country and Harlem, New York. An "African cosmogram" is used for design spacing of links. You can enter each of the five content areas via a Charleston or Harlem doorway. For each of the content areas you will find a narrative essay with graphics and plenty of links to provide biographical and other reference information.

We were delighted to find the careful attention to detail. One example of this is the way the site links Harlem to South Carolina, for example using Cat Anderson the trumpet player with Duke Ellington, William Johnson the artist, and the Mickey Funeral Home.

**Great Migrations**

### *1999*: Mississippi Delta to Chicago

northbysouth.kenyon. edu/1999

The 1999 seminar took what some consider the aorta of the Black migrations, the heart of the population concentration from Mississippi to Chicago. This year space was used as a theme for the content areas. The site's developers saw the key link as one of flight, "of flying home to Africa," and "stealing away" out of slavery. The migrations were a symbolic journey to freedom's land. This is especially clear when two specific places are linked, Mound Bayou Mississippi and Bronzeville on Chicago's South Side.

### *2000*: Birmingham to Pittsburgh

northbysouth.kenyon.edu/2000

This year the site focused on heavy industrial production and the mining of coal, and on the African American working people as part of the industrial working class. Again the now familiar style of the Kenyon seminar continues to layer the information with punctuations of graphic illustration, even sound files to draw you into the actual sensation of the real experience.

This year the newspapers are taken as the design theme. Each content area has a section with several layers of information. For example, the section on women has eleven sub-links of information.

### *2001*: Charleston to the Mississippi Delta

northbysouth.kenyon.edu/2002

This fourth year of the humanities seminar at Kenyon College focused on four areas: education, food, music, and space. It continued with a nuanced analysis of many aspects of popular culture.

### A Philip Randolph Pullman Porter Museum

aphiliprandolphmuseum.com

This is the website for a museum located in Chicago, Illinois. It is a representation of a union and its militant president. These men who rode the rails were the Black working class elite of the great migration. They moved from city to city and absorbed culture and consciousness up and down the line.

A. Philip Randolph was a great trade union leader with a socialist background. He led a fight against segregation and job discrimination in the 1940s and called a national march on Washington to force the government to open up jobs for African Americans. They threatened him and said he was unpatriotic, but he didn't back down even though it was at time of war. His heroic leadership led President Franklin D. Roosevelt to issue Executive Order 8802 that outlawed all race discrimination in federal employment – 80 years from the end of the Civil War! This fight made people realize that the war for democracy had to be fought inside the USA as well.

## General

**Migration and the American South: A Case Study**
oit.vgcc.cc.nc.us/his132/index.html
A good introduction to the general issues of migration, including some curriculum materials.

**Goin' to Chicago (PBS)**
www.pbs.org/gointochicago/index.html
This is a website designed to support a film produced by PBS. The website includes an essay by James Grossman as well as art and poetry by Langston Hughes and Jacob Lawrence.

**The Shifting Patterns of Black Migration 1965–2000**
www.ers.usda.gov/publications/rdrr93
This site is a thorough examination of recent migration patterns, including a return to the South.

## Violence

**The Last Wave from Port Chicago**
www.portchicago.org
Detailed accounts of a great explosion that killed a large number of African American sailors.

**The Port Chicago Disaster**
intergate.cccoe.k12.ca.us/pc
Good account of the disaster that accounted for 15% of all African American casualties in World War II.

**Tulsa Reparations Coalition**
www.tulsareparations.org
This site documents the terror of a genocidal attack against the Black community including using airplanes to bomb Black neighborhoods.

## Desegregation

**The Desegregation of the Armed Forces**
www.trumanlibrary.org/whistlestop/study_collections/desegregation/large/desegregation.htm
This site provides a full archive of documents on the transformation of the armed forces during the great migration years of World War II.

**The USS *Mason* and Her Crew**
www.ussmason.org
The story of the only all-African American naval crew to go into battle in World War II.

## Good books

Adero, Malaika, ed. (1993) *Up South: stories, studies, and letters of this century's Black migrations*. New York: New Press.

Bontemps, Arna Wendell, and Conroy, Jack. (1997) *Anyplace but here*. Columbia: University of Missouri Press.

Grossman, James R. (1989) *Land of hope: Chicago, Black Southerners, and the great migration*. Chicago: University of Chicago Press.

Haskins, James. (1999) *The geography of hope: the black exodus from the South after Reconstruction*. Brookfield, Conn.: Twenty First Century Books.

Isserman, Maurice. (1997) *Journey to freedom: the African-American great migration*. New York: Facts on File.

Lemann, Nicholas. (1992) *The promised land: the great Black migration and how it changed America*. New York: Vintage Books.

Painter, Nell Irvin. (1992) *Exodusters: Black migration to Kansas after Reconstruction*. New York: Norton.

Stack, Carol B. (1996) *Call to home: African Americans reclaim the rural South*. New York: BasicBooks.

Trotter, Joe William, ed. (1991) *The great migration in historical perspective: new dimensions of race, class, and gender*. Bloomington: Indiana University Press.

Woodson, Carter Godwin. (1970) *A century of Negro migration*. New York: AMS Press.

# 8
# Urban Life

James Boggs wrote a very provocative essay titled "The City is the Black Man's Land." He was from a small town down South but had mostly worked as an auto worker in Detroit, so he knew first hand that after the great migrations Black people became more urban than the entire population. The city was a new and different place for Black people. They were transformed from being sharecroppers in the cotton fields to being workers in the industrial cities.

The Harlem Renaissance was the cultural launch of this new stage of African American history, an explosion of cultural production and the emergence of a "New Negro." The deep feelings of the Black community, long held inside to avoid the sting of the lynch rope, now exploded. Booker T. Washington maintained the tactical Southern position that Blacks and whites could work together in the economy like a hand yet remain separate in social and political matters like fingers. This was quite distinct from W. E. B. DuBois and Marcus Garvey who agitated for equality and mass organization of the Black community. When the lynch mob struck in the South, African American militants marched in open protest in the Northern cities.

The full development of the African American urban experience took place after World War II. The war babies were the first generation of African Americans that were majority born in the cities. By the 1960s this generation had grown up and launched their own cultural revolution. The modern Civil Rights Movement had its first impulse just before World War I with the founding of such organizations as the NAACP (1909) and the National Urban League (1911). The second major leap was after World War II with several new organizations: CORE (1942), SCLC (1957), and SNCC (1960). By the 1960s the mass mobilization of

Southern protests ignited the North. The Civil Rights Movement was joined by a new Black Liberation Movement.

The two main icons of these two wings of protest are Martin Luther King and Malcolm X. King was the embodiment of what DuBois was calling for in his "Talented Tenth" argument, a middle class preacher who dedicated his life to serving his community. Malcolm X was a return to the politics of Nat Turner and David Walker, uncompromising counter-attack against racism is all its forms calling for Black people to fight back with whatever weapons were being used against them. This became the dual approach of non-violent resistance as an offense, and violence as self-defense. In fact, while these two options were debated in public, the activists in the North and South practiced both. Most Civil Rights leaders in the South slept with shotguns by their front doors.

### Hartford Black History Project
www.hartford-hwp.com/HBHP/exhibit

This is a documentary history of a Connecticut city from 1638 to the present time. There is an online text organized in six categories (the last one not yet finished). This is very interesting as it puts the history of this city in the context of times when the urban experience was not nearly the modal experience for the majority of people. It is especially useful in discussing the periods 1819 to 1863 and 1863 to 1890 as the first development of classes within the Black community. This embraces the great tradition of scholarship by E. Franklin Frazier, Charles Johnson, Horace Mann Bond, and Abram Harris.

There is also a database of images organized in 14 categories. This is a clear documentation of how life looked then and it helps locate the experience relative to one's own community and generational experience.

### Portrait of Black Chicago
The National Archives
www.archives.gov/exhibit_hall/portrait_of_black_chicago/introduction.html

This website contains the photographs of John H. White, then a 28-year-old African American photographer for the *Chicago Daily News*. He worked on a government project to document city life in Chicago from

1973 to 1974. Twenty photographs and commentary by White make up the content.

This is a useful site because it draws attention to a movement out of the Black arts movement of the 1960s called "Chicago street photography." This school placed its focus on the candid photo in which the cultural act is frozen in time, in which the consciousness within is captured in a look. A shot needed to open a door to what was within the shot but not on the surface. You have to decode what you see and capture its meaning. The OBAC photographers led the way: Billy Abernathy, Robert Sengstacke, Roy Lewis, Onequa, Johnny Simmons, and more.

**The Daily Aesthetic**
University of Kentucky
www.uky.edu/Projects/TDA/welcome-tda.html
This site is about "leisure and recreation in a Southern city's segregated park system." The documentation is of Douglas Park located in Lexington, Kentucky as part of the segregated park system. The activities of this park and associated institutions reveals what urban social and cultural community life was like in the segregated South from the 1920s until the mid 1950s.

There are short essays, photographs, and interviews with people showing and explaining how the community lived its life. In other words, given segregation in the urban South, and the "racial rules" that defined the contact between whites and Blacks, this site opens up the social life of the Black community. Douglas Park included the Charles Young Community Center where major events took place. This was a place that hosted basketball tournaments and formal dances, dinners and meetings of all kinds.

One of the most interesting things about this site is the interplay between text, image, and voice. This is a site that is gentle in letting the Black community tell the story its way, revealing how people adapt and make life worth living even under the conditions of racist discrimination and economic hardship. The photographs reveal the dignity of a people who maintained their beauty and integrity even under the Jim Crow system.

This site is maintained at the University of Kentucky.

**African American History of Cleveland** (Encyclopedia of Cleveland History)

ech.cwru.edu/ech-cgi/search.pl?subject=AFRICAN%20AMERICAN%20HISTORY

This page is a set of links to small essays about the history of Black people in the city of Cleveland. It is a comprehensive set of topics that provides a detailed composite picture of the city. This site is maintained by the History Department at Case Western Reserve University as part of the Encyclopedia of Cleveland History and the Dictionary of Cleveland Biography.

The strength is that there are nearly 250 links to short, hyperlinked essays about the Black experience in Cleveland. The weakness is that there is little topical organization so you have to dive into the material and use the hyperlinks to guide you deeper into the vast amount of information that seems to be here. Our advice is to dig and you will be rewarded.

There are silences however, as the militant nationalist and Black trade unionist traditions don't seem to be covered to the extent that other topics are. For example, there is an essay on the visits of Martin Luther King to Cleveland, but not Malcolm X even though he gave some of his most powerful speeches there.

**African American Community**

Public Library of Charlotte and Mecklenburg County

www.cmstory.org/african/default.asp

This website documents the city of Charlotte and county of Mecklenburg. The site is based on a collection of photographs that are organized into five topical collections: home and family life, education, work, religion, and community life.

**Harlem 1900–1940**

www.si.umich.edu/CHICO/Harlem

This site is a digital exhibition from the Schomburg Center for Research in Black Culture and the School of Information at the University of Michigan. It is the online version of an exhibit and publication.

This is an important site because these years include what is now called the Harlem Renaissance. At this time there was an explosion of artistic and intellectual creativity that impacted the cultural life in every Black community. Most of the key people are featured in this site. Elsewhere in this book there are links to people who first gained fame in the Harlem Renaissance.

This site represents a positive example of cooperation between a public library and a university, in content and form. This is a model that can be repeated in every city.

# Cities

### Home to Harlem
www.hometoharlem.com/Harlem/hthadmin.nsf/harlem/homepage
This is a comprehensive portal to the cultural and commercial life of Harlem, including historical information, maps, and other reference material.

### Virtual Harlem
www.evl.uic.edu/cavern/harlem
This site presents a reconstruction of Harlem as a virtual environment for teaching about the Harlem Renaissance. This project is being led by Bryan Carter.

### The Black Renaissance in Washington DC 1920–1930
www.dclibrary.org/blkren
This site documents artistic creativity and social movement in the city of Washington D.C.

### Boston
www.nps.gov/boaf/home.htm
Extensive documentation of Black Boston including an interactive map of historical places.

### Princeton, New Jersey
princetonhistory.org/aalife/index.html

General site on the Black experience in this campus based community including a timeline and photographs.

**Duke Ellington's Washington**
www.pbs.org/ellingtonsdc
This site documents the places and the times of Ellington in his home town of Washington D.C.

**Black Baltimore in Transition 1840–1920**
www.mdarchives.state.md.us/msa/stagser/s1259/121/6050/html/1000.html
This site has six categories of information about Baltimore and includes pictures and text.

**Champaign County, Illinois (Black History Committee)**
www.prairienet.org/years
This website is a compilation of material covering the Black experience in this university based town. The site is hosted by PrairieNet, a community network supported by the University of Illinois Graduate School of Library and Information Science.

**Great Day in Harlem**
www.harlem.org/greatday.html
This site documents a gathering in Harlem of almost all the great jazz artists in 1958. The site includes links and documentation for all of the musicians.

## Civil rights

**Rosa Parks**
www.rosaparksinstitute.org
Basic information about the life of this civil rights fighter from Montgomery, Alabama to Detroit, Michigan.

**SNCC 1960–1966**
www.ibiblio.org/sncc/index.html

Good historical site on SNCC with short essays on events and people, include online interviews.

**Ordinary People Living Extraordinary Lives**
www-dept.usm.edu/~mcrohb/html/cd/intro.htm
An excellent and moving portrayal of the Mississippi movement that contrasts the views of Southerners and Northerners.

**Greensboro Sit Ins**
www.sitins.com
This site provides an excellent documentation of the first major sit-ins that started a national movement on February 1, 1960 in Greensboro, North Carolina.

**Powerful Days in Black and White**
www.kodak.com/US/en/corp/features/moore/mooreIndex.shtml
Dramatic photographs by a white Southern photographer who captured some of the best candid shots of the diverse experience of being in the Southern freedom movement.

**Photos by Jo Freeman**
www.jofreeman.com
This site contains a collection of photographs and political campaign buttons that come from the freedom movement in the South.

**Civil Rights Movement Veterans**
www.crmvet.org
This site reflects a continuing network of people who worked in the Civil Rights Movement, who continue to document it and carry on their social justice work on new battlefronts today.

**National Civil Rights Museum**
www.civilrightsmuseum.org
Comprehensive site that represents the online collection of this national museum located in Memphis, Tennessee.

**We Shall Overcome: Historic Places of the Civil Rights Movement**
www.cr.nps.gov/nr/travel/civilrights
This site has been developed by the National Park Service to locate significant places in the civil rights history as a list by states and as an interactive map of states.

**Paul Robeson on the Web**
www.princeton.lib.nj.us/robeson/links.html
A comprehensive site containing links to all aspects of his life, from art to politics.

## Good books

Cha-Jua, Sundiata Keita. (2000) *America's first Black town: Brooklyn, Illinois, 1830–1915*. Urbana: University of Illinois Press.

Drake, St. Clair, and Cayton, Horace. (1993) *Black metropolis: a study of Negro life in a Northern city*. Chicago: University of Chicago Press.

DuBois, W. E. B. (1996) *The Philadelphia Negro: a social study*. Philadelphia: University of Pennsylvania Press.

Horne, Gerald. (1995) *Fire this time: the Watts Uprising and the 1960s*. Charlottesville: University Press of Virginia.

Johnson, James Weldon. (1991) *Black Manhattan*. New York, N.Y.: Da Capo Press.

Lewis, David L. (1997) *When Harlem was in vogue*. New York: Penguin Books.

Rich, Wilbur C. (1989) *Coleman Young and Detroit politics: from social activist to power broker*. Detroit: Wayne State University Press.

Wilder, Craig Steven. (2000) *A covenant with color: race and social power in Brooklyn*. New York: Columbia University Press.

Wright, Richard. (1998) *Native son*. New York: HarperPerennial.

# 9
# De-industrialization Crisis

The end of the urban experience for Black people began at the very beginning. Jobs began to leave the cities as Blacks arrived. By the 1960s the Black community was finding some measure of success in getting more equality in jobs and education than ever before, and yet by the 1970s a deep reversal of social motion began to take place. The old saying about Blacks was "last hired and first fired." Now people began to speak of structural unemployment, permanent unemployment, and speculation of a new disadvantaged class, an "underclass," became the focus of policy discourse. Industrial production moved out of the inner city and left many African American workers behind. A social welfare state was created after the Great Depression as the New Deal under President Franklin D. Roosevelt. This broke down as people at the margins became homeless, worked but were often still below the poverty line, and families were torn apart by divorce, children were born out of wedlock, and the average age of motherhood dipped into the teens.

This process produced forms of radicalism as well as anti-social behavior. The radicalism included such organizations as the Black Panther Party, the League for Revolutionary Black Workers, and the National Welfare Rights Union. The anti-social forms were criminal and destructive in the inner city community, and usually called gangs. However, in the mainstream this process also led to the greatest gains in electoral politics. As the cities became fiscally unmanageable and the police were being used more and more as tools of social control, Black mayors were elected to manage the crisis. This took place in the heart of de-industrialization: Gary (Indiana) and Cleveland (Ohio) were the earliest.

At the heart of this process was the transformation of the economy based on new technologies resulting from the application of expanded capacity of computers. The reorganization of the economy meant that unskilled labor was becoming redundant or such jobs were being relocated to other, cheaper labor markets in far away places. For example, jobs went south to Mexico or Mexican workers came to the USA to work at low pay in substandard conditions as undocumented workers. Black people had been brought to the Americas to work, first as slaves, then share-croppers, and finally as wage-workers. Now, the need for their labor was in decline and the quality of life in the Black community was polarized and one section rapidly degenerated. This is the social context for the new drug crisis of crack cocaine, and the devastating impact of HIV.

## Black Panther Party

www.lib.berkeley.edu/MRC/pacificapanthers.html

This website documents the militant Black social protest that emerged after the civil rights movements in the 1960s. The material presented here has been pulled together by the University of California at Berkeley and Pacifica Radio and organized as part of the Social Activism Sound Recording Project. We include this material here because the Black Panther Party emerged out of the Northern urban ghettoes precisely at the time when the society was beginning to experience massive de-indus-trialization and a reorganization of the social policies governing the Black community and large sections of labor.

This site is structured around a chronology from 1960 to 2002. Linking all of the dates together is a chronology narrative, as well as links to text, sound files, and video. The general outline follows key events like the origin of the Black Panther Party, the Free Huey Movement, the trial of the Chicago eight, the Attica struggle, the funeral of Huey Newton, and COINTELPRO activity.

These files include the following people: George Jackson, Huey Newton, Bobby Seale, H. Rap Brown, Stokley Carmichael, Eldridge Cleaver, Kathleen Cleaver, and Angela Davis. There are also files from organizations and key events.

Some of this material is quite remarkable. There is nearly an hour-long interview with George Jackson. He was killed in prison for allegedly hiding a large handgun in his Afro hairstyle while in prison. This interview is evidence of why some people rank him alongside Malcolm X.

**National Law Center on Homelessness and Poverty**

www.nlchp.org

This site is part of an advocacy research program. The site states its intention: "Our mission is to alleviate, ameliorate and end homelessness by serving as the legal arm of the nationwide movement to end homelessness." The site covers four areas of community life: housing, income, education, and civil rights. There are some free downloadable reports.

In 2001 the US Department of Housing and Development (HUD) indicated that 4.9 million people pay more than 50% of their income for rent while they should pay no more than 30% to have secure economic lives. These people are not yet homeless but might well be one or two paychecks away from facing that possibility. The crisis people face involves having access to food, clothing, housing, and health care. Homelessness is really the summation of the worst of all conditions, and it remains an invisible issue in today's policy debates. The homeless face voicelessness and this website is a good contribution to bringing more visibility to the issue. The major shortcoming is that you don't find the voice of the homeless here, you find the data produced by and for social service agencies.

There is a list of press releases that gives something of a current events update.

**The Fabulous Ruins of Detroit**

www.detroityes.com/home.htm

This website is a labor of love by its creator Lowell Forest Boileau. It is a visual feast that turns the de-industrialization and destruction of Detroit neighborhoods and factories into art and social commentary. He states that the Detroit ruins should be thought of along with the great ruins of the world. He presents photo documentation of historic ruins in Zimbabwe, Greece, and Mexico. "Now, as for centuries, tourists behold those ruins with awe and wonder. Yet today, a vast and history laden ruin site passes unvoiced, even despised, into oblivion."

This site presents clear and vivid images of this great automobile city. The basic organization is in sets of annotated slides, including industrial ruins, downtown ruins, and neighborhood ruins. There are also slides about how some rebuilding is going on in Detroit as well. There is a set of interactive maps that enables one to access the annotated slides based on individual choice.

He sees beauty in what the people of Detroit have done. He sees abandoned cars all painted up as well as the walls of closed factories. He calls these the cave painting of Detroit. Tyree Guyton on Heidelberg Street created the most dramatic and historically significant aspect of the art in the ruins of Detroit. He collected everything that people threw away and with paint covered all aspects of a street. There were bikes in trees, gym shoes walking down the street (glued in place) with no people. Painted hub caps were used to provide a skin for houses and trees. He created this in the early 1980s and even though it drew global attention to Detroit the politicians tore it down by 1999. This art had shamed the corporate leadership of Detroit and they brought it to an end.

## GangResearch.Net
University of Illinois at Chicago
www.gangresearch.net

This website documents the organization of unemployed youth into street gangs. The author is John Hagedorn, Professor of Criminal Justice, Great Cities Institute at the University of Illinois-Chicago.

The main focus is on Chicago gangs, but there is much more to this site than that. The context is set in a series of links in the side bar from great social analysts of Chicago: Robert Park, Jane Adams, and more generally Jacob Riis. There is a very dramatic map of the racial make-up of Chicago neighborhoods. The animated version shows this map over time for each census from 1910 to 2000. In this context there is extensive information on three main gangs in Chicago: Blackstone Rangers (renamed as the El Rukins), the Vice Lords, and the Latin Kings.

This site includes interviews with key Black historians of the Chicago scene: Euseni Perkins, Tim Black, and Harold Washington (the first Black mayor of Chicago).

In addition to Chicago there is a special section on gangs in Milwaukee, and on gangs and globalization. The globalization section is important as it puts the local gang problem in the context of world economic and political dynamics.

**Kensington Welfare Rights Union**

www.kwru.org

This is a website run by and for people who are facing and fighting the social crisis of homelessness and the collapse of the welfare system in post-industrial America. Here you can hear the voices of the victims of poverty who have not been demobilized but are fighting back. The message here is that homelessness is not helplessness.

The site is jammed with information. There are lots of video and audio files of the KWRU activities. Much of the context for the work of KWRU is based on the UN document the Universal Declaration of Human Rights. On this basis they launched their "Poor Peoples Economic Human Rights Campaign." They have demonstrated in Philadelphia, their home base, but also they have organized a Freedom Bus Tour during which welfare activists travel to various cities to build alliances with local groups.

To support this they have developed an educational program they call the University of the Poor. They sponsor classes and conferences, as well as make their strategy documents available on this site.

## Racism

**Racial Profiling** (ACLU)

www.aclu.org/RacialEquality/RacialEqualitylist.cfm?c=133

Reports of racism cases taken by the ACLU. It is good on racial profiling, e.g., cases involving the claim of being arrested solely because one is Black.

**World Conference Against Racism**

www.un.org/WCAR

This is the official website of the world conference held in Durban, South Africa in 2001.

**Racism Watch Desk**

www.fair.org/racism-desk/index.html

This site is focused on racism in the media. FAIR (Fairness and Accuracy in Reporting) is the sponsor of this site.

## Violence

**National Archive of Criminal Justice Data**
www.icpsr.umich.edu/NACJD
This site is an archive of crime data. It can be used to study the drug crisis and its social implications.

**Violence in the City** (1965 Watts Rebellion)
www.usc.edu/isd/archives/cityinstress/mccone
This is the full report of the California's Commission of the Watts Rebellion.

**Street Gangs in Los Angeles**
www.streetgangs.com
This site documents gangs in Los Angeles, especially the Bloods and the Crips. There is also a special page on Tupac Shakur (1971–1996).

## Health

**Black AIDS**
www.blackaids.org
Good general site for information about AIDS in the African American community.

**African American Health** (National Institutes of Health)
www.nlm.nih.gov/medlineplus/africanamericanhealth.html
Good government site on the health crisis facing the African American community.

## Good books

Abu-Jamal, Mumia. (1996) *Live from death row*. New York: Avon Books.
Alkalimat, Abdul, Gills, Doug, and Williams, Kate, eds. (1995) *Job?Tech: the technological revolution and its impact on society: proceedings*

*of the Midwest Conference on Technology, Employment and Community*. Chicago, Ill.: Twenty First Century Books and Publications.

Casanova, Ronald. (1996) *Each one teach one: up and out of poverty: memoirs of a street activist*. Willimantic, Conn: Curbstone Press.

Cone, James H. (1992) *Martin & Malcolm & America: a dream or a nightmare*. Maryknoll, N.Y.: Orbis Books.

Peery, Nelson. (1993) *Entering an epoch of social revolution*. Chicago: Workers Press.

Ranney, David C. (2003) *Global decisions, local collisions: urban life in the new world order*. Philadelphia: Temple University Press.

Sales, William W. (1994) *From civil rights to Black liberation: Malcolm X and the Organization of Afro-American Unity*. Boston, Mass.: South End Press.

Wilson, William J. (1990) *The truly disadvantaged: the inner city, the underclass, and public policy*. Chicago: University of Chicago Press.

Zucchino, David. (1997) *Myth of the welfare queen: a Pulitzer prize-winning journalist's portrait of women on the line*. New York: Scribner.

# 10
# Information Society

The end of the industrial system marks the beginning of a new stage of society. The new society is based upon the expanded use of computers and information technologies in the reorganization of social life. This is a period of great change and dynamic social motion. But not everyone is a beneficiary of upgrades in the quality of their social lives. At the birth of this new society the old inequalities are being born anew as some people connect with the new technology and others are isolated in a "digital divide." African Americans are disproportionately on the disconnected side.

People in the USA use computers in three contexts. African Americans are behind in the use of computers at home and at work, but are more on an equal par in using public access computers at school, in the library, and the community technology center. There is general equality for African Americans when their household income is over $100,000. For most Black people access to computers and the Internet is a function of public policy and community activism. There is special importance for organizations like the Community Technology Centers Network (CTCNet), Black Data Processing Associates (BDPA), and National Society of Black Engineers (NSBE).

This book is a good example of the most important aspect of the digital divide, the extent to which people not only use computers and access the Internet, but the extent to which they are able to upload new content and determine what is in cyberspace for everyone to use. For many people in the African American community, as with all others, the World Wide Web is merely another way to access the content created by others, mainly the corporate sector. The critical entry into the information society is when individuals and groups are able to upload their own information. There is a big difference between getting online to visit the NBA and uploading information about your own high school basketball team.

The sites in this book are about the Black experience, and many of them have been created with the participation of the Black community. This is the way of the future. Hopefully this guide will inspire you and others to grab this technology and make it do what you want, what you need.

### H-Afro-Am

www2.h-net.msu.edu/~afro-am

This is the main discussion list for people interested in debating the Black experience via an online discussion process. As part of H-Net it is mainly a list of students and teachers, but many others are also involved. This includes parents, librarians, journalists, writers, and public policy advocates of all kinds. The list is for information purposes and for discourse, often discussing research issues that have arisen from general interest in the field.

One of the very useful aspects of this list is that on the website it is possible to examine the entire archive of email messages that have been distributed since the list began in January 1998. This is a unique resource in the field in that every discussion on the list becomes a permanent resource. This is a new development such that the graduate students of this generation will several years later speak directly to their successors as their voices have been archived and are merely a click away from interested people who come along. Further, this search function can easily extend to all H-Net lists, an archive with well over one million messages from serious people covering most issues in the humanities and social sciences.

**Community Connector** (School of Information, University of Michigan)
www.si.umich.edu/Community

This site has been created and maintained by the School of Information at the University of Michigan. "The mission of the UM-SI Community Connector is to support community-serving organizations, funders, academics, and students who are using technology to enhance geographic communities." This is one of the best sites to access what is happening at the community level to overcome the digital divide and empower communities with information technology.

The site is organized around four sections that focus on how technology impacts communities, how to connect with others active with community level technology programs, tools and ideas for the practitioner, and other research tools. There is an index that gives a very good listing of topics so community level activists can easily find what they need. This includes a database of articles and reports.

There are many community networks around, and this site is a good guide to them. The national hub is CTCNet, and important local networks can be found in Seattle, Washington; Austin, Texas, and Toledo, Ohio.

**AfroFuturism**
www.afrofuturism.net
This site reflects an attempt to nurture a school of thought or a tendency to reflect on and attempt to create the future culture using technology. The site is run by academics Alondra Nelson (Yale) and Kali Tal (Arizona). Their mission is to "explore futurist themes in Black cultural production and the ways in which technology innovation is changing the face of Black art and culture."

The site is organized by art forms (music, film, and literature) and an archive in which they list all of the people they consider part of this tendency, including hyperlinks to sites with related information. Nelson has edited a special issue of *Social Text* that focuses on AfroFuturism with articles by Ron Eglash, Anna Everett, Tana Hargest, Nalo Hopkinson, Alondra Nelson, Tracie Morris, Kali Tal, Fatimah Tuggar, and Alexander G. Weheliye.

**NSBE** (National Society of Black Engineers)
www.nsbe.org/index.html
This organization has the distinction of being the main membership organization for students preparing for professional careers in all aspects of information technology in college and graduate school. This organization has 300 chapters and plays a vital role in mentoring and networking for graduate school and a professional career. Their annual convention is a trade show for Blacks in information technology.

This website is useful for finding a job as it has a digital job information service designed to match a company with qualified African American candidates. Representatives from prospective employers will also get a great deal from this site. This is also true for graduate education. Every administrative team of academic units dealing with engineering and computer science will find this website of great use.

The organization has a community oriented program called TORCH, Technical Outreach Community Help. The main goal is to assist in overcoming the digital divide for low-income inner city Black communities. There are four focus areas: access, skills, values, and content. The NSBE helps to establish and maintain community technology centers.

**BDPA** (Black Data Processing Associates)
www.bdpa.org
This organization was formed in 1975 and has 40 chapters. By its name it is perhaps easy to see that this organization got going early in the information revolution. Its main focus is getting professionals to volunteer and give a helping hand to inner city youth to develop skill and interest in information technology.

There are chapters that prepare their members to compete at the state, regional, and national levels. High school and middle school youth learn very complex software, from building interactive databases to animation on websites. The organization maintains several listserv discussions to keep everyone informed about current developments on community and minority oriented issues. The BDPA is often a vital link between a school system and the local community, linking the school based computer lab with the local library and the local community technology centers.

## Blacks in science

**African American Astronauts**
www.5x5media.com/bhp/pages/astro.shtml
This is a directory of all Blacks who rose through the scientific and military ranks to get into the astronaut program run by NASA.

**Mathematicians in the African Diaspora**
www.math.buffalo.edu/mad
This is a remarkable site about the intellectual history of Black people in math.

**African Americans in the Sciences**
www.princeton.edu/~mcbrown/display/faces.html
This is a mega site giving information about Blacks in all science fields, including biology, physics, chemistry, biochemistry, engineers, geneticists, entomologists, and inventors. There is a special page on Black women in the sciences.

**Philip Emeagwali**
www.emeagwali.com
Personal home page for the Nigerian scientist playing a leading role in the capacity both of computers to compute and of the community to develop students interested in technical careers.

**Black Engineer.com**
www.blackengineer.com/index.shtml
This is a professional site about opportunities for Black engineers.

**Minorities in Engineering and Science**
was.nd.edu/gem/gemwebapp/gem_00_000.htm
This is an organization dedicated to recruiting people of color to graduate programs in engineering and other areas of science.

## Digital divide

**Digital Divide** (PBS)
www.pbs.org/digitaldivide
This is a very useful site that supported a PBS program. Lots of good links, and easy to use design.

**The Digital Divide Network**
www.digitaldividenetwork.org

This is the main general site on the digital divide, including access to its listserv, a must for people interested in the digital divide.

**Closing the Digital Divide** (Tony Brown)
www.tonybrownsites.com/tonybrown
Tony Brown set this site up to promote his work to overcome the digital divide for the Black community.

## Community technology

**Community Technology Centers Network**
www.ctcnet.org
The main national organization for community technology centers.

**Free Software Foundation**
www.fsf.org
This foundation practices the kind of free circulation of knowledge that will greatly benefit the Black community.

**Technology Access Foundation**
www.techaccess.org
This is about a foundation dedicated to supporting technology education for youth in minority communities.

**Playing2Win**
www.playing2win.org
This is the oldest community technology center in a Black community. Antonia Stone established Playing2Win in Harlem in 1980.

**W. J. Murchison Community Center**
www.murchisoncenter.org
This is about one of the leading CTCs in a Black community in the Midwest.

# Academics

### Race/Ethnicity Studies in Science and Technology
www.rpi.edu/~eglash/eglash.dir/ethnic.htm
This page links to the papers of Ron Eglash, a major scholar on the role of culture and math, especially the use of mathematical fractals in African culture.

### The Institute for African American E Culture
www.iaaec.com
This is a research consortium based in the Boston area seeking to encourage research and community development based on the use of information technology.

### Howard University, College of Engineering, Architecture, and Computer Science
www.founders.howard.edu/CEACS
This is the major engineering college at a historically Black campus.

### BRAIN
www.murchisoncenter.org/acrl
This site describes a research program using information technology in the field of Africana Studies.

### African American Studies and Librarianship
www.lsoft.com/scripts/wl.exe?SL1=AFAS-L&H=LISTSERV.KENT.EDU
One of the most active professional groups on the web focused on librarians but of great use for people in all areas of education.

# Good books

Barber, John T., and Tait, Alice, eds. (2001) *The information society and the Black community*. Westport, Conn.: Praeger.
Battle, Stafford L., and Harris, Rey O. (1996) *The African American resource guide to the Internet*. New York: McGraw-Hill.

Ebo, Bosah. (1998) *Cyberghetto or cybertopia: race, class and gender on the Internet*. Westport, Conn.: Praeger.

Eglash, Ron. (1999) *African fractals: modern computing and indigenous design*. New Brunswick, N.J.: Rutgers University Press.

Green, Venus. (2001) *Race on the line: gender, labor and technology in the Bell System, 1880–1980*. Durham, N.C.: Duke University Press.

Jenkins, Timothy, and Om-Ra-Seti, Khafra. (1997) *Black futurists in the information age: visions of a twenty-first century technological renaissance*. San Francisco: KMT Publications.

Jenning, James, ed. "The Information Superhighway and Communities of Color," Special Issue Fall 1995/Winter 1996, *The Trotter Review*, published by the William Monroe Trotter Institute, University of Massachusetts, Boston.

Kolko, Beth E., Nakamura, Lisa, and Rodman, Gilbert B., eds. (2000) *Race in cyberspace*. New York: Routledge.

Mack, Raneta Lawson. (2001) *The digital divide: standing at the intersection of race and technology*. Durham, N.C.: Carolina Academic Press.

Nakamura, Lisa. (2002) *Cybertypes: race, ethnicity, and identity on the Internet*. New York: Routledge.

Nelson, Alondra, and Tu, Thuy Linh N., with Hines Alicia Headlam, eds. (2001) *Technicolor: race, technology, and everyday life*. New York: New York University Press.

# PART TWO
# Guide to the Best Society and Culture Sites

## W. J. Murchison Community Center

Two UT students in the center with produce from the Murchison Community Garden, Lawrence and Fernwood.

1616 Lawrence Toledo, Ohio
242-3466
WJMCC@murch.org
map to the center
our supporters
board and staff
community math academy
editors
NEW! First Saturday
garden
manual
mission
photo album
poetry and song
sosdigitaldivide
tedweb
NEW! donate online
eGroups
google
yahoo
yahooligans
Yes 2 Math, Knowledge is Power!

# Overview

Part One of this guide, on history, dealt for the most part with the 19th and 20th century experiences of African Americans. Part Two is focused on the contemporary situation and details websites that will provide information that directly pertains to everyday life. This is critical because the Internet and the World Wide Web are providing direct assistance to people in real time. When you want information you can get it if it is on the web. This section makes it clear that there is plenty of content about Black people and for Black people on the web. There needs to be more, but there's a lot here already.

We have organized this guide to websites about Black culture and society in 20 topics. Of course this does not cover everything, but as one can see we provide a comprehensive approach to starting you off on your exploration of cyberspace.

The web is alive and part of it is born and part of it dies every hour. As you use this guide make a habit of using your web browser to save all of the sites you visit that have the kind of information you really do use. Share these with a friend. In fact it would be a good idea to share these sites on a weekly or at least monthly basis with friends and family, and hopefully they will get the message and share their findings with you. We can all help each other. It is in this spirit that we have prepared this guide for you. We hope it will help you find what you need, and encourage you to share what you know.

# 11
# Family and Heritage

In 1976, Alex Haley's novel, *Roots* and the subsequent CBS mini-series in 1977 was a powerful story, tracing Haley's lineage back to the days of slavery. Both the book and the enormously successful mini-series initiated a surge of interest in genealogy and African American history. African Americans face a unique set of challenges when it comes to collecting family histories, because of slavery. These challenges include gaining access to primary resources such as manumission papers, plantation records, and church documents. Although a majority of primary resources will always reside in court houses, archives, and historical societies, the digitization of this information has made it accessible to everyone if it has been posted on a web page.

One way in which Americans have embraced and celebrated African American heritage is through several holidays and observances. Important examples include Black History Month, Kwanzaa, Martin Luther King Jr. Day, and Juneteenth.

Juneteenth emerged as the result of the Emancipation Proclamation. On January 1, 1863, US President Abraham Lincoln declared free all slaves residing in territories in rebellion against the federal government. This Emancipation Proclamation actually freed few people. It did not apply to slaves residing in slave states; nor did it affect slaves in Southern areas already under Union control. Naturally, the states in rebellion did not act on Lincoln's order. In Texas, Union General Gordon Granger did not proclaim the slaves of Texas free until June 19, 1865. This day has become known as Juneteenth and has become an occasion for commemoration by African Americans in many parts of the United States.

Black History Month has been a recurring observance thanks to the work of Dr. Carter G. Woodson, a historian who founded the Association for the Study of Negro Life and History in 1915. From the beginnings of the organization, he set out to mark the second week in February as Negro History Week. Woodson's organization, now known as the Association for the Study of Afro-American Life and History, successfully promoted "Negro History Week" to "Black History Month."

Another recent observance that is becoming more known and celebrated is Kwanzaa. Kwanzaa was first introduced in 1965 by Dr. Maulana Karenga and is now celebrated by millions of African Americans. Kwanzaa typically begins on December 26th and ends on January 1st. The celebration was introduced as a value system for "rescuing and reconstructing African American lives as a people" using seven principles, known as Nguzo Saba. The principles "are essential standards of personal and social excellence directed toward building moral community and strengthening the community's capacity to define, defend, and develop its interest in the most positive sense."

Martin Luther King Jr. Day has been the first new American holiday since Memorial Day was created in 1948. MLK Jr. Day was first proposed in 1968, four days after the assassination of MLK Jr. After a tremendous outcry over two decades, President Ronald Reagan signed the legislation in November of 1983 creating the national holiday on the third Monday of January. The King Holiday has become a deeply spiritual day for many Americans who honor the principles of Dr. Martin Luther King Jr.

Weddings, parenting, family entertainment are familial experiences that are celebrated by all ethnic groups and races, however, and there are websites that cater to African American consumers in ways that are unique, historical, and culturally sensitive. This chapter covers these categories and identifies websites that could be definitely useful to anyone planning the ultimate familial experience, be it a wedding, or a culturally rich family outing.

### Afrigeneas: African Ancestored Genealogy
www.afrigeneas.com
This is the major site for Black family genealogical research. To get one started there is a beginner's guide consisting of ten frequently asked questions. This is a user friendly site that should help people interested

in researching family history. The site has search capacity, but if one scrolls down the first screen then there is a site map for a more direct guide. This is a research site with a great deal of information in databases so you have to be careful and patient to find what you need.

You can search many things on this site. You can do a name search in all the known slave narratives. A more general search is possible by surname, including census records. There are also full text materials relating to slavery. The site provides a link to the slave databases constructed by Gwendolyn Midlo Hall for 18th and 19th century Louisiana. There are several full text city directories for the 19th century. There is also an interactive map of the USA that provides contacts to help with research in each state, as well as state related resources that are online.

The entire site is also structured to solicit contributions from the users because new information is becoming available every day. Furthermore, many hard copy materials have not been digitized as of yet so volunteers who can get this job done will create a resource for everyone else. This is an example of how the content of cyberspace is built by users who are creating a greater wealth for everyone. This is a new form of collective knowledge production in which everyone works for a collective end product. You can create something, keep it, and give it away at the same time. There need be no difference between the original and a copy.

The African American community has had to fight to preserve its history, especially the details of family history. There is a great deal of work that is just beginning to construct the databases to cross reference information about people and their relationships. Black people have experienced two great forced migrations that have little systematic documentation, the slave trade that separated them from Africa, and the great migrations that pulled Black people out of the South. We are only now on the way to reconnecting and documenting the connections that can steadily take us back through time.

### The Official Kwanzaa Website
www.officialkwanzaawebsite.org
This is the official website for the Kwanzaa Holiday created under the leadership of Dr. Maulana Karenga. This holiday began in Los Angeles

(1966), the year Black Power emerged as a slogan, after the Watts revolt in 1965. Karenga is a professor of Black Studies at California State University, Long Beach. He is also the Director of the Institute of Pan-African Studies and the National Chairperson of the US Organization. This holiday emerged when people were reacting against the commercialization of Christmas, and trying to find a way to connect with their African heritage. The information on this website will be of use to parents wanting to do the same with their children.

The holiday takes place over a seven day period, from December 26th to January 1st. It is based on the seven principles of Kawaida usually written first in Ki-Swahili and then English: Umoja (Unity), Kujichagulia (Self-Determination), Ujima (Collective Work and Responsibility), Ujamaa (Cooperative Economics), Nia (Purpose), Kuumba (Creativity), and Imani (Faith). Each day is devoted to one principle and guides family gatherings over meals and gift giving.

There is a guide to understanding the original guidelines for family observance in the form of twelve frequently asked questions. The US Postal Service issued a stamp on October 1997 in commemoration of Kwanzaa.

## Juneteenth: Worldwide Celebration
www.juneteenth.com
This site is a full service site for the commemoration of Juneteenth. The holiday began June 19, 1865 in Galveston, Texas and has since spread throughout the world as the day to celebrate the emancipation of Black people from slavery. The other day for this celebration is January 1st when it was supposed to happen for everyone.

This site provides a very good history of the holiday, and lists organizations designed to keep it alive. There is a form on the site to solicit participation in a campaign to have the US Postal Service issue a stamp to commemorate Juneteenth. There is also an opportunity to contribute art and poetry about the holiday and the emancipation.

One of the important historical aspects of the site is an interactive map of the USA that leads to local observances of Juneteenth, from 1997 to 2001. This is an important indicator of public history and the collective memory of the African American people. July 4th is observed as the national day of independence from British colonialism, but such independence left Blacks as slaves. Juneteenth is a holiday of freedom and emancipation for the African Americans. It is a holiday that should be commemorated by everyone, not just the Black community.

## Martin Luther King Holiday

www.thekingcenter.org

President Ronald Reagan signed into law a bill making Martin Luther King's birthday a national holiday. This holiday is officially managed by the Martin Luther King Center, set up in 1968 by his widow Coretta Scott King. The Center is designed to keep the memory of King alive and to organize educational activities for activists to continue the tradition of struggle in search of what King called "the Beloved Community."

The site provides a good deal of information on the King Holiday. It announces the annual theme, and lists activities taking place throughout the USA as well as internationally. The King Center annually hosts a summit of the Civil Rights Movement at that time to explore the application of King's ideas to current problems.

At the heart of the King Center is the library and archive in which the major collection of King's material is held. This is one of the major locations for scholars to study the Civil Rights Movement. In addition to King's the library archive holds some of the papers of other civil rights figures such as Julian Bond, Ben Brown, Fred Gray, Septima Clark, Howard Moore, and Fred Shuttleworth.

This site is a major example of how Black people have achieved a certain amount of equality with the mainstream establishment. The King Center is a rare and important facility.

## Children's Defense Fund

www.childrensdefense.org/index.htm

This organization is the leading organization dealing with the health and well being of children in the USA, and as such it is a major resource for understanding and helping the plight of African American children. Its motto is to "leave no child behind." They want to give children a good start in life: a healthy start, a head start, a fair start, a safe start, and a moral start. Marian Wright Edleman, an African American with a law degree from Yale University, started the Children's Defense Fund in 1973, after working as a civil rights attorney. She writes a weekly column "Child Watch," and selected articles are archived on the site.

The website has a wealth of statistical data on the plight of children in the USA including African American children. There is data on the national level, the state level, as well as in topical fact sheets.

The CDF purchased the 158 acre farm formerly owned by Alex Haley, author of *Roots* and a collaborator on the autobiography of Malcolm X. They continue to use it for education programs and conferences.

## Holidays

**Kwanzaa Information Center**
www.melanet.com/kwanzaa

**MLK Jr. Day.com**
www.mlkday.com

**Kwanzaa on the Net**
www.holidays.net/kwanzaa

**The Holiday Zone: MLK Jr. Day**
www.geocities.com/Athens/Troy/9087/mlk

**The Holiday Zone: Celebrating Black History Month**
www.geocities.com/Athens/Troy/9087/black/black.html

**The 19th of June**
www.19thofjune.com

## Genealogy

**African American Cemeteries Online**
www.prairiebluff.com/aacemetery

**Christine's Genealogy Website**
www.ccharity.com

**Genealogy Resources on the Internet: African Ancestored Mailing Lists**
www.rootsweb.com/~jfuller/gen_mail_african.html

## Family life

**Black Parenting Today (Magazine)**
www.blackparentingtoday.org

**CelebratingChildren.Com**
www.celebratingchildren.com

**Watoto World's Parental Guide**
www.melanet.com/watoto/parents.html

## Weddings

**African Wedding Guide (AWG)**
www.africanweddingguide.com

**Ask Ginka African American**
www.askginka.com

**VIBride.com**
www.vibride.com

## Other

**Bill Pickett Invitational Rodeo**
www.billpickettrodeo.com

**Universoul Circus**
www.universoulcircus.com

# Good books

Abner, Allison, Anne C. Beal, and Linda Villarosa. (1998) *The Black parenting book: caring for our children in the first five years*. New York: Broadway Books.

Burroughs, Tony. (2001) *Black roots: a beginner's guide to tracing the African American Family Tree*. New York: Fireside Books.

Chase, Henry. (1994) *In their footsteps: the American Visions guide to African-American heritage sites*. New York: Henry Holt.

Cole, Harriette. (1996) *Jumping the broom wedding workbook: a step-by-step write-in guide for planning the perfect African-American wedding*. New York: Henry Holt.

Harris, Fran. (1998) *In the Black: the African-American parent's guide to raising financially responsible children*. New York: Simon and Schuster.

Harris, Jessica B. (1995) *A Kwanzaa keepsake: celebrating the holiday with new traditions and feasts*. New York: Simon and Schuster.

Harris, Jessica B. (1995) *The welcome table: African-American heritage cooking*. New York: Simon and Schuster.

Jamison, Sandra L. (1999) *Finding your people: an African-American guide to discovering your roots*. New York: Perigee Books.

Karenga, Maulana. (1998) *Kwanzaa: a celebration of family, community, and culture*. Los Angeles: University of Sankore Press.

Kunjufu, Jawanza. (1995) *Countering the conspiracy to destroy Black boys*. (four volumes) Chicago, Ill.: African American Images.

Logan, Sadye L. M. (2001) *Black family: strengths, self-help, and positive change*. Boulder: Westview Press.

Pemberton, Doris H. (1983) *Juneteenth at Comanche Crossing*. Austin: Eakin Press.

Robinson, Wayne C. (1997) *The African-American travel guide*. Edison, N.J.: Hunter.

Signature Bride Magazine. (2001) *Going to the chapel: from traditional to African-Inspired, and everything in between – the ultimate wedding guide for today's Black couple*. New York: Berkley Books.

Wiggins, William H., Jr. (1987) *O freedom! Afro-American emancipation celebrations*. Knoxville: University of Tennessee Press.

# 12
# Health

Health is the concept we use to discuss our physical and emotional state of being. It reflects levels of economic development and the extent to which people have security in their social lives. Health reflects job status, insurance, neighborhood amenities, access to health care services, and levels of education among other things. Further, health conditions are passed on from generation to generation, including genetic based health conditions like sickle cell anemia. To study the health of a community is to take a biopsy of its total condition. Yes, health is a personal matter, but it is also a matter of social, political and economic substance.

Black people have been an essential source of labor, hence a minimal level of health has been necessary to keep the US economy going. Slavery was the economic foundation of the entire US economy so while slaves were literally worked to death their life span was an important part of determining profit so it was managed very carefully. This was even more true during the recent industrial period as in the end it involved trade union benefits including health insurance and retirement. The current period of de-industrialization has brought an end to this level of health and started a new historical health crisis.

One of the key issues is that Black people are disproportionately on the low end of almost all social indicators of good health. Another is that research has many times confirmed that Black people suffer from racist decisions within the health care industry. But these negative factors have been offset to some extent by the rise of Black health care professionals in both historically Black institutions like Meharry Medical College (Nashville, Tenn.) and Howard University Medical School (Washington, D.C.) as well as mainstream institutions. Black people work in all aspects of health care.

**African American Health** (Medline)

www.nlm.nih.gov/medlineplus/africanamericanhealth.html

This site is a service of the US National Library of Medicine and the National Institutes of Health. There are eleven parts to this site: nutrition, prevention screening for HIV/AIDS, research, specific conditions, organizations, statistics, children, men, seniors, teenagers, and women. Under each one there are entries that range from media articles to government reports. An example is a news report of a study that found that "TV shows aimed at Blacks carry more Junk food ads" (dated 2/27/03).

This is an information service that can usefully be checked on a weekly basis as the reports tend to be from reliable sources and cover a wide range of topics. There is a great deal of information available on health matters and it is important to have more than one reliable source to make sure the information is correct. This site can be a useful place to keep up on current events.

**National Medical Association**

www.nmanet.org

The National Medical Association was founded in 1895 and has a membership of over 25,000 African American physicians. They have had 106 national meetings, only missing a few years over this long history. They have a journal dating back to 1909. Sample issues are available online.

The site lists information of the following national programs: asthma, breastfeeding, clinical trials, HIV/AIDS, immunization, lupus, tobacco, and traffic safety. These national programs are aimed at the main health problems facing Black people. On almost every health indicator Black people are facing more of a health crisis than any other sector of the population except Native Americans. This organization plays a role as a lobbying group to represent the interests of the Black community.

**Office of Minority Health**

www.omhrc.gov

This agency is part of the Department of Heath and Human Services. It was set up in 1985 in response to a government report that signaled the health crisis in minority communities. One of the features is a Resource

Center with lots of information, and for people without access to the web there is a toll free 800 phone number to make inquiries.

The site provides a search function covering a wide variety of sources the agency has gathered, including an extensive listing of press releases and conferences. One of the unique features of this site is a section on full text reports and statistics. This includes a very useful report from 1999: "Improving the Collection and Use of Racial and Ethnic Data in Health and Human Services." This report lays the basis for a revamping of relevant statistics on minority health. Community level health activists and health care professionals in the African American community can use this in determining what statistics can best meet their needs and in what forms they would like access.

### National Black Nurses Association
www.nbna.org

This organization was established in 1971 in Cleveland Ohio. Today there are 150,000 African American nurses in 73 chapters. Several position papers are included on this site: education, Medicare, immunization, violence, reproductive rights, federal funding, nursing shortage, and health care disparities. These are policy statements that sum up the issues from the perspective of the Black nurse, and suggest policy action to impact the general health condition in the Black community.

The NBNA publishes a biannual journal and includes an archive of journal article abstracts on this site. In addition there is a quarterly newsletter with a full text archive. As with most organizations it also includes information on its annual conference.

This organization is very important as nursing is the traditional way that women have been involved as health care professionals. Further, the nurse is in a power relationship with doctors and has had to struggle for professional and social respect. This organization is a very important promoter of equality for women and the democratization of the health care industry.

### National Minority AIDS Council
www.nmac.org

AIDS is a major cause of death for Black people. The National Minority AIDS Council is a major clearing house for relevant information about this dreaded plague and what can be done about it in terms of medical treatment and political action. It was set up in 1987. This website is a general resource for conferences, media, and publications about HIV/AIDS. There is a search function that probes the entire site.

One unique feature is a prison initiative in the section on treatment. There is a major crisis in prisons where HIV/AIDS is rapidly spreading. Many practical guidelines are included for policy changes and practical programs. On this and other issues the site includes many documents and transcripts from professionals who sum up their research and practical experience.

There is a very up to date and comprehensive interactive calendar of national activities. There is an online action center for one stop shopping for action to deal with the lack of funding and political apathy by policy makers. For professional and community activists there is a job bank for openings in the field of care and prevention.

This is a site for families of AIDS victims to study. It can help overcome ignorance and powerlessness. It is a place to hook up with other people and find a community so that dealing with this crisis can be more tolerable.

## General

**Black Health Care.com**
www.blackhealthcare.com

**All About Black Health**
www.allaboutblackhealth.com

**Heart & Soul**
www.heartandsoul.com

**Diversity Rx**
www.diversityrx.org

**National Caucus and Center on Black Aged, Inc.**
www.ncba-aged.org

**African American Health Care Project**
www.med.umich.edu/haahc

**Multicultural Health**
www.med.umich.edu/1libr/multicul/multi00.htm

**Health Quest: Black Health Magazine**
www.healthquestmag.com/healthq/default.asp?source=healthq

## Women

**Office of Minority Health and Research** (National Institute of Neurological Disorders and Stroke)
www.ninds.nih.gov/funding/minorities_and_disabilities.htm#
Specialized

**African Americans and Lung Disease**
www.lungusa.org/diseases/africanlung_factsheet.html

**African Americans and Tobacco**
www.cdc.gov/tobacco/sgr/sgr_1998/sgr-min-fs-afr.htm

**Cancer Rates Higher in African Americans**
www.cancer.org/docroot/nws/content/nws_1_1x_colorectal_cancer_rates
_higher_in_african_americans.asp

**African Americans and Cancer**
www.iccnetwork.org/cancerfacts/ICC-CFS1.pdf

**Improving Cardiovascular Health in African Americans**
www.nhlbi.nih.gov/health/public/heart/other/chdblack/index.htm

**Osteoporosis and African American Women**
www.osteo.org/newfile.asp?doc=r607i&doctitle=Osteoporosis+and+
African%2DAmerican+Women&doctype=HTML+Fact+Sheet

**African American Heart Disease**
www.americanheart.org/presenter.jhtml?identifier=3007879

**Hypertension in African Americans**
www.postgradmed.com/issues/2002/10_02/douglas_intro.htm

## Medical training and research

**Meharry Medical College**
www.mmc.edu

**College of Medicine, Howard University**
www.med.howard.edu

**Morehouse School of Medicine**
www.msm.edu

**The Center of Excellence, COE, in Minority Medical Education and Health**
www.msu.edu/user/coemmeh/index.htm

**Center for Minority Health**
www.cmh.pitt.edu

**Agency for Healthcare Research and Quality: Minority Health**
www.ahrq.gov/research/minorix.htm

**Center for the Study of Race and Ethnicity in Medicine**
wiscinfo.doit.wisc.edu/crem

**Center for Research on Ethnicity, Culture and Health (CRECH)**
www.sph.umich.edu/crech

**Multicultural Health Clearinghouse**
www.mckinley.uiuc.edu/multiculturalhealth/index.html

**Minority Health Project**
www.minority.unc.edu

**Institute on Domestic Violence in the African American Family**
www.dvinstitute.org

**Barbara Jordan Health Policy Scholars Program**
www.bjcsp.com

## Aging

**Center on Minority Aging**
www.unc.edu/depts/cmaweb

**Center for Aging in Diverse Communities**
medicine.ucsf.edu/cadc

## Health professionals

**African American Therapists: Healing the Hearts and Mind of Black People**
www.africanamericantherapists.com

**Association of Black Cardiologists**
www.abcardio.org

**National Dental Association**
www.ndaonline.org

**NIH Black Scientists Association**
bsa.od.nih.gov

## Mental health

**Institute for African American Mental Health** (I AM)
www.has.vcu.edu/psy/iam

# Hair

**Nappy Hair**
www.napptural.com

**Black Beauty & Hair**
www.blackbeautyandhair.com

**Afro Hair**
www.afrohair.com

**Afro Care**
www.afrocare.com

## Alternative

**Taliah Waajid's Natural Hair Center**
www.naturalhair.org

**Organization of African Traditional Healers**
www.mamiwata.com/OATH.html

## Good books

Alcena, Valiere. (2001) *The African American woman's health book: a guide to the prevention and cure of illness.* Fort Lee, N.J.: Barricade Books.

Ashby, Muata Abhaya. (1997) *Egyptian yoga: the philosophy of enlightenment.* Miami: Cruzian Mystic Books.

Bailey, Eric J. (2002) *African American alternative medicine: using alternative medicine to prevent and control chronic diseases.* Westport, Conn.: Bergin & Garvey.

Banks, Ingrid. (2000) *Hair matters: beauty, power, and Black women's consciousness.* New York: New York University Press.

Bell, Geneva E. (1997) *My Rose: an African American mother's story of AIDS.* Cleveland, Ohio: Pilgrim Press.

Braithwaite, Ronald L., and Taylor, Sandra E., eds. (2001) *Health issues in the Black community*, 2nd ed. San Francisco: Jossey-Bass.

Byrd, W. Michael, and Clayton, Linda A. (2000) *An American health dilemma: a medical history of African Americans and the problem of race*. New York: Routledge.

Byrd, W. Michael, and Clayton, Linda A., eds. (2002) *An American health dilemma. Vol. 2, Race, medicine, and healthcare in the United States 1900–2000*. New York: Routledge.

Goosby, Eric, and Appel, Adrianne. (2002) *Living with AIDS/HIV: The African American's guide to prevention, diagnosis, and treatment*. Roscoe, Ill.: Hilton Publishing Inc.

Harris-Johnson, Debra, and Rose, Tony, eds. (2001) *The African-American teenager's guide to personal growth, health, safety, sex and survival: living and learning in the 21st century*. Phoenix, Ariz.: Amber Books.

Hill, Robert B., Billingsley, Andrew, Engram, Eleanor, and Reed, Wornie L., eds. (1993) *Research on the African-American family: a holistic perspective*. Westport, Conn.: Auburn House.

Johnson, Ruth W., ed. (1999) *African American voices: African American health educators speak out*. Sudbury, Mass.: Jones and Bartlett.

Lightfoot, Sara Lawrence. (1988) *Balm in Gilead: journey of a healer*. Reading, Mass.: Addison-Wesley.

Logan, Sadye L., and Freeman, Edith M. (2000) *Health care in the Black community: empowerment, knowledge, skills, and collectivism*. New York: Haworth Press.

Porter, Gayle K., and Gaston, Marilyn H. (2001) *Prime time: the African American woman's complete guide to midlife health and wellness*. New York: One World.

Poussaint, Alvin F., MD., and Alexander, Amy. (2001) *Lay my burden down: suicide and the mental health crisis among African-Americans*. Boston: Beacon Press.

Reed, James W., Shulman, Neil, and Shucker, Charlene. (2001) *The Black man's guide to good health: essential advice for African American men and their families*. Roscoe, Ill.: Hilton Publishing, Inc.

Smith, George Edmond. (2002) *Taking care of our own: a family medical guide for African Americans*. Roscoe, Ill.: Hilton Publishing Inc.

# 13
# Education

The educational experiences of the African American people have always been a leading indicator of the quality of life in the African American community. From a denial of formal education during slavery, to inferior schools starved from resources under Jim Crow segregation, to the inequality of de facto segregation in the industrial city. The situation is even more intense with low education attainment for African Americans in the context of the information revolution.

The teaching profession has been one of the mainstays of the Black middle class, usually providing a government job with decent pay, safe and clean working conditions, and good benefits. The Black middle class could satisfy its need for a good job and serve the community as well. Teachers, social workers, doctors, and lawyers were the core of the "talented tenth" that DuBois focused on in his call for educated Blacks to serve their community. This call is critical today as the education crisis we face approximates that faced in the late 19th century. Then the challenge was to prepare for the industrial system, while now Black youth are preparing for the information society.

In this chapter we continue to focus on using our citations to get you inside the African American experience. Our best sites cover the Historically Black Colleges and Universities, graduate-level and undergraduate Black Studies programs, as well as guides to the web in general, and current research trends.

## United Negro College Fund
www.uncf.org
This site is the major access to the institutions that developed during the period of formal segregation to serve the education needs of the Black

community, now called the Historically Black Colleges and Universities (HBCUs). This organization is under the able leadership of William Gray, minister and former Congressman from Philadelphia, as President and CEO. It represents 39 institutions in a direct way, but actually serves the cause of Blacks in higher education in general.

This site presents a directory to member institutions, searchable alphabetically, by degree offered, and by location via an interactive map. Press releases from the last three years represent a comprehensive set of commentaries on policy issues facing Blacks in higher education. The site includes valuable information on scholarships and internships in general and those particularly targeting minority and low-income students.

One of the great services that these institutions provide is a gateway for first generation college students from the South to have an opportunity to attend college. Of course some of them have generations of graduates who make up the Black middle class, but increasingly the Black middle class sends their children to integrated schools, with the outstanding exceptions of Howard, Fisk, Spelman, Morehouse, and Hampton among others.

### Floyd Ingram's Resource Center
www.coatopa.com/fi-edu.html
Floyd Ingram is a librarian turned web administrator for Benedict College in Columbia, South Carolina. He is a prolific creator of webliographies, organized lists of website URLs on all aspects of the Black experiences and related subjects. His site is a professional site, but gives encouragement to non-professionals because he demonstrates quite ably the importance of a good webliography, and that's something everyone can put together by carefully saving the links on a given subject of interest.

His list on education is particularly good. He has organized it in six major sections: academic organizations, federal and state organizations, education technology and distance learning, grants and funding, higher education, and K–12. But these are merely links to sites without commentary, so as usual (including with this book) you have to remain critical and look at each site just as you would with any information source – always seek multiple sources and seek a consensus without assuming any one site is authoritative.

It is also wonderful to see a scholar/administrator at an HBCU play a leading role with this technology. Too many times it is assumed that the historical elites will always dominate the social construction of knowledge, and that if a Black person is really smart then the "rich white folks" will grab them up to teach their children in some kind of "dream team." This is not so. Prof. Ingram demonstrates that knowledge production can occur in the places serving the Black grass roots.

### eBlack Studies
www.eblackstudies.org
This website is a comprehensive guide to the academic field of Black Studies (African Studies, etc.). It has been developed at the Africana Studies Program at the University of Toledo, the first program established on the basis of eBlack Studies, the use of information technology as the modus operandi of the teaching and research done by faculty and students.

There are four main parts of this site: academic and professional organizations, journals and newsletters, undergraduate degree programs, and graduate degree programs. There are nearly 300 undergraduate programs and over 30 graduate degree programs. This is a comprehensive approach that makes no distinction based on any given narrow ideological definition. From this perspective the integrity of any program is left to the student and faculty to judge, as personnel changes and ideological tendencies come and go, but a focus on the Black experience in the mission of a program is enough to qualify it for its listing.

This site is very useful for students seeking a program that meets their needs. It is also useful to academic professionals looking for a journal to publish in or an organization to join or a national conference to submit a paper for reading.

### Journal of Blacks in Higher Education
www.jbhe.com/index.html
This journal is probably the best source for factoids, sound bites of statistics and quoted information that covers the Black experience in higher education. Its main orientation is to focus on the elite institutions of higher education like the Ivy Leagues, but even with that limitation it is a major source of information that provides a unique service.

In addition to full text articles, this site includes a job bank and a section called vital statistics. If you're giving a talk and need some information on higher education this is a good place to check. Another interesting feature is an affirmative action timeline covering the period from 1990 to the present. This is an easy to download document that graphically presents a case against the racist attacks against affirmative action.

This site is a good example of the kind of site that can represent a hard copy journal. Not all of the articles are posted here, but many are and that makes it an invaluable source. Further, this site will entice you to check the journal out, suggest your library subscribes, or to even take out an individual sub if it meets your particular needs to that extent.

### Commission on Research in Black Education
www.coribe.org

This is a wonderful site in that it is an excellent example of cutting edge work being done by professional Black educators to provide leadership to research and policy development. This group began in 1999 as a group within the American Educational Research Association. The core work has been done by young scholars, in collaboration with a group of senior scholars (elders), and a network of colleagues who joined the process in a variety of ways.

The main content of the site is a report, "Facing the New Millennium," released June 2001. The lead author of the report was Prof. Joyce King (Spelman College). The four main sections of this 54 page report (PDF) are methodology, declaration of intellectual independence, education for human freedom, and a research and action agenda. There are also appendices by participating scholars.

There were six other members of this planning group for this project in addition to Prof. King: Gloria Ladson Billings (University of Wisconsin – Madison), Beverly Gordon (Ohio State University), James Banks (University of Washington – Seattle), William Watkins (University of Illinois – Chicago), L. Scott Miller (National Task Force on Minority High Achievement), and Etta Collins (University of Southern California).

This site includes many papers and commentaries from such senior scholars as Asa Hilliard (Georgia State University) and Frank Bonilla in Riverside. It is a model for what should be done in every major field of study – a collaborative project run by younger scholars working under the guidance of their senior scholar elders to sum up and spell out a research agenda. This was done at the beginning of Black Studies in the 1960s, so it's good to see it starting again at the beginning of the 21st century.

## General

**Quality Education for Minorities Network**
qemnetwork.qem.org

**Separate but Not Equal: Race, Education, and Prince Edward County, Virginia**
www.library.vcu.edu/jbc/speccoll/pec.html

**Center for Diversity Education**
main.nc.us/diversity

**This Site is for My Children** (Ed Whitfield)
home.earthlink.net/~elwhit

**Institute for Peoples Education and Action**
www.peopleseducation.org

## Organizations

**National Council for Black Studies**
www.cas.gsu.edu/ncbs

**National Association for Equal Opportunity in Higher Education**
www.nafeo.org

**Council of Independent Black Institutions**
www.cibi.org

**Black Alliance for Educational Options**
www.baeo.org/home/index.php

**National Association for the Education of African American Children with Learning Disabilities**
www.charityadvantage.com/aacld/HomePage.asp

**National Alliance of Black School Educators**
www.nabse.org

**National Association of African American Studies**
www.naaas.org

## K–12

**K–12 Electronic Guide to African Resources on the Internet**
www.sas.upenn.edu/African_Studies/K-12/AFR_GIDE.html

**African American Teachers Lounge**
members.tripod.com/~teacherslounge

**Watoto World: Websites for Children, Parents, and Educators of African Descent**
www.melanet.com/watoto

**African American Academy**
www.seattleschools.org/schools/aaa

**Harvard University Urban Superintendents Program**
www.gse.harvard.edu/usp

**The Algebra Project**
www.algebra.org

**First Saturday: Yes to Math, Knowledge is Power**
www.murchisoncenter.org/firstsaturday

## Higher education

**Harvard University Urban Superintendents Program**
www.gse.harvard.edu/usp

**Institute for Urban and Minority Education**
iume.tc.columbia.edu

**College Financial Aid for Minority Students**
www.finaid.org/otheraid/minority.phtml

**Black Excel: The College Help Network**
www.blackexcel.org

## Linguistics

**Work of William Labov**
www.ling.upenn.edu/~wlabov/home.html

**Work of John Rickford**
www.stanford.edu/~rickford

**Work of Geneva Smitherman**
www.msu.edu/~smither4

**Ebonics Information Page** (Center for Applied Linguistics)
www.cal.org/ebonics

**African American English**
www.umass.edu/aae

**Work of Salikoko F. Mufwene**
humanities.uchicago.edu/faculty/mufwene

# Publications

**Black Issues in Higher Education**
www.blackissues.com

**The Journal of Negro Education**
www.howard.edu/schooleducation/Programs/JNE/index.htm

## Statistics

**Race Statistics** (National Center for Educational Statistics)
nces.ed.gov/edstats/title.asp?editions=Curr&L1=320&L2=0&L3=0&
Subj=Race%2Fethnicity+%28see+also+topic+of+interest%29

## Good books

Aldridge, Delores, and Young, Carlene, eds. (2000) *Out of the revolution: the development of Africana studies*. Lanham, Md.: Lexington Books.

Anderson, Talmadge. (1993) *Introduction to African American studies: cultural concepts and theory*. Dubuque, Iowa: Kendall/Hunt.

Billings, Gloria Ladson. (1997) *The dream keepers: successful teachers of African Americans children*. San Francisco: Jossey-Bass.

Bowles, Samuel, and Herbert Gintis. (1976) *Schooling in capitalist America: educational reform and the contradictions of economic life*. New York: Basic Books.

Bullock, Henry A. (1967) *A history of Negro education in the South: from 1619 to the present*. Cambridge, Mass.: Harvard University Press.

DuBois, W. E. B. (2001) *The education of Black people: ten critiques 1906–1960*. New York: Monthly Review Press.

Hale, Janice E., and Vincent Franklin. (2001) *Learning while Black: creating educational excellence for African American children*. Baltimore: Johns Hopkins University Press.

Jencks, Christopher, and Phillips, Meredith, eds. (1998) *The Black–white test score gap*. Washington, D.C.: Brookings Institution Press.

Kunjufu, Jawanza. (2002) *Black students – middle class teachers*. Chicago, Ill.: African American Images.

Morgan, Marcyliena H. (2002) *Language, discourse and power in African American culture*. Cambridge: Cambridge University Press.

Moses, Robert P., and Charles E. Cobb, Jr. (2001) *Radical equations: math literacy and civil rights*. Boston: Beacon Press.

Orfield, Gary, Susan E. Eaton, and the Harvard Project on School Desegregation. (1996) *Dismantling desegregation: the quiet reversal of Brown v. Board of Education*. New York: New Press.

Perry, Theresa, Claude Steele, and Asa G. Hilliard III. (2003) *Young, gifted, and Black: promoting high achievement among African-American students*. Boston: Beacon Press.

Watkins, William, James H. Lewis, and Victoria Chou. (2001) *Race and education: the roles of history and society in educating African American students*. Boston: Allyn and Bacon.

Watson, Clifford, and Geneva Smitherman. (1996) *Educating African American males: Detroit's Malcolm X Academy solution*. Chicago: Third World Press.

Woodson, Carter Godwin. (1990) *The mis-education of the Negro*. Nashville, Tenn.: Winston-Derek.

Zaslavsky, Claudia. (1996) *The multicultural math classroom: bringing in the world*. Portsmouth, N.H.: Heinemann.

# 14
# Food

Everyone has to eat, and all human cultures include guidelines for how to acquire, prepare, and consume the food necessary to live. This survival function of foods is often wrapped within cultural rituals that have to do with religion, family, and community, both as we live day today as well as a way to institutionalize community memory. This is particularly evident for African Americans as so much of the food history of Africa was drowned in the holocaust of slavery and colonial domination. On a day-to-day basis Black people then ate minimal quantities, often of the least desirable foods, but were able to apply African cultural values and practices to create a new cuisine, both in terms of its nutritional value and its sustainability under adverse conditions. In terms of historical memory the most obvious use of foods has been the Emancipation Day meal traditionally served on January 1st. Black eyed peas, hogs head cheese, ham, and other Southern foods were served as a celebration of freedom beginning January 1, 1865. As with all people, to understand the food history of African Americans is to discover something very basic about their soul. That's why it's called soul food.

The traditional diet of Black people, from Africa through slavery, was mainly a diet for farmers and hard working people with access to a wide array of fruits and vegetables. In fact, Black people brought African food and food culture with them and infused this into the Southern way of life so even white people in the South, whether they knew it or not, ate African. It was when the African American people left the land and the farming way of life that they faced their most fundamental food crisis. On the one hand this was a crisis of adaptation while on another level it began a crisis of survival. This was, and is, part of a general transformation of world culture based upon buying food not growing it, including both its production and consumption. Because time is also a commodity traditional cultural practices have been replaced by the market ritual of grabbing "fast food" and eating it as fast as possible in between other activities or while watching television. Food as social time, with family conversation and trans-generational rituals (like cooking practices handed down from grandmother to mother to daughter), has declined greatly.

The net result of all of this has produced a health crisis as part of the overall social and economic crisis. The "McDonaldization" of world culture has become a fact. The response has been an effort to increase governmental regulation to protect the public, increased education so people can take better care, and the development of a healthfoods industry to give people a healthy alternative.

### Black Vegetarians
www.blackvegetarians.com
This is an independent site designed to promote vegetarianism in the African American community. Marya Annette McQuirter and Tracye Lynn McQuirter created this site for four types of eating styles: the fruitarian, the live or raw foodist, the vegan, and the vegetarian. They include a page on health where they give some basic reasons for each of these styles and argue the general desirability of sticking close to fruits and vegetables. They deal with heart disease, cancer, stroke, and diabetes.

This is a labor of love and while this is not an encyclopedia of information their very genuine approach is attractive. They include definitions, some delightful recipes (including a smoothie to die for!), and a health quiz with answers easily available on the site.

There are forms to submit your own information, especially your favorite recipe. They are trying to create a community around this basic rethinking of how to be healthy. This is an important concern. So much of this is part of traditional soul food, and yet there are aspects of soul food that need to be changed to impact the types of diseases that impact Black people.

### Heart Healthy Home Cooking African American Style
National Institutes of Health
www.nhlbi.nih.gov/health/public/heart/other/chdblack/cooking.htm

This is an online booklet published by the National Institutes of Health in 1997. It contains 20 healthy recipes for staples of the African American food tradition. There are three categories: breads, vegetables, and side dishes; main dishes; and beverages and desserts.

This is an important intervention into the food-health discourse because it represents the position that it is possible to remain in a food tradition and eat for health and taste. Many people argue that old habits die slowly and even if it's not completely good for you it's hard to leave cooking you've eaten for most of your life. This booklet demonstrates that it is possible to make a few changes and keep on with those same tasty dishes.

### Sylvia's: Queen of Soul Food
www.sylviassoulfood.com
This is the website of the premier soul food restaurant in Harlem, New York. The main restaurant was founded in 1962, and a second one has opened in Atlanta in 1997. They are owned by the Woods family, Herbert and Sylvia Woods, their four children and several grandchildren. It opened with a seating capacity for 35 and now can seat 450. They have expanded now to include a line of soul food products, and two cookbooks.

This website is here to represent the many soul food restaurants that exist in every Black community in the United States. These often started by cooks taking people in their kitchens, especially single men who would pay for a meal plan and come over to eat with the family or alone. This includes Gladys' in Chicago, Gates Bar-b-Q in Kansas City, and Dukey Chase in New Orleans.

One of the great tasks of historical research is to create online archives of these institutions that have been so central to the collective community identity, feeding generation after generation the foods central to African American culture.

### The Congo Cook Book
www.congocookbook.com
This is a major culinary asset in cyberspace. There are over 150 recipes from all over Africa, including detailed information about the foods and the practice of cooking. The website has annoying ads on it, but if you

can manage to navigate around them you will be rewarded. In fact there is a way to download the entire cookbook as a PDF file if you carefully go to the Frequently Asked Questions and find out how to do it. This site was prepared by returned volunteers from the Peace Corps who put it together as a way to build solidarity and understanding with the peoples of Africa.

The full range of vegetables and meats are covered in this comprehensive text. They have recipes for full dinners as well as snacks. There are also cultural essays about the role of food and food preparation in African cultures, as well as how this is carried out relative to gender roles, especially the role of women.

Recipes are available by ingredients, region and country, and by other topics. Listed are the most popular dishes on the site: plantains, chicken in peanut-tomato sauce, fufu, ginger beer, fruit salad, cardamon tea, moyin-moyin, jollof rice, tamarind drink, groundnut stew, chai, elephant soup, akoho sy voanio, muamba nsusu, saka-saka, akara, cane rat, dongodongo, grilled tilapia, and matoke. If you're curious about any of these dishes you can find a full description and the recipe on the website.

**The Soulfood Cookbook**
www.soulfoodcookbook.com
This is an online cookbook with recipes for many kinds of dishes: chicken, beef, pork, fish, vegetables, bread, desserts, beans, and beverages. You can find ways to make hush puppies, deviled crab eggs, and old favorites like cornbread dressing and macaroni and cheese.

This is the kind of online cookbook that young people might want to pay attention to as it can get you started if you haven't yet gotten the family recipes from your elders. You can take these basic recipes to start and adjust them based on your family tradition. The magic in the kitchen is in the details and often the style one uses in getting the job done.

One of the great issues that needs to be considered in any body of information about cooking is the freshness of the ingredients that are used. The main thing is to try and find fresh stuff, produce and meats. This is about learning how to see and smell what is fresh. Soul food came out of an agricultural environment in which all the food was fresh and organic. Now we are living in the biochemical age and we have to learn new ways to select what to cook, and how to cook. But when it comes to recipes there's nothing wrong with sticking to tradition, and this website will get you started.

## General

**A History of Soul Food**
www.foxhome.com/soulfood/htmls/soulfood.html

**Food by Black Entertainment Television**
www.bet.com/articles/0,,c3gb1843–2499,00.html

**The Gumbo Pages**
www.gumbopages.com

## African Diaspora

**African Cooking and Recipes**
www.africaguide.com/cooking.htm

**The Sikunu Cookbook**
sikunu.topcities.com

**The African Cookbook**
www.sas.upenn.edu/African_Studies/Cookbook/about_cb_wh.html

**African Chop: Enjoy the Tropical Foods of Africa**
www.africanchop.com

**Authentic Cuisine from Ghana**
www.africanrecipes.com

**Recipes from Mauritius**
ile-maurice.tripod.com

**Menus and Recipes from the Sudan**
www.sudan.net/society/recipe.html

**Kenyan Recipe Page**
nutford.kijabe.org/recipes.html

**Gambian Recipes**
www.africanculture.dk/gambia/foodmenu.htm

**Ethiopia: Spicy Food from the Cradle of Civilization**
www.globalgourmet.com/destinations/ethiopia/index.html

## Personalities

**Vertamae Grosvenor**
www.pbs.org/wttw/kitchen

**B. Smith**
www.bsmithwithstyle.com/food

## Recipes

**The Chitterling Site: The Soul Food Site**
www.chitterlings.com

**Soul Food**
www.thegutsygourmet.net/soul.html

## Good books

Carter, Danella. (1995) *Down-home wholesome: 300 low fat recipes from a new soul kitchen*. New York: Dutton.

Ferguson, Sheila. (1993) *Soul food: classic cuisine from the Deep South*. New York: Grove Press.

Gaines, Fabiola. (1999) *The new soul food cookbook for people with diabetes*. Alexandria, Va.: American Diabetes Association.

Grosvenor, Vertamae. (1999) *Vertamae cooks again: more recipes from the Americas' family kitchen*. San Francisco: Bay Books.

Height, Dorothy. (1994) *The Black family dinner quilt cookbook: health conscious recipes and food memories*. New York: Simon & Schuster.

Jones, Wilbert. (1998) *The healthy soul food cookbook: how to cut the fat but keep the flavor*. Secaucus, N.J.: Carol Pub. Group.

De Knight, Freda. (1989) *The ebony cookbook*. Chicago: Johnson Publications.

Shange, Ntozake. (1998) *If I can cook/you know you can*. Boston: Beacon Press.

White, Joyce. (1998) *Soul Food: Recipes & Reflections from African American Churches*. New York: HarperCollins.

Woods, Sylvia, and family, with Melissa Clark. (1999) *Sylvia's family soul food cookbook: from Hemingway, South Carolina to Harlem*. New York: William Morrow and Co.

# 15
# Women

Black women make up half the adult population of the Black community and have had to face all of the trials and tribulations faced by Black men and more. Black women face triple oppression: racism, economic problems, and male supremacy. This is a set of problems faced not only outside of the Black community but inside as well. Of course not all Black women face these problems to the same degree, but most are victims of racism, class exploitation, and sexism. As more and more Black women get degrees in higher education, good jobs, and some attainment of power the situation is more diverse and any discussion has to be more finely tuned to the facts.

There have always been outstanding Black women. Against all odds Black women have achieved, even when not recognized they have been there as the core intellects and hard workers to staff community institutions. From the family to the church, from most service professions (teaching, social work, nursing, and domestic service) to entertainment (on stage and as sex workers), Black women have been carrying more than their share of the load to keep the Black community viable. They have birthed and reared the children, and cared for the men against all odds. Moreover they have carried on even when the men were not there or acted in anti-social ways including domestic violence and delinquency in financial support.

Every stage of the struggle for equality has had women speaking their own voices, and being part of the overall community leadership. From Sojourner Truth and Harriet Tubman in the slave period, to Anna Julia Cooper and Ida B. Wells in the rural period, to Shirley Chisholm and Ella Baker in more recent times, women have been leaders.

Today Black women are challenging all obstacles, and fighting to break down all gender restrictions against them. In Black Studies women have emerged as a major topic. Black women writers have started telling their stories and getting proper recognition – Toni Morrison won the Nobel Prize for Literature, Rita Dove won the Pulitzer Prize for Poetry, and Alice Walker the National Book Award. As elected officials Black women have given leadership to the US Congress in both the House of Representatives and the Senate, as well as at the state and local levels. They have emerged as trade union leaders like Addie Wyatt and ministers like Johnny Coleman. Today there is no limit on what Black women can achieve.

**Distinguished (Black) Women of Past and Present**
www.distinguishedwomen.com/subject/BlackHist.html
This site is an online biographical dictionary about outstanding Black women. There are 30 topics within which several hundred women are included with biographical sketches and links to their work, often full text references. They include an annotated list of suggested readings, and a webliography to additional online sources of information.

Two of the largest categories are government and politics (16 women listed) and human rights (14 women listed). The ones that are small are nevertheless of high quality. For example, the anthropology category lists three women: Johnnetta Cole (former President of Spelman College and current President of Bennett College for Women), Niara Sudarkasa (former President of Lincoln University), and Zora Neale Hurston the noted folklorist and creative writer.

This site is a model for a more general approach to Black women on the web. Every woman of note, and this can be as wide or as narrow a definition as one would like, can be included in a database that collects biographical information and works of intellectual scholarship and creativity in any form (text, sound, image, video, etc.). Such a massive undertaking would require the cooperation of all Black Women's Studies programs and scholars, including libraries and archives. Even so, the potential rewards from such an undertaking seem worth the effort. Once comprehensive and inclusive bibliographies are online and available to all then there is no need for students and scholars to keep reinventing the same material. We need to keep expanding the list of women who are given the respect of being part of the permanent record.

## Women of Color Resource Center
www.coloredgirls.org

This center was created in 1990 as a resource center for women of color to study and struggle. The Executive Director is the long time activist and author Linda Burnham. There are five projects: Women's Human Rights, Popular Education, Welfare, Peace and Justice, and Sisters of Fire. The center is inclusive of women from all nationalities, with a focus on women from oppressed communities.

The Center sponsors a listserv discussion online and basically maintains an activist posture with regard to the main policy question impacting women. Most of the Center's written material is not online but available in printed form through this website. We include it here because the structure of this site is a model for what a local women's center can be in terms of education programs and social action. It is based in the San Francisco Bay area, but this can be replicated in every major city in the country.

The Sisters of Fire Program is an awards program to recognize women who best represent the sort of radicalism that this center embodies. The Peace and Justice project emerged after the 9/11 attack against the World Trade Center. The organizers target their political activism against both terrorism and war.

## Black American Feminism: A Multidisciplinary Bibliography
www.library.ucsb.edu/blackfeminism

This site is maintained by Sherri Barnes, a librarian at the University of California at Santa Barbara. It was established in 2002, and is updated quarterly. This is a bibliography of printed texts, but we include it because it is so extensive. There are 30 topics for as many as 1000 references. There is a form on the site to allow readers to submit references for inclusion.

This is an example of how the World Wide Web can be important even if its use in this case is for sharing references to materials that are not available online. For the detailed reference to books currently in print the practice has become for people to go to one of the online book retail companies and check for the full reference from their commercial database. This usually works but does not include articles, self-published material, smaller pamphlets from activists, and organizational reports. This kind of bibliography can be inclusive of all these things and of use to the casual reader as well as the systematic scholar.

This is an opportunity for every doctoral student to add their detailed references, for every academic to routinely submit their publication list just as they do for their annual review, and for journals to send in their tables of content to make sure their material is in the bibliography. This kind of listing should properly be supervised by a committee of scholars and librarians, and organized in such a way that their term appointment might be measured in some way so that appropriate academic credit could be given for this very valuable professional service.

### Women of Color Web
www.hsph.harvard.edu/grhf/WoC
The main purpose of this site is to provide full text material on all kinds of women of color including African Americans. The material is organized in three basic sections: feminisms, sexualities, and reproductive rights. Full text articles and book chapters are included from the following African American women: Pat Hill Collins, Kimberle Williams Crenshaw, bell hooks, Angela Davis, Barbara Smith, and Dorothy Roberts.

There is a section on teaching that includes a set of links to academic units that focus on women of color. Also included are several syllabi on women of color related topics such as race and gender. This is very helpful for students in Black women's studies.

The site also includes activist material. The page on organizations has four sections: activism, health, queer, and feminist/womanist. Community activists will find this section useful for networking with groups and finding people with similar interests. Finally, the site includes links to online discussion lists.

### Black Women's Health
www.blackwomenshealth.com
Dr. David Pryor set this site up in 1999 to be a comprehensive source of information about Black women. He intends to develop a commercial

side of this site, but the information provided makes it a valuable source for everyone. He basically gathered a group of health professionals to write short essays on various topics. There are over 100 short essays under broad headings like health issues, nutrition, and spiritual and mental health, finances, and a catch-all category called "got a minute."

The site encourages people to get involved and participate. The site has online discussion forums on male–female relationships, diet, mental and spiritual health, and health in general. You can also sign up for a newsletter.

## Business

**African Sisters.com**
www.africansisters.com

## Professions

**Black Career Women (BCW)**
www.bcw.org

## Network

**International Black Women's Network**
www.blackliving.com

**Sisternet Online: Health, Healing, Leadership**
www.sisternetonline.org

## Global

**Global Black Woman**
www.globalblackwoman.com

# General

**Blackgirl International**
www.blackgirl.org/index.html

**Premyier.com: Real Woman Real Connections**
www.premyier.com

**Niaonline.com**
www.niaonline.com

**Debrena's World**
www.debrenasworld.com

**National Black Herstory Task Force**
www.blackherstory.org

**African American Feminism**
www.cddc.vt.edu/feminism/afam.html

# Media

**Sister2Sister Magazine**
www.s2smagazine.com/startfw/home.htm

**Today's Black Women Radio Show**
www.jktbw.com/page1.html

**Three Black Chicks**
www.3blackchicks.com

# Individuals

**Sojourner Truth**
xroads.virginia.edu/~HYPER/TRUTH/cover.html

**Mary McLeod Bethune Council House**
www.nps.gov/mamc

**Madame C. J. Walker**
www.madamcjwalker.com

**Elizabeth "Mumbet" Freeman**
www.mumbet.com

**Dr. Charlotte Hawkins Brown** (Palmer Memorial Institute)
www.ah.dcr.state.nc.us/sections/hs/chb/chb.htm

## Lesson plans

**Elizabeth Catlett's Life and Career**
www.clevelandart.org/exhibcef/catlett/html/index.html

**Incidents of the Life of a Slave Girl**
www.scribblingwomen.org/hjincidents.htm

**The Bones of Louella Brown, by Ann Petry**
www.scribblingwomen.org/aplouella.htm

**Hate is Nothing, by Marita Bonner**
www.scribblingwomen.org/mbhatenoth.htm

## Literature

**African American Women Writers of the 19th Century**
digital.nypl.org/schomburg/writers_aa19

**African-American Women On-line Archival Collections**
scriptorium.lib.duke.edu/collections/african-american-women.html

**Mostly Menfolk and a Woman or Two: A Virtual Exhibit of 18th and 19th Century African American Literature**
www.metalab.unc.edu/afam_authors/homepage.html

**Selected Women Writers of the Harlem Renaissance: A Resource Guide**
www.nku.edu/~diesmanj/guides

## Miscellaneous

**Conjure Women**
www.rebekahfilms.org

**Nursing Old Wounds**
www.af.mil/news/airman/0498/nurse.htm

## Good books

Bennett, Michael, and Dickerson, Vanessa D. (2001) *Recovering the Black female body: self-representations by African American women*. New Brunswick, N.J.: Rutgers University Press.

Byrd, Ayana D., and Tharps, Lori L. (2001) *Hair story: untangling the roots of Black hair in America*. New York: St. Martin's Press.

Bambara, Toni Cade, ed. (1970) *The Black woman: an anthology*. New York: Penguin.

Collier-Thomas, Bettye, and Franklin, V. P. (2001) *Sisters in the struggle: African American women in the civil rights–black power movement*. New York: New York University Press.

Craig, Maxine Leeds. (2002) *Ain't I a beauty queen? Black women, beauty, and the politics of race*. Oxford: Oxford University Press.

Gilkes, Cheryl Townsend. (2001) *If it wasn't for the women: Black women's experience and womanist culture in church and community*. Maryknoll, N.Y.: Orbis Books.

Guy-Sheftall, Beverly. (1995) *Words of fire: an anthology of African-American feminist thought*. New York: New Press.

Harley, Sharon, and the Black Women and Work Collective. (2002) *Sister circle: Black women and work*. New Brunswick, N.J.: Rutgers University Press.

Harris-Lopez, Trudier. (2001) *Saints, sinners, saviors: strong Black women in African American literature*. New York: Palgrave.

Hine, Darlene Clark, ed. (1997) *Facts on File encyclopedia of Black women in America*. New York: Facts on File.

Hine, Darlene Clark, and Gasper, David Barry, eds. (1996) *More than chattel: Black women and slavery in the Americas*. Bloomington: Indiana University Press.

hooks, bell. (1989) *Talking back: thinking feminist, thinking Black*. Boston: South End Press.

hooks, bell. (1992) *Ain't I a woman: Black women and feminism*. Boston: South End Press.

Hull, Akasha Gloria. (2001) *Soul talk: the new spirituality of African American women*. Rochester, Vt.: Inner Traditions.

Jacobs, Harriet Ann. (2000) *Incidents in the life of a slave girl, written by herself*. Cambridge, Mass.: Harvard University Press.

James, Joy, and Sharpley-Whiting, T. Denean, eds. (2000) *Black feminist reader*. Malden, Mass.: Blackwell Publishers.

Moody, Joycelyn. (2001) *Sentimental confessions: spiritual narratives of nineteenth-century African American women*. Athens, Ga.: University of Georgia Press.

Roses, Lorraine Elena, and Randolph, Ruth Elizabeth. (1990) *The Harlem Renaissance and beyond: literary biographies of 100 Black women writers, 1900–1945*. Boston, Mass.: G. K. Hall.

White, E. Frances. (2001) *Dark continent of our bodies: Black feminism and the politics of respectability*. Philadelphia: Temple University Press.

# 16
# Politics and Civil Rights

Black people have always been at the heart of the greatest moral choices and issues of power in US politics. The US Constitutional Convention in 1788 failed to take the high ground to end slavery, and used the infamous 3/5 clause to mask moral failure. President Lincoln failed to take the high ground when his 1863 "Emancipation Proclamation" only condemned the slave states that were in rebellion, but not the institution of slavery. The Supreme Court failed to take the high ground in 1955 when they tangled up the speed of school integration with the planned ambiguity of "with all deliberate speed." The clarity of freedom without any limitations has yet to be clearly articulated as public policy.

Politics is about power and the forces that change and maintain the economy, social life, and international relations. Mainstream politics are based in the electoral system in which the people as voters have a role to play. This has been one of the main themes of Black politics, the fight for the right to vote and the use of that vote to advance political policy and program that meets the needs of the Black community.

The main arena for Black politics is in the community outside of the electoral arena. The Civil Rights Movement and various forms of Black Power, from Marcus Garvey to Malcolm X, have dominated Black politics in the 20th century.

### Rainbow/Push Coalition
www.rainbowpush.org
This site is a showcase for the activities of its founder and president Rev. Jesse Jackson. He is one of the major visible leaders of the civil rights establishment representing the most progressive views of the Black middle class. He is the most consistent activist on picket lines throughout

the country marching with trade unions, and people struggles from Maine to Mississippi. His most consistent focus is on building Black economic development by building Black capitalism. His most recent initiative has been to build a coalition between Black business leaders and Wall Street.

This site gives you the work of Jesse Jackson in every medium. It advertises video transmission of his weekly Saturday speeches from Chicago, as well as other audio, video, and hard copy text of speeches and press releases. You can also sign up for a free "JacksFax," a weekly fax that will be sent to you with his latest views and policy initiatives.

Push/Rainbow has eight regional offices throughout the country including the national headquarters located in Chicago. There are six national programs that mainly focus on economic development such as a program to enlist 1000 churches in efforts to build local economic bases of power. The organization has posted the proceedings of its "Silicon Valley Digital Connections 2001 Conference" that is an important part of the national discourse on overcoming the digital divide.

**Black Radical Congress**
www.blackradicalcongress.org
This website is one of the most visible reflections of the radical Black tradition struggling to survive at the beginning of the 21st century. There are echoes that go back to the 1960s including surviving members of the Black Panther Party, the League of Revolutionary Black Workers, the Congress of African Peoples, the African Liberation Support Committee, the Student Organization for Black Unity, SNCC, and Peoples College. Almost all socialist groups have cadres who are activists in the BRC. The core leadership is made up of Black Studies faculty and students, with local chapters in many cities.

The BRC's two main documents are posted on this site, "Principles of Unity" and a "Freedom Agenda". The five founding members were Abdul Alkalimat (University of Toledo), Bill Fletcher (Trans-Africa), Manning Marable (Columbia University), Leith Mullings (CUNY Graduate Center), and Barbara Ransby (University of Illinois-Chicago). The founding Congress in 1998 was attended by several thousand activists from over 25 states. There are several special interest caucus groups, the most active being the caucus of militant Black women.

One of the great distinctions of the BRC is that it was one of the first organizations to employ the strategic method of cyberorganizing, using the Internet to build a protest movement. The 1998 Congress was organized mainly on the Internet using a website and email. The BRC maintains an active listserv discussion group. This list is not only the place to stay informed about the BRC, but press releases and commentary comes through about all aspects of the Black liberation movement. Currently the BRC has published policy positions on a variety of international issues. A BRC delegation played an active role in the World Conference Against Racism held in Durban, South Africa in 2001. The organization is currently active in the anti-war movement.

### NAACP Online
www.naacp.org

The NAACP is the oldest and the largest civil rights organization. It has 2200 organizational units in every state and several countries, including more than 500,000 members. This is significant as adult membership is annually $30, and for youth it is $10. Kwesi Mfume, a former member of Congress, serves as the national leader of the NAACP. He has led the organization into every major policy area that impacts the quality of life of African Americans. Almost every Black community has a chapter of the NAACP. It serves as the shadow government to represent the Black community, hence most major ministers are active. It is a training context for political leadership.

Given the age of the organization one of the significant documents on the site is an annotated chronology of the NAACP from its founding date of 1909. And for the future it includes a document that contains the proposed strategic priorities and goals covering 2002–06. In addition there is a full description of the national organization and requirements for membership.

Jeff Johnson heads the Youth and College Councils. He is a graduate of the University of Toledo, who began his political career by leading a protest to create the Africana Studies Program while he was head of the Black Student Union. There are 600 Youth Councils.

## Congressional Black Caucus

www.house.gov/ebjohnson/cbcmain.htm

The supreme legislative body in the US government is the Congress. Black members of Congress have formed a Black caucus, and that body is the leading force among Black elected officials in the USA. This website will give you very useful information on the role of Black people as members of Congress as well as current and past issues of relevance to the African American community that come up for Congressional action.

This site provides biographical information on every African American who has ever been in Congress. This includes four Senators, and 102 members of the House of Representatives. There are links to the home pages of every current member of the Congressional Black Caucus, and these pages usually contain information about their home districts as well as information regarding the committees on which they serve.

The website includes essays on the history of Blacks in Congress in general, and on the Congressional Black Caucus in particular since its formation in 1971. It presents five special issues as foci for sub-committees: health, justice and voting, housing, technology, and the environment and agriculture. Information is also available from their non-profit arm, the Congressional Black Caucus Foundation, **www.cbcfinc.org**.

## Malcolm X: A Research Site

www.brothermalcolm.net

This site focuses on Malcolm X, the major Black figure to emerge from the Black nationalist movement since World War II. It is comprehensive and includes family history, an extensive chronology, a bibliography of books by and about him, and a webliography including various sites and institutions named after him. There is also a set of full audio speeches available for listening or downloading.

But this site contains more than this. It is the main site for listening to the activists of the militant anti-imperialist tradition that has maintained the legacy of the last couple of years of Malcolm X's life. This was a time when he evolved beyond the narrow nationalism of the Nation of Islam and its leader Elijah Muhammad, and took his place among the world's leaders of the post-World War II national liberation movements.

All 24 sessions of the 1990 conference "Malcolm X: Radical Tradition and Legacy of Struggle" are included on this site as audio files. The participants cover all aspects of militant Black activism. Featured in the opening session were Margaret Burroughs, Alex Haley, C. Eric Lincoln, Amiri Baraka, and Betty Shabazz.

The site also contains audio files of a seminar held in Cuba that focused on Malcolm X and the Cuban Revolution. A special feature of this site is a ten minute video of Fidel Castro speaking with the US participants of this seminar. Participants included Muhammad Ahmed, Kwame Toure (Stokely Carmichael), James Turner, William Strickland, William Sales, Tony Monteiro, Abdul Alkalimat, Akinyele Umoja, and many others.

The sound files from the 1991 conference that featured the concerns of Black women are here, including such people as Jayne Cortez, Sonja Sanchez, Donna Coombs, and Vicky Garvin. There are also important sessions on youth, culture, and socialism.

## History

**Leadership Conference on Civil Rights**
www.civilrights.org/index.html

**Civil Rights 1860–1980**
www.spartacus.schoolnet.co.uk/USAcivilrights.htm

**Civil Rights Oral History Bibliography**
www-dept.usm.edu/~mcrohb

**Greensboro Sit-Ins: Launch of a Civil Rights Movement**
www.sitins.com

**Civil Rights in Mississippi**
www.lib.usm.edu/~spcol/crda

**Civil Rights Timeline 1954–91**
www.infoplease.com/spot/civilrightstimeline1.html

**Martin Luther King Papers Project**
www.stanford.edu/group/King

**The Martin Luther King Center**
www.thekingcenter.com

**Huey Newton**
www.pbs.org/hueypnewton

**Fred Hampton**
www.providence.edu/afro/students/panther/hamptonsr.html

**Race and Ethnicity**
www.eserver.org/race

**Ralph Bunche**
www.ralphbunchecentenary.org
www.ralphbunche.com/index.html

**John Brown**
history.furman.edu/~benson/docs/jbmenu.htm
www.iath.virginia.edu/jbrown/master.html
www.johnbrown.org
www.iath.virginia.edu/jbrown/sources.html

**The Sojourn to the Past Project**
www.sojournproject.org

**The Sixties Project**
lists.village.virginia.edu/sixties

## Electoral politics

**The Color of Money: Campaign Contributions and Race**
www.colorofmoney.org

**National Conference of Black Mayors**
www.blackmayors.org

**Al Sharpton**
www.nationalactionnetwork.org

**National Coalition on Black Civic Participation**
www.bigvote.org

## Movement politics

**National Urban League**
www.nul.org

**Project South**
www.projectsouth.org

**Center for Third World Organizing**
www.ctwo.org

**Leadership Conference on Civil Rights**
www.civilrights.org/index.html

**National Civil Rights Museum**
www.civilrightsmuseum.org

**Civil Rights Documentation Project**
www-dept.usm.edu/~mcrohb

**National Black United Front**
www.nbufront.org

**N'COBRA: National Coalition of Blacks for Reparations in America**
www.ncobra.com

**Malcolm X Grassroots Movement**
www.mxgm.org/main.htm

**ANSWER: Act Now to Stop War and End Racism**
www.internationalanswer.org

**Greensboro Justice Fund**
www.gjf.org/gjf_main.html

**The Peoples Institute for Survival and Beyond**
www.thepeoplesinstitute.org

**War Without End? Not in Our Name!**
www.notinourname.net

**National Civil Rights Movement**
www.ncrm.org.uk/index.html

**New York Civil Rights Commission**
www.nycivilrights.org/about/begin.jsp

**Freedom Road Socialist Organization**
www.freedomroad.org/index.html

## Government

**National Black Caucus of State Legislators**
www.nbcsl.com

**State Legislative Black Caucuses**
California www.assembly.ca.gov/lbcweb/lbchisty.htm
Michigan www.housedems.com/blackcaucus
Louisiana www.legis.state.la.us/llbc
South Carolina www.usca.edu/aasc/blackcaucus.htm
Maryland www.blacklegislatormd.org
Missouri www.duboislc.org/blackcaucus
Georgia www.glbcinc.com
Mississippi www.diversepro.com/afro/showOrg.asp?id=210
Florida www.fbc-leo.com

**THOMAS: Legislative Information on the Internet**
(search for words like race, African American, and Black)
thomas.loc.gov

**US Commission on Civil Rights**
www.usccr.gov

## Government surveillance

**COINTELPRO**
www.icdc.com/~paulwolf/cointelpro/cointel.htm

**FBI – Freedom of Information Act Online**
foia.fbi.gov/foiaindex.htm
Includes:

Atlanta Child Murders
Josephine Baker
Black Panther Party – Winston Salem
Cointelpro
Deacons for Defense and Justice
W. E. B. DuBois
Wallace D. Fard
Five Percenters
Highlander Folk School
Jonestown
Martin Luther King
Ku Klux Klan
Stanley Levison
Malcolm X (Little)
Viola Liuzzo
Thurgood Marshall
Mississippi Burning
Moorish Science Temple of America
Elijah Muhammad
Muslim Mosque Inc.
NAACP
National Negro Congress
Organization of Afro-American Unity
Mack Charles Parker
A. Philip Randolph
Paul and Eslanda Robeson
Jackie Robinson
SCLC
Clarence 13X Smith
SNCC
Roy Wilkins
Richard N. Wright

**US Civil Rights Division** (Department of Justice, US Government)
www.usdoj.gov/crt/crt-home.html

## Academic research

**Joint Center for Political and Economic Studies**
www.jointcenter.org

**Civil Rights Project of Harvard University**
www.civilrightsproject.harvard.edu

## Good books

Alkalimat, Abdul, and Gills, Doug. (1989) *Harold Washington and the crisis of Black Power in Chicago*. Chicago: Twenty First Century Books and Publications.

Barker, Lucius Jefferson, and Jones, Mack H. (1994) *African Americans and the American political system*. Englewood Cliffs, N.J.: Prentice Hall.

Dawson, Michael. (2001) *Black Visions: The roots of contemporary African American political ideologies*. Chicago: University of Chicago Press.

Henry, Charles P. (1992) *Culture and African American politics*. Bloomington: Indiana University Press.

Jennings, James. (1994) *Understanding the nature of poverty in urban America*. Westport, Conn.: Praeger.

Marable, Manning. (1988) *Black American politics: from the Washington marches to Jesse Jackson*. London: Verso.

Nelson, William E. (2001) *Black Atlantic politics: dilemmas of political empowerment in Boston and Liverpool*. Albany, N.Y.: State University of New York Press.

Pinderhughes, Dianne Marie. (1947) *Race and ethnicity in Chicago politics: a reexamination of pluralist theory*. Urbana, Ill.: University of Illinois Press.

Reed, Adolph L., Jr. (1999) *Stirrings in the jug: Black politics in the post-segregation era*. Minneapolis: University of Minnesota Press.

Rich, Wilbur C. (1996) *Black mayors and school politics: the failure of reform in Detroit, Gary, and Newark*. New York: Garland Pub.

Ture, Kwame, and Hamilton, Charles. (1992) *Black Power: the politics of liberation in America*. New York: Vintage Press.

Walters, Ronald W., and Smith, Robert C. (1999) *African American leadership*. Albany, N.Y.: State University of New York Press.

Walton, Hanes, Jr. (1997) *African American power and politics: the political context variable*. New York: Columbia University Press.

# 17
# Religion and the Church

The most fundamental beliefs encoded in all human cultures include religious beliefs. People cling to their religious beliefs to stabilize the meaning of life in an otherwise confusing world of conflict and ambiguity. This is certainly true for African American people who have their religion to anchor the foundation of community cultural and social life. The Black church is where Black music is based, where cultural practices are mastered from such diverse activities as cooking, organizing meetings, and leadership skills. The Black church is the universal meeting place for the community, and the minister is almost always a leader in the community, both for internal matters and out in the wider society. To know the Black community it is imperative to know the Black church and its related activities.

The Black church has always adopted new communications technologies. From word of mouth, to various uses of printed texts, to radio and television the Black church has embraced every major technological advance to consolidate and serve its membership as well as to spread the word to the community. This is true today as the Black church is adopting the new information technologies of computers, the Internet, and the World Wide Web.

Black religious life has everything one might expect to find – local churches, organizations on all levels covering a variety of issues, music, a diverse set of academic institutions, and the most all encompassing leadership training tradition. The Black church has always been in every major movement for social justice and peace, and that continues today in cyberspace.

**CyberChurch**
www.cyber-church.us

This important project has the goal of creating a web page for every African American church in the USA. The Toledo Spiders, a group organized at the Africana Studies Program of the University of Toledo, initiated this process by building a website for every Black church in Toledo, Ohio. The amazing feature of this process is that these web pages are being created for the churches for free.

A full set of web links are included to cover Black academic theologians, church denominations and related organizations, and links to religious music of all kinds. In addition there are links to the religions of the African Disapora, especially the New World religious tradition that links back to the Yoruba of Nigeria including Voodoo (USA), Vodun (Haiti), Santeria (Cuba), and Candomble (Brazil).

The main content of the site is a focus on churches in the USA. A national network of students and faculty in Africana Studies programs are collecting data to build this site. There are four levels being built for each church in the database.

1. Church directory: basic information on the church including a picture.
2. Institutional church: full description of church organization and activities, including profiles of ministers and leadership.
3. Church Voice: audio files of a sermon and the church choir, including at least one interview with a senior church leader.
4. Wired Church: establishment of a community technology center within the church to serve the congregation and the local community.

The website has links to forms for churches and church members to submit their information to be included in this important site.

**The North Star: A Journal of African American Religious History**
northstar.vassar.edu
This is a full text online journal covering all aspects of the African American religious experience. It was launched in 1997 and every back issue is available in an archive on the site, in addition to the current issue. They produce two issues per year. The editor is Judith Weisenfeld at Vassar College.

There are two features that make this an outstanding site in addition to the full text articles. The first is a listing of dissertations underway and completed. This is very useful as a networking tool for graduate students to find peers working on similar topics and to facilitate the sharing of research information. The second feature is a section dealing with web resources. The organizers write short annotations of key websites they determine to be of interest to their readers.

As the costs of print publications increase it is difficult for many library budgets to afford keeping up even with the number of journals that one might have found in the past. This is not only the case in the sciences, but extends to the humanities as well and that includes the study of religion. Online journals are a necessity if scholarship is to be peer reviewed and circulated to all interested professional scholars. Otherwise, scholarship is increasingly imprisoned in a class structure that links knowledge to wealth, both individual and institutional.

**African American Religion: A Documentary History Project**
www.amherst.edu/~aardoc/menu.html
This is a project under the direction of Albert Raboteau (Princeton) and David Wills (Amherst). The site is about the preparation of a 13 volume set of books to be published by the University of Chicago Press. This set of volumes is organized in three main periods:

1. African American Religion in the Atlantic World 1441–1808
2. The Continental Phase 1808–1906
3. The Global Phase 1906–Now

There are many useful aspects to this site, even without the full text of all 13 volumes. It does include some sample documents, and there are interpretive essays written in preparation for the complete series. In addition there are course syllabi that take different approaches to the Black religious experience that will be particularly interesting to students and faculty alike.

This site is a great advertisement for the impact of the Black Studies movement since the 1960s. Earlier generations of scholars also had their own impetus to gather up documents for the study of intellectual and cultural history. Clearly leaders of this include librarians, and scholars who have organized a program of research. The best example of this is Carter G. Woodson. In addition to Woodson scholars of the Black church who have made great contributions include Benjamin Mays, E. Franklin Frazier and Arthur Fauset. This particular set of volumes and this website have been propelled with the wind from Black Studies driving their sails. The rebirth of history that breathes life into a people's tradition can begin when the archives are opened and people have access to all that has gone before. This is a good place to begin sharing such a process.

### School of Divinity, Howard University
www.howard.edu/schooldivinity

This is the oldest institution established for the training of religious professionals in the African American community. It was established in 1867 and has been operating for 136 years. The current Dean is Professor Clarence Newsome. He continues a long line of distinguished scholars and great preachers. This is demonstrated in two biographical statements posted on the site about two of his predecessors, Howard Thurman and Benjamin Mays. These men are the foundation scholars and theologians for Black religious thought in the 20th century, rivaled by the activist ministries of Martin Luther King and Malcolm X.

The site gives a very good summation of the academic program at the school. This includes three main degrees: MA in Divinity, MA in Religious Studies, and a PhD in Ministry. This is a program designed to continue the applied studies of an activist ministry in the social gospel tradition. Also included is a list of speakers at the school and at the weekly chapel services on campus. This reads like a who's who of modern Black religious activism and theological scholarship.

This is the institution that guided the Black minister from an inspired but unlettered champion of faith to a professional organizer grounded in modern theology and academic excellence. The danger has always been the tendency critiqued by Carter G. Woodson in his book *The Miseducation of the Negro*. He describes such an unlettered preacher who so inspired his congregation that they sent him to theology school. He came back and had adopted a formal style outside of the oratorical tradition of the Black church and a language not of the people. This is the historical struggle of such institutions as Howard University: how to maintain academic excellence and social relevance. Each generation has had to fight this battle, and sometimes it goes more one way than another.

## Black and Christian

www.blackandchristian.com

This is a comprehensive site that covers the Black church in the Christian tradition. It is a dynamic site with a full screen offering you choices for multiple paths to what is offered. It looks exciting and is fast and easy to navigate. It is organized around five basic sections: the pulpit, the pew, academy, the Black church, and global.

This site is of interest to both the professional clergy as well as the general public. It is a virtual religious community and enables one to communicate with religious leaders and thinkers, as well as one another. All of the standard Internet tools are available including email and chat, and you can sign up for a free newsletter. There is a search function on the site and links to a wide variety of websites of related interest.

## Holy texts

**Bibles**
www.bibles.net

**Quran** (Koran)
www.noi.org/study/quran.htm

**Holy Koran of the Moorish Science Temple**
www.geocities.com/Athens/Delphi/2705/koran-index.html

**Sacred Texts of African Religions**
www.sacred-texts.com/afr

## Organizations

**African Methodist Episcopal Church**
www.amecnet.org
www.ame-church.org

**Christian Methodist Episcopal Church**
www.cmesonline.org
www.c-m-e.org

**National Baptist Convention, USA**
www.nationalbaptist.org/congress/index.shtml

**The Progressive National Baptist Convention**
www.pnbc.org

**The Congress of National Black Churches**
www.cnbc.org

**Full Gospel Baptist Church Fellowship**
www.fullgospelbaptist.org

**Black Jews, Hebrews, and Israelites**
members.aol.com/Blackjews

**All Africa Conference of Churches**
www.aacc-ceta.org

**National Black Catholic Evangelization Forum**
www.bcn.net/~wsavage

**Union of Black Episcopalians**
www.afroanglican.org/ube

**Church of God in Christ**
www.cogic.org

**Presiding Bishop, Church of God in Christ**
www.bbless.org

**African American Mennonites**
www.thirdway.com/menno/FAQ.asp?F_ID=10

**The African and African American Nichiren Shoshu Buddhist Website**
www.proudblackbuddhist.org/may_pbb_index/Page_1x.html

**Nation of Islam Online**
www.noi.org

**African American Ministers Leadership Council**
www.aamlc.net

## African Diaspora

**Santeria**
www.religioustolerance.org/santeri.htm

**African Religion**
www.shikanda.net/african_religion/index.htm

**African Traditional Religion**
www.afrikaworld.net/afrel

**OrishaNet**
www.seanet.com/Users/efunmoyiwa/welcome.html
www.seanet.com/Users/efunmoyiwa/welcome.html

**Botanicas: African and Latin American Spirituality in Southern California**
www.humnet.ucla.edu/humnet/folklore/gallery/botanica

## Social justice

**Southern Christian Leadership Conference**
www.sclcmagazine.com/index.htm

**Interreligious Foundation for Community Organization**
www.ifconews.org

**Veterans of Hope Project**
www.iliff.edu/about_iliff/special_veterans.htm

**American Friends Service Committee**
www.afsc.org

**Sojourners: Christians for Justice and Peace**
www.sojo.net

**Word and World: A Peoples School**
www.wordandworld.org

**Jubilee Institute**
www.belovedcommunitycenter.org/jubilee_institute1.htm

**Church Fires/Rebuilding Burned Churches**
gbgm-umc.org/advance/Church-Burnings/index.html

**African Christian Fellowship Youth**
www.acfyouth.org/index.shtml

## Music and art

**The Spirituals Project**
www.spiritualsproject.org

**Gospel Music Workshop of America**
www.gmwa.org

**Black Jesus Picture Collection**
laughingjesus.50megs.com/blackjesus/blackjesus.htm

**Thomas Dorsey**
www.africanpubs.com/Apps/bios/0554DorseyThomas.asp?pic=none

**Mahalia Jackson**
www.geocities.com/BourbonStreet/2675

## Theologians

**James Cone**
www.uts.columbia.edu/fac/cone.html

**Dwight Hopkins**
divinity.uchicago.edu/faculty/profile_dhopkins.html

**Cheryl Giles**
www.hds.harvard.edu/dpa/faculty/area2/giles.html

**Cain Felder**
www.husdsupport.org/faculty_directory.htm#felder,%20Dr.%20Cain%Oh

**Delores Williams**
www.uts.columbia.edu/fac/williams.html

**Vincent Harding**
www.iliff.edu/about_iliff/faculty_vincent.htm

**Yolanda Smith**
www.yale.edu/divinity/fac/faculty/SMITH.htm

**Robert Paris**
www.ptsem.edu/meet/Faculty01/paris.htm

**Joan Martin**
www.episdivschool.org/academic/Faculty/martin.html

## Academic courses

**Interdenominational Theological Center**
www.itc.edu

**Paine Theological Seminary**
www.payne.edu

**Shaw University Divinity School**
www.shawuniversity.edu/SUDS/index.html

**University of Birmingham (UK)**
www.theology.bham.ac.uk/postgrad/black.htm

**Program of Black Church Studies**
candler.emory.edu/ACADEMIC/BCSP/courses.html

**Institute for Black Catholic Studies**
www.xula.edu/IBCS.html

**Black Church Studies**
www.divinity.duke.edu/production/ProjectsAndPrograms/BlackChurch/
index.aspx

**Kelly Miller Smith Institute on Black Church Studies**
divinity.library.vanderbilt.edu/kmsi/default.htm

**Course Syllabi (African and African American Religion)**
www.aarweb.org/syllabus/browse.asp

## Publications and media

**Black Gospel Radio**
www.blackgospel.com

**The Journal of Religious Thought**
iibp.chadwyck.com/infopage/publ/jrt.htm

**AME Today**
www.ame-today.com

**Black Theology**
www.continuumjournals.com/journals/index.asp?jref=3

**The Star of Zion**
www.thestarofzion.org

## History

**Slavery and Religion in America: A Time Line 1440–1866**
www.ipl.org/div/timeline

## Good books

(1993) *The original African heritage study Bible: King James Version: with special annotations relative to the African/Edenic perspective.* Nashville, Tenn.: J.C. Winston.

Billingsley, Andrew. (1999) *Mighty like a river: the Black church and social reform.* New York: Oxford University Press.

Collier-Thomas, Bettye. (1998) *Daughters of thunder: Black women preachers and their sermons, 1850–1979.* San Francisco: Jossey-Bass.

Cone, James H., and Wilmore, Gayraud S. (1993) *Black theology: a documentary history.* Maryknoll, N.Y.: Orbis Books.

Frazier, Edward Franklin. (1964) *The Negro church in America.* New York: Schocken Books.

Fulop, Timothy E., and Raboteau, Albert J., eds. (1997) *African-American religion: interpretive essays in history and culture.* New York: Routledge.

Hopkins, Dwight N. (2002) *Heart and head: Black theology – past, present, and future.* New York: Palgrave.

Lincoln, C. Eric, and Mamiya, Lawrence H. (1990) *The Black church in the African American experience.* Durham, N.C.: Duke University Press.

Sernett, Milton C., ed. (1999) *Afro-American religious history: a documentary witness.* Durham, N.C.: Duke University Press.

Thurman, Howard. (1984) *Jesus and the disinherited*. Richmond, Ind.: Friends United Press.

Woodson, Carter Godwin. (1992) *The history of the Negro church*. Washington, D.C.: Associated Publishers.

# 18
# Business

The promise of the 19th century emancipation that ended slavery was that African Americans would become equal members of the society. In the United States one of the major aspects of this should have been for a substantial number of Black people to become capitalists in belief and in ownership of businesses. What Black people got was belief but little ownership. The first gains by Black people after emancipation and since has been driven by public policy and the force of government sanction. However, the beginning of the 20th century saw the rise of a movement for Black business led by Booker T. Washington. This was the expression of the segregated Black community having a business market, consisting of personal services, food, and other retail outlets. The 1960s opened up the mainstream economy to Black participation, from the Boards of Directors to CEOs, from the Fortune 500 companies on down. This is not a large class, but it is a Black presence. They network, in organizations and conferences, and they continue to fight racism and all forms of discrimination.

There is a national community of overlapping networks that make up Black business. There are many academic programs, from Black oriented business schools to Black students' organizations in mainstream institutions. However, the majority of Black businesses are small and operate at the neighborhood level. The Black community is largely segregated on a de facto basis, and therefore there the geographical basis for businesses in the Black community continues to exist. The current political/economic trend includes a new form of globalization to keep the lid on indigenous Black business development. Global capital has begun to take control of hair care and nail care, as well as food and pharmaceutical sales.

The most exciting potential involves innovative (hardware or software) applications of information technology to the reorganization of the Black community and the realization of various forms of cyberpower.

**Black Enterprise**
www.blackenterprise.com
This site is focused on business activities by African Americans, both within the Black community as a market for small business as well as African American participation in the business mainstream. This is a full service business site based on the *Black Enterprise* magazine founded in 1968. It includes information on financial markets and searchable access to stock quotes. There are pages to guide the user on issues of small businesses, investing, personal finance, and career planning, and information on the book publishing division of Black Enterprise. The site also provides headline news information on various topics, especially topics of interest to African Americans, as well as information on conferences and seminars.

This site is an interesting contrast to the historical origin of organizing Black businesses undertaken by Booker T. Washington with his National Negro Business League. Washington was limited basically to businesses that served the Black community. Earl Graves, the founder and editor of *Black Enterprise*, has far surpassed this by representing Black business in an era when African Americans are on the boards of Fortune 500 corporations and Black-run businesses operate in the mainstream more than ever before. This is still a small percentage of Black businesses, as most remain small owner-run businesses with few employees. However, we are past the era when being the first Black person to achieve something is big news. The focus has changed to a proper percentage of the market and each job category. There is still a long way to go before there is full equality in the private sector.

This site provides a page called Teenpreneur devoted to information about business for young people. The organizers sponsor an annual conference aimed at four age groups: 4–6, 7–10, 11–13, and 14–18. In these conferences they advise the youth on developing business plans and setting realistic goals. On the website they provide a twelve lesson curriculum aimed at young aspiring teenpreneurs. They also provide a portal to higher education, as well as feature articles aimed at professional business students.

## National Black MBA Association
nbmbaa.org
This is a professional association for African Americans with a Master of Business Administration (MBA) degree. It was formed in 1970 and currently has 40 chapters and 6000 members in the USA. In 2000 a comparable Black MBA UK group was formed in England. This is a highly select group of African Americans in business. The membership has a much higher income than the general population of African Americans, with 21% of members' households having incomes of over $100,000. Most of their chapters have active websites linked to this national site.

The main thrust of this site is to provide professional services and networking for Black holders of or students seeking the MBA degree. One of the main assets is a virtual networking function to bring together businesses and Black MBA job seekers. The Association hase 400 business partners who participate in its national conference and provide support. The virtual networking links a job bank with resumés of job seekers with company recruiters. This is a wonderful use of cyberspace, to have one stop shopping for a highly skilled and selective job market.

In addition, the site has other features of more general interest. This includes a set of press releases about current events in the business world, especially regarding issues of interest to African Americans in business. The Association's big annual event is a conference during which major personalities in the business world give speeches and seminars, as well as provide an opportunity for networking on a face to face basis.

## 1992 and 1997 Survey of Minority Owned Businesses
www.census.gov/csd/mwb
The Census Bureau collects information on the general population as well as business and other aspects of the society. It issued a press release explaining the data on this site: "African American businesses in the United States totaled 823,500, employed 718,300 people and generated

**Business**                                                          **173**

$71.2 billion in revenues in 1997, according to a report released today by the Commerce Department's Census Bureau." The full statistical details for this survey and a comparable one in 1992 are on this site. There is no other body of statistical data that describes Black businesses like this.

Over 50% of all African American businesses are in seven states: New York (10.5%), California (9.6%), Texas (7.3%), Florida (7.2%), Georgia (6.8%), Maryland (5.8%), and Illinois (5.0%). Washington D.C. had the highest percentage of Black businesses, with 24% of businesses there being African American owned.

Of all these businesses half had sales of $10,000 or under, while 1% had sales of $1 million or more. Only about 11% had paid employees, but that 11% accounted for 79% of total gross receipts. In general the number of Black businesses grew by 25% from 1992 to 1997.

This site is very useful as it provides aggregate statistics as well as data by state and by major cities (Standard Metropolitan Statistical Areas). This is one of the aspects of what the Census Bureau provides as an online service. Students at all levels, really beginning at least in high school, should be introduced to this site. In addition, every community level activist and organizational leadership will find this useful because such information is needed for proposals and policy analysis.

**Minority Business Development Agency**
www.mbda.gov
This agency is part of the Department of Commerce and has been set up to assist minority business development. This website is dedicated "to becoming an entrepreneurially focused and innovative organization, committed to empowering minority business enterprises for the purpose of wealth creation in minority communities." The site has four foci for its services: new businesses, home businesses, small businesses, and medium businesses. For each it provides suggestions and guidelines for starting and carefully planning a business.

Its main feature is to be a free consultant service for minority business developers. This includes detailed guidelines for the following: access to markets (including both business to business as well as business to government opportunities), access to capital, management and technical assistance, and education and training. A good aspect of this website is an interactive calendar of relevant activities searchable by date.

It is also possible to register with this agency and get access to a password protected part of the site. This gives you access to more direct information about grant applications and specific services provided by the Agency.

## US Small Business Administration
www.sba.gov

This is the main government agency for small businesses. It is not specifically focused on minority or African American businesses, but certainly does cover them as well as all others. It is important because most Black businesses are small and therefore are in need of the services offered by this agency.

This is the first place to start if one is interested in starting a business. It is designed as a very user friendly site, with immediate access to what is needed. A good example is the information provided for developing a business plan – an easy to read few pages with bullet points that guide you through the process in clear and easy steps. There are many other resources, including shareware and online resources to carry out business related functions that are free downloads. These kinds of free resources are essential to offset start-up costs.

# Organizations: General

**National Black Chamber of Commerce**
www.nationalbcc.org

**The Ebony Cactus: An African American Perspective on Business in Arizona**
www.theebonycactus.com

**National Black Business Council**
www.nbbc.org/nbbc/about.htm

**The National Black Expo**
www.nationalblackexpo.com/index.html

**National Coalition of Black Meeting Planners**
www.ncbmp.com

**The Network for African American Technology Entrepreneurs**
www.nateli.org/index.htm

**African American Students Union**
sa.hbs.edu/aasu

**Black Business Students Association at Stanford**
sa-gsb.stanford.edu/clubs/bbsa

**Black Management Association**
www.kellogg.northwestern.edu/student/club/bma

**African American MBA Association**
gsbwww.uchicago.edu/student/aambaa/2003/index1.htm

**Black Business Students Association**
www.gsb.columbia.edu/students/organizations/bbsa

## Organizations: Industries

**International Black Buyers and Manufacturers Expo and Conference**
www.ibbmec.com

**National Bankers Association**
www.nationalbankers.org/default.asp

**National Minority Mortgage Bankers Association**
www.nmmbainc.org/index.php

**American League of Financial Institutions**
www.alfi.org

**Black Farmers and Agriculturalists Association**
www.coax.net/people/lwf/bfaa.htm

**National Association of Black Accountants**
www.nabainc.org

**National Organization of Minority Architects**
www.noma.net

## Small businesses

**National Center for Neighborhood Enterprise**
www.ncne.com

## Media

**Black Business Journal**
www.bbjonline.com

## Academic programs

**School of Business, Howard University**
www.bschool.howard.edu

**National Economics Association**
www.ncat.edu/~neconasc/index.html

## Women

**Madam C. J. Walker**
www.madamcjwalker.com

## Business ethics

**Wall Street Simulation** (World Council of Churches)
www.ecumenicalyouth.org/wall_street.html

**Corporations Watch**
www.corpwatch.org

**Minority Business Enterprise Legal Defense and Education Fund**
www.mbeldef.org

## Statistics

**Federal Data and Information Resources**
www.ncat.edu/~neconasc/federal.html

## Good books

Bell, Gregory S. (2002) *In the Black: a history of African Americans on Wall Street*. New York: John Wiley.

Boston, Thomas D., ed. (2002) *Leading issues in Black political economy*. New Brunswick, N.J.: Transaction Publishers.

Bundles, A'Lelia. (2002) *On her own ground: the life and times of Madam C. J. Walker*. New York: Washington Square Press.

Graves, Earl G. (1998) *How to succeed in business without being white: straight talk on making it in America*. New York: HarperBusiness.

Harris, Abram Lincoln. (1970) *The Negro as capitalist: a study of banking and business among American Negroes*. New York: Haskell House Publishers.

Jackson, Jesse, Sr., and Jackson, Jesse, Jr., with Gotschall, Mary. (2000) *It's about the money! How you can get out of debt, build wealth, and achieve your financial dreams*. New York: Times Business.

Lewis, Reginald F., and Walker, Blair S. (1997) *Why should white guys have all the fun? How Reginald Lewis created a billion dollar empire*. New York: John Wiley.

Walker, Juliet E. K. (1999) *Encyclopedia of African American business history*. Westport, Conn.: Greenwood.

Walker, Juliet E. K. (1998) *The history of Black business in America: capitalism, race, and entrepreneurship*. New York: Macmillan Library Reference USA.

# 19
# Labor

Labor is the key category for any historical understanding of the African American experience. Slavery was a system for the exploitation of labor, and its legacy has locked Black people more often than not into the lowest levels of income, the most dangerous and dirty jobs, and with the least job security. The current crisis facing an increasing number of Black youth is that they will not have the opportunity for long-term job security because their labor is no longer needed to sustain production and often new immigrants provide the low-paid domestic labor Blacks used to do when they were recent arrivals in the city from the Southern cotton fields. New immigrants are coming into the USA and being forced to accept even lower wages than what would be paid to African Americans, or the jobs are being migrated to regions with cheaper production costs, especially wages for labor.

African American folklore narrates the historical development of Black labor. No greater hero exists in the collective memory of the Black experience than the folk hero John Henry, "a steel driving man." Even unemployment was a labor category in that people were the surplus labor to be pulled into production when needed. However, today this has become permanently unemployed labor with no expectation of a normal secure job. The inner cities have become forbidden zones with homeless workers set adrift in the ruins of urban blight.

On the other hand Black people make up a substantial portion of the employed working class. Black workers are unionized at a rate higher than the national norm and have a long history of being militant fighters for workers' rights.

**Coalition of Black Trade Unionists**
www.cbtu.org

This is a website of an organization formed in 1972 to increase the union-ization of Black workers, to increase the quality of their lives, and to increase their political power. Five key national trade union leaders formed this organization: Bill Lucy of the American Federation of State Country and Municipal Workers; Nelson "Jack" Edwards of the United Auto Workers; William Simons of the Washington Teachers Union; Charles Hayes of the United Food and Commercial Workers Union; and Cleveland Robinson of the Distributive Workers of America District 65. The CBTU's members come from 50 unions with over 50 chapters in the USA and Canada.

The organization makes a clear statement of its intent on the website: "CBTU is not a Black separatist or civil rights organization. It is a fiercely independent voice of Black workers within the trade union movement." The website is as clear as this self-definition. It is easy to navigate with a site map to all the topics covered.

It has information on five key committees: women, youth, retirees, international affairs, and environmental justice. The other national focus is on politics, with information on the Political Empowerment Network. CBTU meets annually in a national convention and information for this event is always posted on this website.

### African American Labor History Websites
www.afscme.org/about/aframlink.htm
This is a compilation of links to labor sites maintained by the American Federation of State County and Municipal Employees (AFSME). It has content but one has to navigate carefully to get the full content of what is being offered. There are four categories of links about the African American experience: general history, labor history, Martin Luther King, and books and films. These links are good but they indicate that lots of work needs to be done for Black labor to be represented fully in cyberspace.

One of the strengths of the site is its focus on Black labor in the South. The following are included as full text articles: Michael Honey on Black factory organizing in the Jim Crow era; Barbara Jean Hope on Hosea Hudson, a Black communist labor organizer in Birmingham; and Howard Zinn on Charleston (South Carolina) Black waterfront workers. There are also several links to primary documentation of Martin Luther King and the Memphis sanitation workers strike.

There are a number of links to biographical sketches of Black labor leaders from various trade unions as well as in the mass movement. One of the rare gems in this collection is a link to an essay by A. Muhammad Ahmed on the history of the League of Revolutionary Black Workers, a militant rank and file organization of workers in Detroit.

The trade union movement is making an effort to get its rank and file online as well as locals to bring organizational communications into the 21st century. The AFL-CIO has a program for the members to purchase computers and get connected for a reduced price, as do several unions. In fact, even some companies (e.g., Ford Motor Company) are offering their employees an opportunity to purchase computers in a plan to employ the Internet to help streamline and cut costs. The test of e-democracy will be for workers to be online and part of the network society to the same extent as the owners and managers of the corporations where they work.

### A. Philip Randolph Institute

www.aprihq.org

This organization is designed to work for a lack-labor alliance. It was founded in 1965 and currently has 150 chapters in 36 states. The current president is Norman Hill, a long-time activist in the labor movement and activities for social justice. One of the useful features of this site is a set of biographical sketches of Hill and two of the main founding leaders of the Institute, A. Philip Randolph (1889–1979) and Bayard Rustin (1912–1987).

This site includes details of the annual conference schedule. An annual national conference is held as well as regional conferences and education conferences. These are useful supplements to the meetings of Black workers within their unions. The Institute also provides job training to assist young workers in gaining the qualifications to enter certain technical fields. This is an institution with offices in the Black community making it easier to outreach to Black youth who otherwise might not have direct access to the contacts necessary to get a good job.

**Equal Employment Opportunity**
Department of Labor
www.dol.gov/dol/topic/discrimination/ethnicdisc.htm
This is a site that assists both workers and employers with issues of discrimination and abuses of various kinds in the workplace. It provides a clear guide to rights of workers and specific references to the laws that govern the workplace. It also provides information for small businesses with guidelines for diversity training. The Department provides free workshops as a routine process in an attempt to prevent problems from arising.

One of the most interesting aspects of this site is the statistics it provides. It lists detailed statistical data on the charges files by Blacks, women, the physically challenged, and older workers. It also provides the data on how these charges were resolved. The Department defines the context for these actions with statistical information about job patterns for the various categories of workers covered by the legislation it enforces.

**Statistics on Minority Workers**
Bureau of Labor Statistics
www.bls.gov/cps
The Bureau of Labor Statistics is the main federal source for statistical information about workers in the US economy. This is the one stop shopping place for labor statistics, and as many of its data tables have comparative data it is also an essential site for information about Black labor. They present data that compares whites, Blacks, and Hispanics.

This site is user friendly as it provides a glossary of terms to assist those unfamiliar with this kind of statistical data. The Bureau's surveys report data annually and on a monthly basis. One interesting fact concerns union membership. As of 2002 Black adult workers were the most unionized: Blacks 16.9%, whites 13.0%, and Hispanics 11.1%.

This is not a site filled with animation and exciting color graphics, but it is one of the most important sites one can visit if searching for information vital to the well being of the African American community. You can answer key questions with the data it presents: What kind of

**Labor**

jobs do people have? How much money do they make? How much difference is there between Black, Hispanic, and white workers?

## History

**Black Workers and the Labor Movement**
www.murchisoncenter.org/rahul/introbook/chapter7.htm

**African Americans in the Youngstown Steel Industry**
www.as.ysu.edu/%7Ecwcs/AmandaR.htm

**African Americans in Food Service**
anacostia.si.edu/food/index.htm

## Organizations: General

**Coalition of Black Trade Unionists Canada**
www.cbtu.ca

**Coalition of South African Trade Unions (COSATU)**
www.cosatu.org.za

**The Labor Party**
www.thelaborparty.org

**AFL-CIO**
www.aflcio.org

**Coalition of Labor Union Women**
www.cluw.org

**The Affirmative Action Association**
www.affirmativeaction.org

## Organizations: Trade unions

**United Domestic Workers of America**
www.udwa.org/leadership.htm

**The Black Flight Attendants of America**
www.bfaoa.com

**The National Alliance of Postal and Federal Employees**
www.napfe.com

**Minority Caucus** (International Brotherhood of Electrical Workers)
www.ibew.org/stories/01journal/0110/010908_mc1.htm

## Struggle

**Black Panther Caucus – UAW**
sunsite.berkeley.edu/calheritage/panthers/caucus.htm

**A. Philip Randolph**
www.aphiliprandolphmuseum.com
www.pbs.org/weta/apr/aprbio.html
www.spartacus.schoolnet.co.uk/USArandolph.htm

**National Interfaith Committee for Worker Justice**
www.nicwj.org/index.html

**Sweatshop Watch**
www.sweatshopwatch.org

**The Strike Page**
www.thebird.org/strikes

**Justice for Janitors**
www.seiu.org/building/janitors

**Solidarity Center AFL-CIO**
www.solidaritycenter.org

## Diversity and equity

**National Association of Social Workers**
www.socialworkers.org/diversity/default.asp

**Employment Discrimination: An Overview** (Legal Information Institute)
wwwsecure.law.cornell.edu/topics/employment_discrimination.html

## Culture

**Union Songs**
www.crixa.com/muse/unionsong

## Academic study and research

**School of Industrial and Labor Relations**
www.ilr.cornell.edu

**African Labor**
www-sul.stanford.edu/depts/ssrg/africa/labor.html

## Statistics

**US Bureau of Labor Statistics**
www.bls.gov

## Media

**H-Labor** (H-Net Discussion List)
www2.h-net.msu.edu/~labor

## Good books

Arnesen, Eric. (2001) *Brotherhoods of color: Black railroad workers and the struggle for equality*. Cambridge, Mass.: Harvard University Press.

Foner, Philip Sheldon. (1982) *Organized labor and the Black worker, 1619–1981*. New York: International Publishers.

Georgakas, Dan, and Surkin, Marvin. (1998) *Detroit: I do mind dying*. Cambridge, Mass.: South End Press.

Harley, Sharon, and the Black Women and Work Collective, eds. (2002) *Sister circle: Black women and work*. New Brunswick, N.J.: Rutgers University Press.

Harris, William. (1991) *Keeping the faith: A. Philip Randolph, Milton Webster, and the Brotherhood of Sleeping Car Porters*. Champaign, Ill.: University of Illinois Press.

Minchin, Timothy J. (2001) *The color of work: the struggle for civil rights in the Southern paper industry, 1945–1980*. Chapel Hill: University of North Carolina Press.

Needleman, Ruth. (2003) *Black freedom fighters in steel: the struggle for democratic unionism*. Ithaca, N.Y.: ILR Press.

Obadele-Starks, Ernest. (2000) *Black unionism in the industrial South*. College Station, Tex.: Texas A & M University Press.

Spero, Sterling, and Harris, Abram. (1968) *The Black worker: the Negro and the labor movement*. New York: Atheneum.

Winslow, Calvin, ed. (1998) *Waterfront workers: new perspectives on race and class*. Champaign, Ill.: University of Illinois Press.

# 20
# Science and Technology

There have been four major types of contribution that Black people have made in the realm of science and technology. By this we mean Black scientists have made serious contributions to create a body of knowledge and a related set of social practices that together represent science and technology in this society. The four are as follows:

1. Retention of African science: the African people brought advanced knowledge of working with metals, of growing crops, of cooking, of medicine, and of astronomy among other things. These African knowledge systems have made a major impact on social life in the USA.
2. Transformation of technology in the workplace and in social life: the intimate relationship between workers and their tools was the crucible for Black creativity from the cotton gin to the assembly line.
3. Technologies of survival from slavery till the present: Black people have been leaders in the tactics of everyday resistance to increases in exploitation and health risks.
4. Mainstream science: the achievements of African Americans in academic programs and professional associations.

Our primary concern in this directory is with mainstream western science. We focus on the role of African Americans in both the academic study and research front of science, and also on those in professional careers in the public and private sector. Of course the role of public policy and the fight for social justice in science is a constant theme.

One of the main ways that racism has been expressed is in pseudo-scientific arguments to prove the racial inferiority of African Americans and others. So it is very interesting that what is at stake in this field is not merely how science views the issue of race, but what in the end science actually is. The Bell Curve split the scientific community over the racial inferiority of the African. Bad science became a power rationale for a system that treated Black people as if their supposed inferiority were a proven fact. In this era of globalization there is a great deal to be learned about what might make up global science, legitimate in every society and of free use for everyone.

### African Americans in the Sciences
www.princeton.edu/~mcbrown/display/faces.html
This site contains a massive listing of biographical information about scientists in a wide variety of scientific fields of research. The information is accessible by name or by discipline. There is also a special listing of women scientists in all of these fields. The following disciplines are included: Biochemistry, Biology, Chemistry, Computer Science, Engineering, Entomology, Genetics, Geology, Mathematics, Medicine, Meteorology, Microbiology, Oceanography, Physics, Protozoology, and Zoology. The people included here are the major figures, the path breakers who led the way and established a record of excellence. These scientists struggled against racism by achieving excellence in their chosen fields of study.

One of the unique historical features of this site is that it lists the first Black PhD in every one of the fields covered, including name, institution, and date of degree.

It includes information about the degrees awarded to Blacks. Between 1870 and 1960 there were 587 African Americans awarded the PhD degree, with the breakdown as follows: Biosciences 43%, Chemistry 32%, Physical Sciences 16%, Agricultural Sciences 6%, and Pharmaceutical Sciences 3%.

### Mathematicians of the African Diaspora
www.math.buffalo.edu/mad
The main focus of this site is on Black mathematicians. Dr. Scott Williams maintains this site as part of his long-standing work as a mathematician and historian of Blacks in science. He is a cofounder of two

key organizations that promote Black research in mathematics: the National Association of Mathematics (1969) and the African American Research Group in Mathematics (1997). His site includes information on 450 people, including an extensive listing of Black women holders of the PhD in math. Less than 1% of all mathematicians are Black, but, of those, 25% of all Black mathematicians are women!

He presents a chronological listing of facts about Blacks in math, with links to information about individuals, awards, and other topics. There are extensive links to math in the African Diaspora, including journals, conferences, academic institutions, and leading scholars.

But there is more to this site than math. There are special pages on the following: physicists, astronomers, awards received by Black mathematicians, job openings, HBCU math departments, obituaries, organizations, and journals. He also includes several of his full text articles on the history of Blacks in science.

This site is a model for the intellectual history of African Americans in an academic field of study.

## Women and Minorities in Science and Engineering
www.mills.edu/ACAD_INFO/MCS/SPERTUS/Gender/wom_and_min.html

This site is mainly about women in general, but includes a great deal of information about the Black experience as well. It is especially useful for young Black women interested in pursuing a career in a scientific field. It is essentially a webliography that has two sections of particular interest to African Americans: Women and Minorities in Science and Engineering, and Racial Minorities in Science and Engineering.

In the 21st century the role of science and technology will be center stage more than ever before. Gender roles are being redefined and it is critical that this be continued in the fields of science and engineering. Young Black women can be encouraged to pursue scientific fields of study if the librarians and teachers they encounter can guide them to the information that will reveal role models, provide guidelines for how to combat male supremacy in the labs and classrooms, and how to think of themselves in new terms and not be held back by the experiences of previous generations.

This site is very good for male teachers of science and engineering. They are the gate keepers to these fields and can play a positive role if they are informed and motivated to do so. This site is a good place to start.

## National Black Graduate Students Association
www.nbgsa.org
This site is about a national organization founded in 1989. It is composed of Black graduate students throughout the USA. The site gives information about their annual conferences during which there are opportunities for networking and the sharing of experience. The main feature of this site is that graduate students have a context in which to interact with peers. This provides the opportunity to have cross-disciplinary discussions, and for students from mainstream campuses and HBCUs to connect and share experiences.

## History of Race in Science
MIT
www.racesci.org
This is an important site in that it focuses on racism within science, the fight for maintaining the highest standards of scientific scholarship in the study of peoples around the world, especially Africa and the African Diaspora. The site in maintained under the leadership of Prof. Evelyn Hammonds, Professor of the History of Science and African American Studies at Harvard University.

The site includes bibliographies that contain over 1000 references organized in 40 topical areas. There are syllabi of courses taught on many aspects of race in science, as well as articles in the news media that indicate the issues being discussed in public discourse. The site provides the interactive opportunity for people to contribute to the site by submitting items for the bibliography, course syllabi, and news articles. This feature is important because without the help of a wide network of contributors, keeping such a site current would not be possible.

A major feature of this site is the webliography. There are links for the following topics: health, genetics, reproductive rights, scientific racism, anthropology, and exhibitions and world fairs. There is also a link to material about information concerning professional associations.

This is a site of great value for many courses that focus on racism.

# History

**Blacks in Technology: Past and Present**
www.users.fast.net/%7Eblc/xlhome2.htm

**African Americans Do Science**
www.ericse.org/bhm.html

**Ronald McNair**
www.aad.berkeley.edu/uga/osl/mcnair/Ronald_E._McNair.html

**African American Astronauts**
quest.nasa.gov/qchats/special/mlk00/afam_astronauts.html

## Women

**Women and Minorities in Science and Engineering**
www.mills.edu/ACAD_INFO/MCS/SPERTUS/Gender/wom_and_min.
html

**Women, Minorities, and Persons with Disabilities in Science and Engineering: 1996**
www.nsf.gov/sbe/srs/nsf96311

**Black Women in Mathematics**
www.math.buffalo.edu/mad/wmad0.html

## Genetics

**Minorities, Race and Genomics**
www.ornl.gov/hgmis/elsi/minorities.html

**Communities of Color and Genetics Policy Project**
www.sph.umich.edu/genpolicy/current/index.html

# Inventors

**African American Inventors**
www.invention.org/culture/african/index.html

**Black Scientists and Inventors**
www.infoplease.com/spot/bhmscientists1.html

**African American Inventors**
www.enchantedlearning.com/inventors/black.shtml

# Organizations

**National Society of Black Physicists**
nsbp.org/cgi-bin/nsbp.cgi?page=home

**American Chemical Society Minority Affairs**
www.chemistry.org/portal/Chemistry?PID=acsdisplay.html&DOC=
minorityaffairs\index.html

**National Association of Mathematicians**
jewel.morgan.edu/~nam

**National Action Council for Minorities in Engineering**
www.nacme.org

**The Benjamin Banneker Association**
www.math.msu.edu/banneker

**Student National Medical Association**
www.snma.org

**Council for African Americans in the Mathematical Sciences**
www.math.buffalo.edu/mad/CAARMS/CAARMS-index.html

**National Organization for the Professional Advancement of Black Chemists and Chemical Engineers**
www.nobcche.org

**Black Wings** (Blacks in Aviation)
www.ssbinc.com/b_wings

## African Diaspora: Africa

**African Scientific Network**
www.physics.ncat.edu/%7Emichael/asn

**Physicists of the African Diaspora**
www.math.buffalo.edu/mad/physics/index.html

**Science in Africa**
www.scienceinafrica.co.za

**Chemistry in Africa**
www.webanalytes.com/cheminafrica.html

**African Mathematical Union**
www.math.buffalo.edu/mad/AMU/index.html

**History of Science and Technology in Islamic Civilization**
www.ou.edu/islamsci

## African Diaspora: Caribbean

**Caribbean Journal of Science**
caribjsci.org

**Ministry of Commerce, Science and Technology**
www.mct.gov.jm

**The Institute of Jamaica**
www.instituteofjamaica.org.jm

**Trinidad and Tobago, Science and Environment**
www.caribbeansitedirectory.com/links/trinidadandtobago-science
andenvironment.html

**General Directory to the Caribbean**
(Click on country, then on science and the environment for a set of links)
www.caribbeansitedirectory.com

## Academic study

**Strategies for Teaching Science to African American Students**
www.as.wvu.edu/~equity/african.html

**Minority Introduction to Engineering, Entrepreneurship, and Science Program**
web.mit.edu/mites/www

**Office of Minority Student Education**
www.msa.caltech.edu

**Minority Students**
web.mit.edu/admissions/www/undergrad/freshman/minority

**Office of Minority and Special Programs**
www.coe.gatech.edu/omsp

**Office of Minority Student Affairs**
www.rpi.edu/dept/omsa

**College of Engineering, Architecture, and Computer Science**
www.founders.howard.edu/CEACS

**Institute for the Study of Academic Racism**
www.ferris.edu/htmls/OTHERSRV/ISAR/homepage.htm

## Publications

**African Technology Forum**
web.mit.edu/africantech/www/index.html

**African Journal of Mathematics**
www.african-j-math.org

**Afrika Matematica**
www.math.buffalo.edu/mad/AMU/Afrika-Matematica.html

## Good books

Christian, Marcus. (1972) *Negro ironworkers in Louisiana, 1718–1900*. Gretna, La.: Pelican Pub. Co.

Jones, James Howard. (1993) *Bad blood: the Tuskegee syphilis experiment*. New York: Free Press.

Krapp, Kristine M., ed. (1999) *Notable Black American scientists*. Detroit, Mich.: Gale Research.

Lewontin, Richard C., Rose, Steven, and Kamin, Leon J. (1984) *Not in our genes: biology, ideology, and human nature*. New York: Pantheon Books.

Manning, Kenneth R. (1983) *Black Apollo of science: the life of Ernest Everett Just*. New York: Oxford University Press.

Sullivan, Otha Richard. (2002) *Black stars: African American women scientists and inventors*. New York: Wiley.

Van Sertima, Ivan, ed. (1983) *Blacks in science: ancient and modern*. New Brunswick, N.J.: Transaction Books.

Warren, Wini. (1999) *Black women scientists in the United States*. Bloomington: Indiana University Press.

Wynes, Charles E. (1988) *Charles Richard Drew: the man and the myth*. Urbana, Ill.: University of Illinois Press.

# 21
# Military

African Americans have been involved in every war fought by the USA, but at every point the participation of Blacks in the armed forces has been conditioned and limited by the prevailing norms of institutional racism. Black soldiers were not given special treatment by racist white America, but they had one major advantage in that they were armed and trained to use their weapons. Black soldiers who fought in foreign wars always returned home and had to continue fighting for social justice in their own home country.

Benjamin O. Davis became the first regular officer in the US Army in 1901. Colin Powell became Head of the Joint Chiefs of Staff in 1989 making him the top office in all the US armed forces. This history is filled with heroism and struggle, and recognition for the contributions of these military feats has not yet been completed.

Racism has been a factor at every stage of US history. One of the unusual aspects of this military history is the Civil War. This war is celebrated in many ways and has the result of giving status and honor to the Confederacy. Most Americans do not know the real history of the war and how the Black Union soldiers were repeatedly slaughtered when surrendering and given no decent treatment. In World War II the captured German soldiers were often given better treatment than Black soldiers in the US Army. Imagine the psychology of US Black troops being trained in segregated facilities in the South while in Southern communities Black people were still being lynched. The preparation of fighting a war for democracy was full of tension for them: were they preparing to fight a war in Europe and Africa or in Mississippi?

Today there are Black students enrolled in the academic institutions that serve every branch of service. Black people are stationed all over the world, but are often over-represented in frontline combat units likely to have serious casualties.

## African Americans in Army History
www.army.mil/cmh-pg/topics/afam/afam-USA.htm
This is an official site of the US Army. It is full of photos and essays about the African American experience in the history of the Army. There is a feature on the first General, Brigadier General Benjamin Davis who served for 50 years. His son continued on to become the second General. There is a feature on the first Black graduate of the Military Academy at West Point, Lt. Henry Ossian Flipper (1856–1940). He ended his life in disgrace, but was cleared of false charges against him by President William Clinton. These three men were fighters against many historical obstacles in a very bureaucratic context.

The Army has been disproportionately based on the recruitment of Southerners so a fair amount of regional racism has been transplanted among both enlisted men and officers. However, war is an objective process in which one wins or loses, lives or dies. This has led the military leadership to make decisions that sometimes are in advance of the national norms but serve pragmatic military interests. Jefferson Davis, president of the confederacy after resigning as Secretary of War for the US (Union), in one of his last acts signed an order to recruit more Black soldiers into the Confederate Army than were fighting for the Union. This was a desperate act to place guns in the hands of slaves to fight for the preservation of slavery. It happened to a very limited extent, but it is incredible to think that the Confederates would take such a risk. One wonders what the slaves would have done with those guns.

This site details the process by which the Army integrated, from 1940 to 1965. There is also detailed information on specific military units (battalions, regiments, and divisions) in the Civil War, World War I, and World War II.

## African (American) Military History
www.fatherryan.org/blackmilitary
This site is titled African Military History and is about the African American experience in the US military. It is a wonderful example of

young people helping to build meaningful content in cyberspace. This site has been maintained by students in the Honors Computer Science classes at Father Ryan High School in Nashville, Tennessee. They started it in 1997 and continue to add new content each year.

There are four parts to this site. Pre-World War II contains pages on the 54th Massachusetts, the first all-Black unit to fight for the Union in the Civil War; Buffalo Soldiers, African Americans who fought in the US Cavalry (called that by the Indians who likened Black hair to that of the Buffalo); and Black soldiers in World War I. The part on World War II includes pages on the Tuskegee Airmen, the first Black pilots; and the Red Ball Express, the heroic Black soldiers in the transportation corps who kept the fuel supplied to the vehicles making up the 1944 Allied advance towards Germany. The remaining two parts are on important individuals and other aspects of the military including the US Coast Guard, Blacks in military art, and Black Medal of Honor recipients.

**Department of Defense Celebrates African American History Month**
www.defenselink.mil/specials/AfricanAm2003
This is an official site of the US Department of Defense, and focuses on all branches of the military in honor of the annual February celebration of Black History Month. The site begins with a presidential proclamation made every year to direct all branches of government to honor the contributions of African Americans. There are also links to other agencies like the Smithsonian Institution.

Each branch of the military has some information on this site. The Army provides detailed biographical information on the 81 African Americans who so distinguished themselves in combat that they were awarded the Medal of Honor, the highest medal awarded for military service. It is interesting that half of these medals were awarded for service in the Civil War or Vietnam, when the Black community was politically mobilized in the fight to end slavery in the 1860s and in the Black liberation movement of the 1960s. It seems Black men were in a fighting mood and the military command found it useful to be fair in giving them proper respect for their accomplishments.

There are pages on Black astronauts, the Coast Guard, and other topics. The Navy provides information on the eight major ships named after African Americans. The Marines section provides biographical sketches on the eight Black Generals currently serving as of 2002.

## African American Military History
www.coax.net/people/lwf/aa_mh.htm
This is perhaps the most comprehensive site on Blacks in the US military. Bennie McRae, an independent cyber-scholar who has compiled links and posted content, maintains this site. He has pages on the Black experience organized around these topics: the Revolutionary War, the War of 1812, the Civil War, the Western Frontier, the Spanish American War, World War I, World War II, the Korean War, and the Vietnam War.

When reviewing the comprehensive approach to the topic taken by McRae it leads one to think about how content on the same topic can be aggregated so that all of it can be more easily accessed. The current stage of building cyberspace follows the pattern of individual authorship, keeping content separate like books as individual units. But cyberspace offers the possibility of collective intelligence by which content can be more like a library in which all the books can be accessed as one big book. Hyperlinking everything together will be the ultimate realization of what can be done in cyberspace. In fact this book is but one step toward the reorganization of cyberspace into one big BRAIN, a Black Research Archive on the Internet in which all web content dealing with the African American experience is linked together.

This process will require a full discussion of the key values for Black liberation in the information age: cyber democracy, collective intelligence, and information freedom.

## African American Military History
www.geocities.com/mclane65/black-heroes.html
This website is an excellent compilation of links and web content. It is similar to the site by Bennie McRae, but has new content. It is organized by wars and gives interesting information about each.

There is a feature on Peter Salem, one of the Black veterans of fighting in the American Revolution. He has the distinction of fighting in the Battle of Bunker Hill. He killed Major Pitcairn, the military commander of the British troops. This site includes photos of his grave.

The site gives useful data about the Black participation in the Civil War in which over 200,000 African Americans fought. Seventeen per cent (38,000) were killed. They fought in 449 battles. Black troops were organized into 166 all-Black units, but only had 75 Black officers. Twenty-two Black Civil War soldiers won the Medal of Honor.

This site also contains pages on two contemporary Black leaders with military distinction, Colin Powell and Francis Taylor. General Powell served as Head of the Joint Chiefs of Staff and now is the Secretary of State. General Taylor is now the State Department's Ambassador at Large and Coordinator for Counter-Terrorism.

## History: General

**Real African American Heroes**
www.raaheroes.com

**African American Warriors**
www.aawar.net/default.htm

**Historical Context of the African American Military Experience**
www.denix.osd.mil/denix/Public/ES-Programs/Conservation/Legacy/AAME/aame1.html

**African Americans in the Military: A Historical Perspective**
www.africanamericans1.homestead.com

**African American Soldier Posters**
www.jodavidsmeyer.com/combat/posters/nBlackSoldiers.html

**Minorities in the Military**
www.texans-r-us.com/minorities.htm

**African-Americans Proudly Serving in United States Armed Forces**
www.jodavidsmeyer.com/combat/bookstore/blacksinWWII.html

**Fort Des Moines Memorial Park**
www.fortdesmoines.org/index.html

**Private George Watson**
Quartermaster Museum
www.qmfound.com/watson.htm

## History: American Revolution

**African Americans in the American Revolution**
www.wsu.edu/~dee/DIASPORA/REV.HTM

**The Revolution's Black Soldiers**
www.americanrevolution.org/blk.html

**America's Forgotten Patriots**
afroamhistory.about.com/library/prm/blforgottenpatriots1.htm

## History: US colored troops in the Civil War

**Siege of Fort Blakeley, Alabama**
www.siteone.com/tourist/blakeley/index.html

**United States Colored Troops Institute for Local History and Family Research**
info.hartwick.edu/usct/usct.htm

## History: Buffalo Soldiers

**The Buffalo Soldiers on the Western Frontier**
International Museum of the Horse
www.imh.org/imh/buf/buftoc.html

**Buffalo Soldiers and Indian Wars**
www.buffalosoldier.net

**Buffalo Soldiers.net5**
www.buffalosoldiers.net

## History: World War II

**World War II: African Americans**
bss.sfsu.edu/tygiel/Hist427/1940sphotos/blacks/WWIIblacks.htm

**The Maritime Administration Salutes African Americans for War Time Service in the US Merchant Marine and Maritime Service**
www.marad.dot.gov/education/history/BlackHistory/salutes_to_african_americans.htm

**The Invisible Cryptologists: African Americans, WWII to 1956**
www.nsa.gov/wwii/papers/invisible_cryptologists.htm

**African Americans in World War II**
www.coax.net/people/lwf/ww2.htm

**Photographs of African Americans in World War II**
www.powerpointart.com/powerpoint-backgrounds-pages/powerpoint-background-themes/african-americans-1.html

## History: Tuskegee Airmen

**Tuskegee Airmen, Inc.**
www.tuskegeeairmen.org

**The Tuskegee Airmen: A Tribute to My Father**
www.geocities.com/Pentagon/Quarters/1350

**The Tuskegee Airmen**
nasaui.ited.uidaho.edu/nasaspark/safety/history/tusk.html

## History: Korea

**African Americans in the Korean War**
korea50.army.mil/history/factsheets/afroamer.shtml

**Koreas and the Integration of the Armed Forces**
www.nationalhistoryday.org/03_educators/2000/koreaarmed.htm

**When Black is Burned: The Treatment of African American Soldiers During the Korean War**
mcel.pacificu.edu/as/students/stanley/thesistitle.html

## History: Vietnam

**Vietnam Veterans Against the War**
www.oz.net/~vvawai/index.html

**National Coalition for Homeless Veterans**
www.nchv.org/index.cfm

**SNCC Position paper on Vietnam**
lists.village.virginia.edu/sixties/HTML_docs/Resources/Primary/Manifestos/SNCC_VN.html

## Armed services

**African Center for Strategic Studies**
National Defense University
Department of Defense
www.africacenter.org

**African Americans in the US Army**
www.army.mil/cmh-pg/topics/afam/afam-usa.htm

**Black Wings**
www.ssbinc.com/b_wings/index.htm

**African Americans and the US Navy**
www.history.navy.mil/photos/prs-tpic/af-amer/afam-usn.htm

## Good books

Allen, Robert L. (1989) *The Port Chicago mutiny*. New York: Warner Books.

Astor, Gerald. (1998) *The right to fight: a history of African Americans in the military*. Novato, Calif.: Presidio.

Buckley, Gail Lumet. (2001) *American patriots: the story of Blacks in the military, from the Revolution to Desert Storm*. New York: Random House.

Cornish, Dudley Taylor. (1987) *The Sable Arm: Black troops in the Union Army*. Lawrence, Kans.: University Press of Kansas.

Ellis, Mark. (2001) *Race, war, and surveillance: African Americans and the United States government during World War I*. Bloomington: Indiana University Press.

Homan, Lynn M., and Reilly, Thomas. (1998) *The Tuskegee Airmen*. Charleston, S.C.: Arcadia.

Johnson, Jesse. (1974) *Black women in the armed forces: 1942–1974*. Hampton, Va.: Jesse Johnson.

Lanning, Michael Lee. (1997) *The African-American soldier: from Crispus Attucks to Colin Powell*. Secaucus, N.J.: Carol Publ.

Nalty, Bernard C. (1989) *Strength for the fight: a history of Black Americans in the Military*. New York: The Free Press.

Smith, Graham. (1988) *When Jim Crow met John Bull: Black American soldiers in World War II Britain*. New York: St. Martin's Press.

Stillwell, Pail, ed. (1993) *The Golden Thirteen: recollections of the first Black naval officers*. Annapolis, Md.: Naval Institute Press.

Trudeau, Noel Andre. (1999) *Like men of war: Black troops in the Civil War, 1862–1865*. Boston: Back Bay Books/Little, Brown.

Wright, Kai. (2002) *Soldiers of freedom: an illustrated history of African Americans in the armed forces*. New York: Black Dog & Leventhal.

# 22
# Law

The law has been a very important part of the Black experience. Black people were the victims of US law until the 13th, 14th, and 15th Constitutional amendments. Until the end of the Civil War and these new laws were passed and ratified African Americans were legally slaves with no rights, no citizenship rights, and no human rights either! With these amendments they were no longer slaves, were declared citizens and given the right to vote in federal elections. Many party primary elections were segregated until 1944, and voting rights were not secure until the 1965 Voter Rights Act. Because of this process the political control of the USA has been disproportionately in the hands of Southerners whose political careers were based on excluding potential Black voters.

In addition to the legislative and executive branches of government the law is maintained in a judicial system of lawyers and judges in the court systems. One of the great developments has been the African American legal professional. Black lawyers have been key, as individuals and in national networks like the NAACP Legal Defense Fund. The main training ground until the 1960s was Howard University Law School with such leaders as Charles Houston who served as Dean, and who masterminded the legal campaigns that along with mass protests ended legalized (de jure) segregation. Now Black law professors and Black judges are at all levels of the legal system.

The law regulates all aspects of society, hence the law in a dimension that covers everything. This has been especially true in fighting racism, whether in the form of segregation or more subtle forms of discrimination. When looking at this chapter one might also check the sites listed in the Politics and Civil Rights chapter as well.

**National Black Law Students Association**

www.nblsa.org

This is a national organization of Black law students founded in 1968. It currently has 6000 members in 200 chapters. A good historical feature is the listing of all former officers. This list demonstrates that many current leaders in academic law, politics, and other aspects of the legal profession have been groomed by their leadership in this organization.

It provides several services via this website to serve Black law students. There is a free newsletter available via the Internet, as well as press releases that comment on current events. The Association encourages community service and has a downloadable Community Service Handbook that contains many guidelines for service projects and outreach strategies that can help the local community.

The organization sponsors a National Moot Court Competition with regional qualification competitions. There is also a Mock Trial Competition. The annual topic is listed with accompanying documentation so participants can prepare. This is a wonderful opportunity for law students to develop in active real life simulations. The undergraduate and even high school students can learn from this site. When one has a parent or close family member in the legal profession there is a distinct advantage in planning a law career. This kind of site can be of great service for someone without those family resources. Next to hanging out in the local Law School library this site can help give one a good idea of what it's like to be a lawyer.

**National Bar Association**

www.nationalbar.org

This is the largest organization of Black lawyers, founded in 1925 when segregation prevented Black lawyers from full participation in the American Bar Association. There are four parts to this site: news, conferences and meetings, resources, and President's message.

These lawyers are a major resource for the Black community, not only in terms of providing legal representation, but as a group they have interests that advance the legal and political general conditions for all African Americans.

**National Conference of Black Lawyers**

www.ncbl.org

This organization was established in 1968. They state their mission on the website: "Our mission is to serve as the legal arm of the movement for Black liberation, to protect human rights, to achieve self-determination of Africa and African communities in the diaspora and to work in coalition to assist in ending oppression of all peoples." The site includes press releases, and a list of the organization's leadership. There are chapters listed from many part of the USA as well as affiliates in three other countries.

The Civil Rights Movement in the USA has had different historical stages in which new organizations were formed that represented the new politics based on the changes in social and political experiences of the community. This organization emerged two years after the emergence of Black Power and represented that militant perspective by young lawyers. It continues as the most radical legal arm of the Black liberation movement.

**School of Law, Howard University**

www.law,howard.edu

This is the oldest law school for Black lawyers, and still continues to be the largest academic concentration of Black law professors and law students. Kurt Scmoke, former mayor of Baltimore, is the new Dean of the Law School as of 2002. Every faculty member has a website, and in some cases they include their academic scholarship online as well as helpful links for students. In the tradition of Black higher education the site is user friendly and full of practical advice for students.

One of the special features of this site is "In the Steps of Giants." Historically speaking the School of Law is where most Black lawyers went to school up until well after World War II, and it continued to be the national leader after that. This feature is a monthly recognition of outstanding alumni, including a biography of career achievements. This is a unique resource for everyone interested in African Americans in the legal profession.

The *Howard Law Journal* is the official publication of the law school. It is a record of research and legal action that relates to the condition of

Black people in the USA. The students have a journal called the *Howard Scroll: The Social Justice Law Review*.

## NAACP Legal Defense Fund

www.naacpldf.org

Thurgood Marshall established this organization as part of the NAACP in 1940, and it went on to become an independent organization years later. This is the organization that most African American lawyers worked with because the fight against segregation was a collective task of building up cases in lower courts on the way to major cases before the US Supreme Court. The legal mastermind was Charles Houston, a Harvard trained African American lawyer who orchestrated this national campaign for desegregation. As Dean of Howard Law School he used the Moot Court to prepare a generation of Black lawyers for this task.

This organization has been before the Supreme Court more than any other besides the US Justice Department. Its most famous case was the *Brown* v. *Board of Education* that resulted in the famous 1954 decision to end the legal segregation of schools. This was received by the Black community as if it was a second Emancipation Proclamation.

There is a timeline on this site that covers the history of the Black legal battles against segregation from 1933 to 2001. The timeline is interactive in that people and events are hot links to short essays and biographical sketches. This site includes a lot of full text material. It covers the organization's current litigation, including press releases and some briefs. There are annual reports online as well as newsletters.

There is a current focus on the death penalty as Black people are disproportionately sentenced to die. A quarterly report called "Death Row, USA" is issued and archived on the site.

# History

## Charles Houston

www.law.umkc.edu/faculty/projects/ftrials/trialheroes/charleshouston
essayF.html
www.africanamericans.com/CharlesHamiltonHouston.htm

**Thurgood Marshall**
www.thurgoodmarshall.com

**Constance Baker Motley**
www.cwhf.org/browse/motley.html

**Black Women Lawyers Association of Greater Chicago**
www.bwla.org/Flash_index.htm

**The Dred Scott Case**
Washington University Libraries
library.wustl.edu/vlib/dredscott

**Freedom Suits and Slavery**
St. Louis Circuit Court Historical Records Project
stlcourtrecords.wustl.edu/resources.cfm

**From Slavery to the Supreme Court: The African American Journey Through the Federal Courts**
www.jtbf.org

**The Damon Keith Law Collection of African American Legal History**
keithcollection.wayne.edu

**Law and Race in the United States: An Outline for Understanding**
usinfo.state.gov/usa/infousa/crights/reports/lawrace.htm

## Organizations

**Lawyers Committee for Civil Rights Under Law**
www.lawyerscomm.org

**National Lawyers Guild**
www.nlg.org

**Southern Poverty Law Center**
www.splcenter.org

**Commission on Racial and Ethnic Diversity in the Profession**
American Bar Association
www.abanet.org/minorities

**National Black Police Association**
www.blackpolice.org

## Social justice

**The Injustice Line**
home.earthlink.net/~ynot/index.html

**The Sentencing Project**
www.sentencingproject.org

**Prison Activist Resource Center**
www.prisonactivist.org

**October 22nd Coalition Against Police Brutality**
www.october22.org

**Black Youth Criminalization of a Generation**
www.rwor.org/s/crim.htm

**Race and Law**
New York State Defenders Association
www.nysda.org/Hot_Topics/Race___Law/race___law.html#Research
Links

## Academics

**Saturday School Program**
www.law.harvard.edu/students/saturday_school

**Harvard Law School Honors Black Alumni**
www.news.harvard.edu/gazette/2000/09.28/lawalums.html

**United Law Students of Color Council**
www.law.upenn.edu/groups/ulscc

## Journals

**National Black Law Journal**
www.columbia.edu/cu/nblj

**Howard Law Journal**
www.law.howard.edu/student-org/lawjournal/index.html

**Michigan Journal of Race and Law**
students.law.umich.edu/mjrl

**Margins: Maryland's Law Journal on Race, Religion, Gender, and Class**
www.law.umaryland.edu/margins

**Race and Ethnic Ancestry Law Journal**
real.wlu.edu

## Good books

Churchill, Ward, and Van der Wall, Jim. (2002) *Agents of repression: the FBI's secret wars against the Black Panther Party and the American Indian movement*. Boston, Mass.: South End Press.

Guinier, Lani. (1994) *The tyranny of the majority: fundamental fairness in representative democracy*. New York: Free Press.

Kent, Deborah. (1997) *Thurgood Marshall and the Supreme Court*. New York: Children's Press.

Lynn, Conrad J. (1979) *There is a fountain: the autobiography of a civil rights lawyer*. Westport, Conn.: L. Hill.

McNeil, Genna Rae. (1985) *Groundwork: Charles Houston and the struggle for civil rights*. Philadelphia: University of Pennsylvania Press.

Marshall, Thurgood. (2002) *Supreme Justice: Speeches and Writings*. Philadelphia: University of Pennsylvania Press.

Motley, Constance Baker. (1998) *Equal justice...under law: an autobiography*. New York: Farrar Straus and Giroux.

Smith, J. Clay. (1998) *Rebels in law: voices in history of Black women lawyers*. Ann Arbor, Mi.: University of Michigan Press.

Smith, J. Clay. (1993) *Emancipation: the making of the Black lawyer, 1844–1944*. Philadelphia: University of Pennsylvania Press.

Weatherford, Carol. (2003) *Great African American lawyers*. Berkeley Heights, N.J.: Enslow Publishers.

Williams, Juan. (2000) *Thurgood Marshall: American revolutionary*. New York: Times Books.

Wright, Bruce. (1996) *Black justice in a white world: a memoir*. New York: Barricade Books.

# 23
# Language and Literature

Every culture is encoded in stories that are told to the children and shared by the entire community. African Americans brought African stories with them and in the New World began to transform those stories based on new experiences. This even involved transforming cultural forms from Europe and Native Americans. Literature begins by simply writing the stories of a culture down into its fairy tales, folklore, and narratives that contain the national myths and core values. African American literature has this element.

The first special genre of African American literature is the slave narratives. Slaves simply resisted racism that denied them their humanity by telling their life history. They plainly and simply proclaimed their humanity in stories that any empathetic human being could appreciate. They laughed and cried, loved their children and cared for each other, and experienced the full range of human emotions and ambiguities. Moral judgments had to be made, and some were good and others bad. They were human and their stories forced an otherwise racist world to pay attention. Following this form the autobiography has remained a special form of literary expression and every generation has produced its share of life stories.

There have been at least four major moments in Black literature in the 20th century. The Harlem Renaissance produced writers in the context of celebrating the arrival of Black people in the city, sort of a Black counter-part to the so-called Roaring 20s of mainstream America's celebration of the city and the automobile. This included Langston Hughes, Zora Neale Hurston, Countee Cullen, and many others. The Chicago Renaissance emerged out of the Great Depression and had its roots in economic and political radicalism. The main writer to emerge here was Richard Wright. The biggest movement of literary production was the Black Arts Movement of the 1960s, including Amiri Baraka as its main literary voice, along with Larry Neal, Sonja Sanchez, Nikki Giovanni, and Jayne Cortez. The fourth movement has been the explosion in writing by Black women in the last two decades of the 20th into the 21st centuries.

In addition to this original literary writing the Black Studies movement in academic circles has helped a new generation of literary critics to take on this work and codify its many dimensions into a body of scholarship. Almost every major college-level English literature program has one or more people who critically focus on Black literature. The canon of "must read" works now frequently includes writing by Black writers, from Frederick Douglass and Frances Harper to James Baldwin and Alice Walker.

### African American Writers: Online E-texts
falcon.jmu.edu/~ramseyil/afroonline.htm
This is a mega site that focuses on about 50 writers with links to biographical sketches and links to full text reproductions of their work. There are 18 women writers in this group. The entire site is searchable. This is maintained by the Internet School Library Media Center.

This is a good example of how building a meaningful site can combine what others have done and what you can do. There are links that cover biography, criticism, lesson plans, and e-texts for these 50 writers.

This is a list that covers the entire history of Black writing and should be a useful resource for teachers at all levels of education.

### African American Literature Book Club
www.aalbc.com
This is an extensive site that provides several hundred biographical sketches of Black writers. It is very current and covers all genres. This is a commercially oriented site but there is a great deal of information so it has a solid educational role to play.

There are databases of information covering a number of important topics, from a national list of Black bookstores accessible by state, as well as publishers, literary agents, writers workshops, online news-letters, and links to other relevant online archives.

## Voices from the Gaps: Women Writers of Color
voices.cla.umn.edu

This site is maintained at the University of Minnesota as a joint collaboration between the Department of English and the Program in American Studies. The heart of the website is a list of authors organized by four factors: name, location of birth or residence, significant dates, and ethnicity/racial identity. It cites the example of Toni Morrison. She is listed under M for Morrison, under her birthstate of Ohio, alongside the years 1927 (her year of birth) and 1933 (the year she won the Nobel Prize for Literature), and under the heading for African Americans.

The organizers plan to use volunteers to continue to expand the site so they provide clear guidelines for people to get involved. Students working on research projects that feature a particular African American Woman writer might get in touch with this project, especially graduate students. The site includes a byline for each entry so it will generally be accepted as a professional publication if you can contribute an essay.

## Black Issues Book Review
www.bibookreview.com

This is the main source of book reviews that focus on the Black experience. When you go to this site a window will prompt you to subscribe to a free online newsletter that is a useful source of current information about Black oriented book publishing.

Some of the articles published in the hard copy magazine are reproduced here in full text, as well as regular columns that concern the publishing industry and news concerning writers. It also lists recent titles in four categories: poetry, fiction, non-fiction, and children's literature.

The site has an index in PDF format covering all past five volumes. You can also find a list of current events, at this time limited to Border book stores.

## Anthology of Modern American Poetry (companion site by UIUC)
www.english.uiuc.edu/maps

This website contains a major collection of online poetry by over 25 major African American poets. It is billed as "An Online Journal and Multimedia Companion to Anthology of Modern American Poetry" edited by Cary Nelson, Professor of English at the University of Illinois. There is an advisory board of scholars.

The following African American writers are included in this compilation: Ai, Amiri Baraka, Arna Bontemps, Gwendoyln Brooks, Sterling Brown, Jayne Cortez, Countee Cullen, Rita Dove, Henry Dumas, Paul Lawrence Dunbar, Alice Dunbar Nelson, Angelina Emily Weld Grimke, Michael Harper, Robert hayden, Langston Hughes, James Weldon Johnson, Bob Kaufman, Etheridge Knight, Audre Lorde, Claude McKay, Dudley Randall, Ishmael Reed, Carolyn Rodgers, Patricia Smith, Melvin Tolson, Jean Toomer, and Margaret Walker.

For each writer there are full texts online, including interviews and in some cases reproductions of book jackets. Literary critics contribute brief comments as well as full text critical articles.

## Book clubs

**African American Literature Book Club**
www.aalbc.com

**Black Literature.com**
www.blackliterature.com

## Texts

**African American Literature: Digital Images Database**
special.lib.umn.edu/rare/givens/IMAGES/scgsearch.html

**Mostly Menfolk and a Woman or Two: A Virtual Exhibit of 18th and 19th century African American Literature**
www.ibiblio.org/afam_authors

# Mystery

**Mystery Noir**
mystnoir0.tripod.com/MystNoirDir

**African American Mystery Page**
www.aamystery.com

## General references

**African American Writers: A Celebration**
www.mtsu.edu/~vvesper/afam.html

## Chronology

**A Brief Chronology of African American Literature**
www.accd.edu/sac/english/bailey/aframlit.htm

## Women

**Rawsistaz: Reading and Writing Sistaz**
www.rawsistaz.com

## Online literature and zines

**FYAH!!!**
www.fyah.com

**Mosaic Books**
www.mosaicbooks.com

**Black Book Network.com**
www.blackbooknetwork.com

**Quarterly Black Review: The Black Book Review Online**
www.qbr.com

**African American Literature Online**
www.geocities.com/afam_literature

## Authors

**The Progress of Colored Women by Mary Church Terrell**
lcweb2.loc.gov/ammem/aap/aapwomen.html

**Paul Laurence Dunbar Digital Text Collection**
www.libraries.wright.edu/dunbar

**Zora Neale Hurston**
i.am/zora

**Virginia Hamilton**
www.virginiahamilton.com/home.htm

**E. Lynn Harris Homepage**
www.elynnharris.com

**Incidents in the Life of a Slave Girl**
xroads.virginia.edu/~HYPER/JACOBS/hjhome.htm
digilib.nypl.org/dynaweb/digs/wwm97255
docsouth.unc.edu/jacobs/jacobs.html

**Nelson George Homepage**
www.nelsongeorge.com/index.html

**Narrative of Sojourner Truth**
www.PageByPageBooks.com/Sojourner_Truth/The_Narrative_of_
Sojourner_Truth

**Anniina's Alice Walker Page**
www.luminarium.org/contemporary/alicew

**Anniina's Toni Morrison Page**
www.luminarium.org/contemporary/tonimorrison/toni.htm

**The Jean Toomer Pages**
www.math.buffalo.edu/~sww/toomer/jean-toomer.html

**Richard Wright Homepage**
home.gwu.edu/~cuff/wright

**From the Archives of the New York Times Book Section: James Baldwin**
partners.nytimes.com/books/98/03/29/specials/baldwin.html

**Amiri Baraka Homepage**
www.amiribaraka.com

**Rita Dove Homepage**
www.people.virginia.edu/~rfd4b/home.html

**Margaret Walker**
www.ibiblio.org/ipa/walker

**The Unofficial Gloria Naylor Homepage**
www.lythastudios.com/gnaylor/index.html

**A Look into Maya Angelou**
www.empirezine.com/spotlight/maya/maya1.htm

## Harlem Renaissance

**Poetry and Prose of the Harlem Renaissance**
www.nku.edu/~diesmanj/harlem_intro.html

**PAL: Perspectives in American Literature – A Research and Reference Guide; Harlem Renaissance (Chapter 9)**
www.csustan.edu/english/reuben/pal/chap9/CHAP9.HTML

**Selected Resources for the Harlem Renaissance: List of Primary/ Secondary Resources, Anthologies and Bibliographies**
www.fishernews.org/hrresources.htm

**Rhapsodies in Black**
www.iniva.org/harlem

**Harlem: Mecca of the New Negro**
etext.lib.virginia.edu/harlem

**Harlem Renaissance**
www.cc.colorado.edu/Dept/EN/Courses/EN370/EN3707117Garcia
www.fatherryan.org/harlemrenaissance

**Harlem 1900–1940: An African American Community**
www.si.umich.edu/CHICO/Harlem

**The Black Renaissance in Washington**
www.dclibrary.org/blkren/index2.html

## Black Arts and 1960s

**Black Arts Movement**
www.umich.edu/~eng499

**American Literature Book Club: Black Arts Movement**
www.aalbc.com/authors/blackartsmovement.htm

**Modern American Poetry – "The Black Arts Movement"**
www.english.uiuc.edu/maps/blackarts/blackarts.htm

**Visual Art Gallery of Black Arts Period**
xroads.virginia.edu/%7EUG01/hughes/gall.html

**Women in the Black Arts Movement**
www.personal.psu.edu/users/j/l/jlp345/index.htm

## Poetry

**Academy of American Poets: Langston Hughes**
www.poets.org/poets/poets.cfm?prmID=84&CFID=12047761&
CFTOKEN=60672469

**The Original Manuscript of Langston Hughes's Ballad of Booker T.**
www.infoplease.com/spot/bhm1.html

**20th Century African American Poetry**
www.public.iastate.edu/~savega/afampoet.html

**Book of American Negro Poetry** (BoondocksNet Editions)
www.boondocksnet.com/editions/anp/index.html

**Nubian Poets.com**
www.Nubianpoets.com

**The George Moses Horton Society for the Study of African American Poetry**
www.unc.edu/campus/sigs/horton

## Organizations

**Black Alliance Writers**
www.blackwriters.org

**Organization of Black Screen Writers (OBS)**
www.obswriter.com

## Novels

**Project on the History of Black Writing (PHBW)**
www.ku.edu/~phbw

## Bookstores

**Jokeae's African American Books**
www.jokaes.com

**Black Images Books**
www.blackimages.com

**Just Us Books**
www.justusbooks.com/index.html

**The Timbuktu Book Company**
www.timbuktubooks.com

## Publishers

**Black Books Galore**
www.blackbooksgalore.com

## Language

**Writings on the "Ebonics" Issue Since December, 1996**
www.stanford.edu/~rickford/ebonics

**Center for Applied Linguistics: Ebonics**
www.cal.org/ebonics

**African American Vernacular English (AAVE)**
www.une.edu.au/langnet/aave.htm

**Phonological Features of African American Vernacular English**
www.ausp.memphis.edu/phonology/features.htm

**African American English**
www.ic.arizona.edu/~lsp/AAEnglish.html

## Good books

Anadolu-Okur, Nilgun. (1997) *Contemporary African American theater: Afrocentricity in the works of Larry Neal, Amiri Baraka, and Charles Fuller*. New York: Garland.

Bailey, David A., et al, contributors. (1997) *Rhapsodies in Black: art of the Harlem Renaissance*. London: Hayward Gallery, the Institute of International Visual Arts.

Baugh, John. (2000) *Beyond ebonics: linguistic pride and racial prejudice*. New York: Oxford University Press.

De Santis, Christopher C., ed. (1995) *Langston Hughes and the Chicago Defender: essays on race, politics, and culture, 1942–62*. Urbana, Ill.: University of Illinois Press.

Frankovich, Nicholas, and David Larzelere, eds. (1999) *The Columbia Granger's Index to African-American poetry*. New York: Columbia University Press.

Gates, Henry Louis, Jr., and McKay, Nellie Y. eds. (1997) *The Norton anthology of African American literature*. New York: W. W. Norton & Co.

Giovanni, Nikki. (1996) *Shimmy shimmy shimmy like my sister Kate: looking at the Harlem Renaissance through poems*. New York: H. Holt.

Govenar, Alan B. (2000) *African American frontiers: slave narratives and oral histories*. Santa Barbara, Calif.: ABC-CLIO.

Hatch, James V., and Leo Hamalian, eds. (1996) *Lost plays of the Harlem Renaissance, 1920–1940*. Detroit: Wayne State University Press.

Honey, Michael K. (1999) *Black workers remember: an oral history of segregation, unionism, and the freedom struggle*. Berkeley: University of California Press.

Knupfer, Anne Meis. (1996) *Toward a tenderer humanity and a nobler womanhood: African American women's clubs in turn-of-the-century Chicago*. New York: New York University Press.

Labov, William. (1973) *Language in the inner city: studies in the Black English vernacular*. Philadelphia: University of Pennsylvania Press.

Locke, Alain, ed. (1997) *The new Negro*. New York: Simon and Schuster.

Mitchell, Verner D., ed. (2000) *This waiting for love: Helene Johnson, poet of the Harlem Renaissance*. Amherst: University of Massachusetts Press.

Moody, Joycelyn. (2001) *Sentimental confessions: spiritual narratives of nineteenth-century African American women*. Athens, Ga.: University of Georgia Press.

Pettis, Joyce Owens. (2002) *African American poets: lives, works, and sources*. Westport, Conn.: Greenwood Press.

Rand, Donna, Toni Trent Parker, and Sheila Foster. (1998) *Black books galore! Guide to great African American children's books*. New York: Wiley.

Rickford, John R. (1999) *African American vernacular English: features, evolution, educational implications*. Malden, Mass.: Blackwell.

Rodgers, Marie E. (1998) *The Harlem Renaissance: an annotated reference guide for student research*. Englewood, Colo.: Libraries Unlimited.

Smith, Valerie, ed. (2001) *African American writers*. New York: Charles Scribner's Sons.

Smitherman, Geneva. (2000) *Talkin that talk: language, culture, and education in African America*. New York: Routledge.

Thompson, Julius E. (1998) *Dudley Randall, Broadside Press, and the Black Arts movement in Detroit, 1960–1995*. Jefferson, N.C.: McFarland.

Young, Kevin, ed. (2000) *Giant steps: the new generation of African American writers*. New York: Perennial.

# 24
# Music

The music of the African American people comes closest to a universal expression of their soul. The making of music is the most unbroken continuity of African culture, through the slave trade and slavery, that contains within it experiences that stretch back to the beginning of our species and before. Black music connects with you in terms of natural rhythms – the heartbeat, breathing, and the physical motions of walking, talking, and making love. People all over the world love the music of African American culture.

There is both continuity and change in this music. The historical periodization of the general African American experience also sets the framework for understanding African American music. Africans brought their own music into the slave experience and then created the work songs and the spirituals. Out of this into the rural period emerged the Blues and all related forms. Into the urban experience we get Jazz in the 20th century and now in the 21st century we have the hip hop/rap revolution.

Naming music types is very subjective and usually related to marketing strategies of music business. In fact, the AACM calls jazz "Black classical music." In fact when one things of Ray Charles, Stevie Wonder, or Nina Simone there are no neat labels that make any sense at all. They are in African American culture and emerge as originals. This was true of Charlie Parker and many others. One of the vital features of African American culture is the improvisational dynamic, an irreverent twisting and turning of reality without regard to authority or any standards that define what is beautiful or right or just. The main thing is that everyone has a voice to be heard, and everyone can contribute creativity to the collective whole. Listen to a jazz group play a tune and then think about this way of thinking about African American music in general.

## Center for Black Music Research

www.cbmr.org

This is one of the major research institutions on music of any kind in the USA. Samuel Floyd is the center's founder and director emeritus, having guided it since it was founded in 1983. Rosita Sands is the current director. This is a research unit of Columbia College Chicago. The Center currently has a branch in St. Thomas, Virgin Islands.

This site contains a great deal of information. There are short essays on 20 musical styles from blues to zydeco including hip hop, reggae, and salsa. The organizers are focused on documenting the history of Black music, and have organized performance groups to keep these styles alive. They also have a full documentation of Black composers in all genres, including classical music from Europe and the African Diaspora. Their performance groups specialize in performing these compositions.

The site is active and features a composer of the month and a player of the month. The site is full of great links, so if you want one stop shopping for serious Black music this is the place you should start.

## Soulful Detroit

www.soulfuldetroit.com

This site is the result of international cooperation to celebrate the history of soul music that was created in the city of Detroit, the town that came to be called Motown because that was where people made automobiles. David Meikle (Glasgow) and Lowell Boileau (Detroit) have collaborated to build this very important site. Many greats are mentioned here, including the legendary Barry Gordy of Motown Records.

This site is built around what they call "webisodes," mini multi-media presentations based on text, and photographs. These take you inside and show the recording studios, the ads and posters, the styles of clothes and hair, and details about the personalities. The webisodes created so far include Sixties Studios of Detroit, the Rose Battiste Story, the 20 Grand, Tera Shirma Story, Northern Soul Tour, and the Soulful Detroit Tour.

It is dramatic to see the hope and strength of these cultural forces, celebrating the Black community becoming urban, becoming secure in factory jobs that gave them a higher standard of living than ever before. On the other hand, in the extensive data base of recording studios you

**Music** 227

can see photos of how many of the buildings look today. Mostly these buildings are deserted and boarded up, with no indication of what had happened there two generations ago. This is a site not to be missed if you ever appreciated or have any interest in the soul music that was once the pride of Motown.

### Institute of Jazz Studies
Rutgers University
www.libraries.rutgers.edu/rulib/abtlib/danlib/jazz.htm
Marshall Stearns (1908–1966) started this Jazz Institute that is now headed by Dan Morgenstein, former editor of *Down Beat* magazine. The Institute maintains a library and archive as well as an academic program that grants an MA in Jazz Studies. There is a weekly radio program on WBGO 88.3 FM (Newark, N.J.). Also featured are monthly meetings of a Jazz Research Round Table.

This site has a "Jazz Greats Digital Exhibit." Currently there are excellent pages on Fats Waller, Mary Lou Williams, and Benny Carter. These include short essays by jazz historians and critics on various aspects of their lives, as well as a listing of books and recordings by and about them. As this section grows it will become a more and more important source of information for jazz lovers.

### Ancient to the Future
Association for the Advancement of Creative Musicians
www.aacmchicago.org
This site is about one of the most important vanguard musical organizations in the history of American music. The AACM was formed in 1965 as a musicians cooperative for the promotion of what they called "Great Black Music." Originally formed by Richard Muhal Abrams and Phil Cohran, and others, this organization continued the tradition in Chicago by their immediate predecessor Sun Ra. They formed groups with overlapping membership, and when one group was preparing for a concert the others would do the publicity, set up the hall, and generally be supportive. They worked together as a cooperative.

This tradition continues even though many of the original players have gone on to world renown. Some of the names are the Art Ensemble of

Chicago and 8 Bold Souls. Players like Anthony Braxton, Joseph Jarman, Lester Bowie, Henry Threadgill, Fred Anderson and others have been winning awards all over the world. The site lists all the members and gives a rundown of their activities. The groups are also listed.

The spirit of the groups is revolutionary. They specialize in featuring multi-instrumentalists. Some of the groups wear the costumes of ancient times, and paint their bodies when they perform as if doing a spiritual war dance calling forth gods to intervene in our social lives. The site is alive with images and with sound files that are provided for most of the individuals and groups.

### The Hip Hop Archive
www.hiphoparchive.org

This website sets out to document hip hop in all its many aspects. Dr. Marcyliena Morgan is the founder of this website that is based at the W. E. B. DuBois Institute for Afro-American Research at Harvard University. This is an excellent model for the collaborative creation of a resource in cyberspace that can be useful to a wide variety of people.

The site is wrapped in the language and imagery of hip hop but aims to be an archive of the material. You have to be patient with its navigational tools but it is worth the effort. A straightforward site index would be helpful. If you click on "power moves" and go to "hip hop zones" you will find an extensive set of links that cover the hip hop scenes in Atlanta, Boston, Los Angeles, Miami, New York City, and Philadelphia. This is very important because the commercial market does not allow for this kind of close-to-ground view of what's going on.

One of the strengths of the site is its extensive links (found under "the word") including a real directory into hip hop around the world. Under the rubric "hip hop university" you can find course syllabi and associated references to the entire scope of hip hop as a cultural force in American popular culture. Finally, under "roundtables" you can find the documentation of a conference held on "Hiphop community activism and education" in 2002. The site encourages contributions. Take the time to check it out, as it's well worth the effort.

# History

**Composers of African Descent**
chevalierdesaintgeorges.homestead.com/Others.html

**African American Sheet Music 1850–1920**
memory.loc.gov/ammem/award97/rpbhtml

**Fisk Jubilee Singers** (PBS)
www.pbs.org/wgbh/amex/singers

**William Grant Still**
scriptorium.lib.duke.edu/sgo/start.html

**Marian Anderson**
www.library.upenn.edu/special/gallery/anderson/index.html
www.library.upenn.edu/special/photos/anderson

**Florence Mills: The Little Blackbird**
www.tip.net.au/~wegan/index.htm

**Life Every Voice: Music in American Life**
www.lib.virginia.edu/speccol/exhibits/music

# Organizations

**Ancient to the Future**
Association for the Advancement of Creative Musicians
www.aacmchicago.org

**International Association of African American Music**
www.iaaam.com

**National Association of Negro Musicians**
www.edtech.morehouse.edu/cgrimes

**Jazz Institute of Chicago**
www.jazzinstituteofchicago.org

## African Diaspora

**African Music Encyclopedia**
www.africanmusic.org

**African Hip Hop**
www.africanhiphop.com

**South Africa**
www.music.org.za

**Bob Marley**
www.bobmarley.freeserve.co.uk

**The Gateway to Reggae Music on the Internet**
www.niceup.com

**The Steelbands of Trinidad and Tobago**
www.seetobago.com/trinidad/pan/bands_tt.htm

**Mighty Sparrow**
www.listen.to/kaiso

## Blues

**Bessie Smith**
alt.venus.co.uk/weed/bessie/welcome.htm

**Ray Charles**
www.raycharles.com

**Delta Blues Museum**
www.deltabluesmuseum.org

**Trail of the Hellhound**
(Delta Blues of the Lower Mississippi Valley)
www.cr.nps.gov/delta/blues

**It's Biscuit Time for the Blues**
www.island.net/~blues

**Beale Street** (Memphis, Tenn.)
www.bealestreet.com

**Rock and Roll Hall of Fame and Museum**
www.rockhall.com/home

**Stax Museum of American Soul Music**
www.soulsvilleusa.com

**Blues Online**
mathrisc1.lunet.edu/blues/blues.html

**The Blue Highway**
www.thebluehighway.com/intro.html

## Jazz

**Duke Ellington**
www.dellington.org
www.washingtonpost.com/wp-srv/style/music/features/ellington/front.htm

**Sun Ra Research**
www.sunraresearch.com

**Louis Armstrong**
www.satchmo.net

**Charlie Parker**
www.cmgww.com/music/parker/parker.html

**John Coltrane**
www.johncoltrane.com

**Miles Davis**
www.wam.umd.edu/~losinp/music/miles_ahead.html

**Billie Holiday**
www.cmgww.com/music/holiday
www.ladyday.net

**Thelonious Monk**
home.achilles.net/~howardm/tsmonk.shtml

**Charles Mingus**
www.mingusmingusmingus.com

**Horace Silver**
members.tripod.com/~hardbop/silver_discography.html

**Swing Through Time: The Story of Detroit Jazz**
www.ipl.org/div/detjazz

**Jazz: A Ken Burns Film** (PBS)
www.pbs.org/jazz

**Interviews about A Love Supreme**
www.jerryjazzmusician.com/mainHTML.cfm?page=lovesupreme.html

**Jerry Jazz Musician**
www.jerryjazzmusician.com/index.cfm

**Red Hot and Cool**
hometown.aol.com/Jlackritz/jazz/index.html

# Rap/hip hop

**Davey D**
www.daveyd.com

**Rapstation**
www.rapstation.com

**Hip Hop Congress**
www.hiphopcongress.org

**Original Hip Hop Lyrics**
www.ohhla.com

**Art Crimes**
www.graffiti.org

**Canadian Hip Hop Online**
www.hiphopca.com

**Hip Hop Infinity**
www.hiphopinfinity.com

**Turntable Lab**
www.turntablelab.com

**Soul Strut**
www.soulstrut.com

**D J Shadow**
www.djshadow.com

**Blackalicious**
www.blackalicious.com

**Boombox Museum**
www.pocketcalculatorshow.com/boombox

# Good books

Davis, Miles, with Troupe, Quincy. (1990) *Miles, the autobiography*. New York: Simon and Schuster.

Ellington, Duke. (1988) *Music is my mistress*. Cambridge, Mass.: DaCapo Press.

Floyd, Samuel A. (1996) *The power of Black music: interpreting its history from Africa to the United States*. New York: Oxford University Press.

Griffin, Farah Jasmine. (2001) *If you can't be free, be a mystery: in search of Billie Holiday*. New York: Free Press.

Mingus, Charles. (2000) *Beneath the underdog*. Edinburgh: Mojo.

Omeally, Robert, ed. (1998) *The jazz cadence of American culture*. New York: Columbia University Press.

Southern, Eileen. (1997) *The music of Black Americans: a history*. New York: W. W. Norton.

Werner, Craig. (1998) *A change is gonna come: music, race, and the soul of America*. New York: Plume.

# 25
# Performing Arts

This section focuses on theater, dance, and film as forms of artistic creation and cultural production. This is a set of activities that emerges out of the traditional culture of a people as the activities involved are to some extent part of everyday life, especially holidays and recurring special occasions (e.g., birthdays, weddings, and funerals). Partly it's the psychological attraction of make-believe as all cultures have created costumes and masks to portray their religion, fairy tales, and the historical narrative of their collectivity. It is also part of the organic educational process, to convey meaning in a dynamic fashion in which the curriculum is contained in a story performed as a play or a dance, live or virtually in a film/video.

Out of Africa and within the slave quarters the Black community continued to celebrate life and entertain each other with song and dance. They were used to entertaining their white slave masters as well, and for that they began to cover up what they really thought with expressions that would satisfy the expectations of their owners. They played it differently than they lived it. They exaggerated the comic while they felt the tragic – laughter covered pain. Paul Lawrence Dunbar captured this in his poem "We wear the mask."

As with every sphere of human activity African Americans have excelled in all areas of the arts, and major figures have achieved status as founders of a tradition. Often Black people have gone to Europe and made careers that would have been impossible within the segregation practiced in the USA. The impact of the Black Studies movement has led to research on many of these people so that their experiences can be preserved and used to clarify how racism was overcome. There are archives being compiled so that their art can be preserved although much of it has been lost.

The performing arts in the contemporary Black community are widespread and full of diverse approaches. Every major city has amateur theater and dance groups, while professional regional groups regularly have full seasons of production in their own facilities as on national tours. Black filmmakers have also become more of a force as Blacks enroll in film schools, as Hollywood begins to target the Black community as part of its mass market, and as video technology makes it less costly to practice this art.

### Alvin Ailey American Dance Theater
www.alvinailey.org

This is the premier modern dance company that has dominated the scene since it was founded in 1958 by Alvin Ailey, a major dancer in his own right. The company is now being run by his lead dancer and protégée Judith Jamison.

This site is a full statement of the company and will be of interest to anyone interested in dance. The history is presented in a year-by-year chronology with photographs and captions that suggest the diverse performances and success it has enjoyed. The site includes full information on its professional touring companies, its schedule and master dance classes offered throughout the country, and its school that includes both a professional and junior level.

This is a dynamic site that gives full information on every aspect of this company. One can see them in action in a very interesting photo gallery. Dance programs on all levels should encourage their students to check this out, and use the standard of Alvin Ailey as the model to aspire to.

### Katherine Dunham Center for Arts and Humanities
www.eslarp.uiuc.edu/kdunham

Katherine Dunham is one of the grande dames of African American culture. She earned all her degrees in Anthropology from the University of Chicago (BA, MA, and PhD). From 1931 when she formed her first dance company she has been a force in dance, based on what has come

**Performing Arts**                                                    237

to be called "The Dunham Technique of Modern Dance." Her research was in Africa and Haiti, and her technique used the movement of the African Diaspora with the discipline and choreography of modern schools of dance. She forced the dance world to accept the power of an African tradition being reborn in the 20th century.

This website celebrates her and her contribution to dance in this cultural center she established in East St Louis. She established a museum based on the art and costumes she collected from her years of research. These materials are exhibited on this website. This is the only cultural center in the mainly Black city of East St Louis, located in Illinois across the river from St Louis, Missouri. They offer a full program of education for youth.

### Dance Theatre of Harlem
www.dancetheatreofharlem.com
Arthur Mitchell created this world-class "neo-classical dance company" to use African American dancers to perform the world's great ballets, especially new and challenging works. The website lists the company's full repertoire, with many entries linked to a short explanation and photo of a DTH performance. One can find information about the Theatre's school as well as full information about the touring schedule.

This company is part of a long history of Black people who have lived in the full reality of being Black and yet are able to bring that perspective to the mastery of bourgeois European culture making it their own and accessible to a wide diversity of people. This goes back as far as Ira Aldridge, the great Shakespearean actor, and is as recent as the Black conductors and performers in the great symphony orchestras of the world. All culture is for the people to take and fashion in their interests and every great African American artist has been open to global influences. Turning to Africa is necessary, but as Randy Weston has explored North Africa, John Coltrane the eastern systems of music, and the Modern Jazz Quartet took on J. S. Bach, so the Dance Theatre of Harlem has danced their way across the great ballets of Europe. The artist has never accepted isolation or segregation of art, nor should anybody else.

**Black Film Center Archive**
University of Indiana
www.indiana.edu/~bfca/index.html
This is an archive set up for people to come and do research in its
extensive holdings. However this website has some very valuable information. It does indicate what the Center holds and has forms for requesting
access to material, either to be viewed on site or copied and sent by mail.
But there is more.

One of the unique features is a set of seven short film clips shot between
1897 and 1900. These clips are excellent documentary examples of the
imagery of Blacks living under the ruthless hand of segregation and racial
domination. In these clips one can see the Black genius of "putting the
Massa on," playing the game of "on my face I laugh while inside I cry."

The Center has special programs about which the site presents information. There are special features on the films of Richard Pryor and
Melvin Van Peeples. For each there are photos, quotes and a related
filmography.

Perhaps the most generally useful aspect of this site is the extensive
listing of film related links. The webliography on Black film is the best
on the web and should be used extensively by students of African
American culture. It covers the following categories: actors, directors,
and producers; animation, organizations, archives and libraries, distrib-
utors, film festivals, film reviews, and posters.

**National Black Theater Festival**
www.nbtf.org
This has become the site for the major annual Black theater event of the
year. Larry Leon Hamlin created this week-long festival with the help
of Maya Angelou in 1989 and it has become a smashing success. In its
schedule there are over 30 plays performed by Black professional
companies from all over the USA. Now there is a fringe festival that has
developed with amateur and college groups sharing performances.

Live theater is a special event, a gathering of audience and performers
who imagine themselves into an experience and share a human moment
called for by the script, orchestrated by a director, but lived by the
performers and the audience in that moment. Every live performance is

**Performing Arts**                                               **239**

different. This festival is a rare moment as many of the audience members are performers in their own right and the emotional energy is at a very high level. This website only begins to share this experience.

## Theatre

**Women of Color, Women of Words**
www.scils.rutgers.edu/~cybers

**Black Theater Network**
www.btnet.org/home.html

**Black Theater**
www.bridgesweb.com/blacktheatre.html

## Musicals

**The Development of an African-American Musical Theatre 1865–1910; American Memory; African-American Sheet Music**
memory.loc.gov/ammem/award97/rpbhtml/aasmsprs1.html

**Blackface Minstrelsy 1830–1852**
www.iath.virginia.edu/utc/minstrel/mihp.html

## Dance companies

**Ballethnic Dance Company Inc.**
www.ballethnic.org

**Alvin Ailey American Dance Theater**
www.alvinailey.org

**Katherine Dunham Center for Arts and Humanities**
www.eslarp.uiuc.edu/kdunham

**The African American Dance Ensemble**
users.vnet.net/aade/main.html

**Rennie Harris Pure Movement**
www.puremovement.net

**Bill T. Jones/Arnie Zane Dance Company**
www.geocities.com/Broadway/Balcony/3252

**The Official Fayard Nicholas Website**
www.nicholasbrothers.com

## Dance

**PBS: Free to Dance** (PBS)
www.pbs.org/wnet/freetodance/about/index.html

**Absolute BreakDancing**
www.scarybubs.com/bboy/break2.html

**African-American Contributions to Theatrical Dance**
www.theatredance.com/mhist01.html

**Archives of Early Lindy Hop**
www.savoystyle.com

**Official Site of Josephine Baker**
www.cmgww.com/stars/baker

## Film

**BlackFilm.com**
www.blackfilm.com

**Black Americans and Silent Film**
www.silentsmajority.com/SpecialFeature/feb97.htm

**Midnight Ramble: African Americans in Film from the 1920s through the 1940s**
www.moderntimes.com/palace/black/index.html

**African Americans in Motion Pictures, the Past and Present**
www.liunet.edu/cwis/cwp/library/african/movies.htm

**African Americans in the Movies: A Bibliography of Materials in the UC Berkeley Library**
www.lib.berkeley.edu/MRC/AfricanAmBib.html

**Separate Cinema**
www.separatecinema.com

**Oscar Micheaux Society**
www.duke.edu/web/film/Micheaux

**Oscar Micheaux Homepage**
www.shorock.com/arts/micheaux/index.html

**Black Film Center/Archive Home Page**
www.indiana.edu/~bfca/index.html

**Urban Entertainment**
www.urbanentertainment.com/0/default.asp?aff_id=0

**Independent African American Film Pioneers**
www.temple.edu/fma/laveta/index.html

**OscarMicheaux.net: A Celebration of Black Independent Cinema**
www.oscarmicheaux.net

**Black FilmMakers Hall of Fame, Inc.**
www.blackfilmmakershall.org

**Sisters in Cinema.com: A Resource Guide about African American Women Filmmakers**
www.sistersincinema.com/index.html

**Hollywood Black Film Festival**
www.hbff.org

**Blaxploitation.com**
www.blaxploitation.com

**Blackflix.com**
www.blackflix.com

**The Black Hollywood Education Resource Center**
www.bherc.org

**BadAzz MoFo Magazine**
www.badazzmofo.com

## Good books

Dunham, Katherine. (1994) *A touch of innocence: memoirs of childhood*. Chicago: University of Chicago Press.

Dunning, Jennifer. (1998) *Alvin Ailey: a life in dance*. New York: DaCapo Press.

Fabre, Geneviève. (1983) *Drumbeats, masks, and metaphor: contemporary Afro-American theatre*. Cambridge, Mass.: Harvard University Press.

Fraden, Rena. (1994) *Blueprints for a Black federal theatre, 1935–1939*. Cambridge; New York: Cambridge University Press.

George, Nelson. (1994) *Blackface: reflections on African-Americans and the movies*. New York: HarperCollins Publishers.

George-Graves, Nadine. (2000) *The royalty of Negro vaudeville: the Whitman Sisters and the negotiation of race, gender and class in African American theatre, 1900–1940*. New York: St. Martin's Press.

Gottschild, Brenda Dixon. (1998) *Digging the Africanist presence in American performance: dance and other contexts*. Westport, Conn.: Praeger.

Harrison, Paul Carter, Walker, Victor Leo II, and Edwards, Gus. (2002) *Black theatre: ritual performance in the African Diaspora*. Philadelphia: Temple University Press.

Molette, Carlton W., and Molette, Barbara J. (1986) *Black theatre: premise and presentation*. Bristol, Ind.: Wyndham Hall Press.

Stark, Seymour. (2000) *Men in blackface: true stories of the Minstrel show*. Philadelphia: Xlibris Corp.

Thomas, Lundeana Marie. (1997) *Barbara Ann Teer and the National Black Theatre: transformational forces in Harlem*. New York: Garland Pub.

Woodard, Komozi. (1999) *A nation within a nation: Amiri Baraka (LeRoi Jones) and Black power politics*. Chapel Hill, N.C.: University of North Carolina Press.

Young, Earl James. (2002) *The life and work of Oscar Micheaux: pioneer Black author and filmmaker, 1884–1951*. San Francisco: KMT Pub.

# 26
# Visual and Applied Arts

The African American visual artist has shared with the musician an unbroken tradition linking all the way back to the traditional arts of Africa. On the slave ship and the slave plantation people could not be stopped from expressing themselves, and all the musician or artist needed for tools were natural parts of the body. The artist only needed hands and eyes as tools to construct art, material representations of cultural meaning. Research has shown that the images and symbols of African culture were reproduced and then improvised in the American context. One good example of this is in the slave graveyards of the South in which one can find African inspired sculpture to commemorate the dead. The iconography of the Yoruba religion has been improvised on in the religious transformations of Santeria, Voodoo, and Candomble. This is not limited to Black artists as the well known appropriation of African imagery to create cubism by Picasso and others attests.

All cultures have a visual aesthetic that manifests itself every day, in the choices people make to create beauty in clothes, in a home environment, in public spaces. The visual artist is a concentration of this cultural dynamic, but also is an innovator who can improvise on what is in the culture to expand it and extend its limits, sometimes to negate and other times to absorb the contributions of other cultures. A two or three dimensional work of art is constructed with layers of meaning that can only be decoded by understanding its historical context, the visual language of the culture, and the content of the subject matter.

The visual artist in the African American community has more opportunities to create and exhibit than ever before. There are Black oriented art galleries in every major city and all museums have some outstanding African American work. African American art historians and critics like David Driskell and E. Barry Gaither have maintained a high standard of criticism and set important guidelines for collections development. In addition to painting, sculpture, and mural making, photography has emerged as one of the most important visual arts.

**The Studio Museum in Harlem**
www.studiomuseuminharlem.org/
This museum was started in 1968 and is the main exhibition space for Black art in New York. The site lists all present, past, and some future exhibitions. There are images on the site from the current exhibitions. These images can give one a sense of artistic trends and the online commentary articulates the key critical issues related to the theme of the exhibits. There is an interactive calendar that provides instant access to ongoing events, including education programs for people of all ages. For residents of New York, as well as visitors, this is a good site to check and keep Black art on your schedule.

Another good feature of this site is the online museum store which gives an annotated listing of its publications, especially exhibit catalogues that can be ordered online. This includes such collectors items as "The Studio Museum in Harlem: 25 Years of African American Art." Art teachers and students, as well as librarians and hobbyists will find this service valuable.

This site helps to raise the question of when virtual online exhibits will become more common as a supplement to viewing the actual, physical work of art. Eventually there will be virtual art that one can only see online, art as an online image. There are technical issues of screen size, bandwidth, and pixels for sharpness of image and color. But as these issues are removed with new generations of technology, this will become one of the great uses of cyberspace, to enjoy the art of the world on your computer screen whenever you feel like it.

**African American Art**
www-unix.oit.umass.edu/~afriart/
Nelson Stevens, Professor of Art at the University of Massachusetts – Amherst, established this website for his students and the general public. It is alive with color and gives one a sense of celebrating life. There is

a gallery of ten artists: Akili Ron Anderson, Adriene Cruz, Louis Delsarte, Calvin Jones, Jon Onye Locakard, Valerie Maynard, Carl Owens, James Phillips, Nelson Stevens, and Pheoris West. There is a small biography of each and examples of their work. There is also a page that includes the work of younger artists, usually Professor Stevens' students. There are images of Malcolm X that present his image through the eyes of a younger generation. Very exciting stuff indeed.

Special attention is given to the mural. This has been a long-standing project for Professor Stevens and his students, painting murals that celebrate the Black experience and provide narrative insight into Black history as a way to invade and transform public space. Murals turn a physical community into an explicit cultural environment in which one has an asynchronous dialogue with images and aesthetics. A mural is an act of public education. There are two essays on this site about murals, by E. Barry Gaither and Michael Harris.

**National Conference of Artists**

www.ncanewyork.com/index.html

Margaret Burroughs, a multi-talented artist poet and organizer of cultural institutions, founded this organization in 1959. She founded the DuSable Museum of African American History in her home in Chicago and it is now one of the leading such museums in the country.

This is the major organization for African American artists and art educators. There is a photo gallery of members at various NCA meetings so one can see the camaraderie shared by these artists and their friends. The site has a list of links to websites maintained by members so this is a portal to some of the most exciting African American art being created.

The site contains a great deal of information for the professional artist, art students, and the general public. For collectors there is a unique listing of websites for over 30 galleries selling Black art. For artists there are links for technical advice and supplies.

There is an NCA newsletter that is available full text online.

**African Americans in the Visual Arts**

Long Island University

www.liunet.edu/cwis/cwp/library/aavaahp.htm

This is a comprehensive site that is of value to anyone interested in learning about African American art. The site is built around 25 notable artists and four historical experiences. There are short essays about art in Africa, the Harlem Renaissance, the WPA, and the 1960s called Changing Times.

For each artist there is a biographical essay including critical comments on their art. This makes this site the most inclusive for one stop shopping on information about Black artists. One of the artists featured here is Henry Ossawa Tanner (1859–1937) who distinguished himself as a master painter in both Europe and the USA. There are several of his paintings reproduced on the site, especially his classic 1893 painting *The Banjo Lesson*.

There is a full set of links to other sites as well. The list of museums and associations is the most complete one available online.

### African American Photographers Guild
www.aapguild.org/
This is "a site celebrating the accomplishments of the African American Photographer." There is a strange combination of commercial material here, but if one can sort through it this is an excellent introduction to Black photography. There is a timeline of Black photographers from 1840 to the present. This is an interactive listing of biographical sketches of the major photographers.

There is an online gallery of 30 photographers, and the work by one of the Guild members is featured on the first screen of the site. There is a free listserv for people interested in a discussion that includes Guild members.

## Visual arts and artists

### African Americans in the Visual Arts A Historical Perspective
www.liunet.edu/cwis/cwp/library/aavaahp.htm

### The Papers of African American Artists
artarchives.si.edu/guides/afriamer/afamguid.htm

**Faith Ringgold**
www.faithringgold.com/

**The Web of Life: The Art of John Biggers: An ArtsEdNet Online Exhibition and Discussion**
www.getty.edu/artsednet/resources/Biggers/index.html

**Romare Bearden Foundation Website**
www.beardenfoundation.org/

**Betye Ireen Saar**
www.bisaar.com
www.netropolitan.org/saar/saarmain.html

**Marshall Arts Presents: Romare Bearden**
www.courses.vcu.edu/ENG-mam/

**Narratives of African American Identity: The David C. Driskell Collection**
www.artgallery.umd.edu/driskell/

**Breaking Racial Barriers: African Americans in the Harmon Foundation Collection – The Harmon Collection**
www.npg.si.edu/exh/harmon/index.htm

**Dox Thrash: An African American Master Printmaker Rediscovered**
209.235.192.90/exhibitions/exhibits/thrash/flash.html

**ArtNoir**
www.artnoir.com

**African American Art: A Los Angeles Legacy**
www.getty.edu/artsednet/resources/African/

# Photographs and prints

**The American Image: Portrait of Black Chicago**
www.archives.gov/exhibit_hall/portrait_of_black_chicago/introduction.
html

**Reflections in Black: A History of Black Photographers, 1840 to the Present**
www.si.edu/anacostia/reflections_in_black2.htm

**Small Towns, Black Lives: African American Communities in Southern New Jersey**
(Photographs and text by Wendel A. White)
www.blacktowns.org

**Through the Lens of Time: Images of African Americans from the Cook Collection of Photographs**
www.library.vcu.edu/jbc/speccoll/cook/

**The Holsinger Studio Collection**
www.lib.virginia.edu/speccol/collections/holsinger/

**The (Roy) Decarava Archives**
www.decarava.com

**Creative Americans, Portraits by Carl Van Vechten**
memory.loc.gov/ammem/vvhtml/vvhome.html

**Jackson Davis Collection of African American Educational Photographs**
www.lib.virginia.edu/speccol/jdavis/

**200 Photographs from the Documentary One Shot – The Life and Work of Teenie Harris**
www.oneshotcharlesharrisphotos.com/

**Gordon Parks, Photographer**
memory.loc.gov/ammem/fsahtml/fachap07.html

**Images of African Americans from the 19th Century**
digital.nypl.org/schomburg/images_aa19/

**Mirror Images: Daguerreotypes at the Library of Congress;
American Colonization Society**
memory.loc.gov/ammem/daghtml/dagamco.html

## Good books

Conwill, Kinshasha, et al. (2001) *Testimony: vernacular art of the African-American South: the Ronald and June Shelp collection*. New York: Harry N. Abrams in association with Exhibitions International and the Schomburg Center for Research in Black Culture.

Driskell, David C. (2001) *The other side of color: African American art in the collection of Camille O. and William H. Cosby, Jr.* San Francisco: Pomegranate.

Gaither, Edmund B. (introduction). (1970) *Afro-American artists: New York and Boston*. Boston, Mass.: The Museum School.

Herzog, Melanie Anne. (2000) *Elizabeth Catlett: an American artist in Mexico*. Seattle: University of Washington Press.

Mathews, Marcia M. (1994) *Henry Ossawa Tanner, American artist*. Chicago: University of Chicago Press.

Nesbett, Peter T. (2001) *Jacob Lawrence: the complete prints, 1963–2000: a catalogue raisonné*. Seattle: Francine Seders Gallery, in association with University of Washington Press.

Patton, Sharon F. (1998) *African-American art*. Oxford: Oxford University Press.

Porter, James Amos. (1992) *Modern Negro art*. Washington, D.C.: Howard University Press.

Prigoff, James, and Dunitz, Robin J. (2000) *Walls of heritage, walls of pride: African American murals*. San Francisco: Pomegranate.

Sims, Lowery Stokes. (1993) *Romare Bearden*. New York, N.Y.: Rizzoli Publications.

Thompson, Robert Farris. (1984) *Flash of the spirit: African and Afro-American art and philosophy*. New York: Vintage Books.

Wahlman, Maude Southwel. (2001) *Signs & symbols: African images in African American quilts*. Atlanta, Ga.: Tinwood.

Willis, Deborah. (2000) *Reflections in Black: a history of Black photographers, 1840 to the present*. New York: W. W. Norton.

# 27
# Gays and Lesbians

African Americans have always been both straight and gay/lesbian, but this has only recently been accepted and celebrated. There were areas of life where it was expressed more openly, for example in the arts or single sex environments like men's or women's colleges. But generally, until recently, the prevailing social norms were against homosexuality in the Black community. Gay/lesbian people were forced to live two lives, one in the straight world and the other in a world of their own making in which love and social relationships could transcend those social constructions of gender.

More and more people are coming out and living their lives openly, refusing to accept the shame or ridicule of the past. Moreover as a community there are needs to be served and social activities to plan. The social and legal aspects of long term relationships are being worked out – marriage, insurance, inheritance, adoption of children, etc. There are specific health concerns, and psychological issues. In general terms each community has to develop its own spaces in which the full expression of homosexuality is the norm.

Gay scholarship has emerged within Black Studies so that the hidden history of gays and lesbians in the African American community is beginning to come to light. While it might be shocking to many to find out all of the historical figures who lived two lives it is in fact an important process of finding out the truth and learning about the full diversity that has always been part of the Black community. Straight homogeneity has been a manufactured lie, and diversity of sexual preference has been as true in the past as it is today.

Today one can find a growing Black gay/lesbian presence in cyberspace. These sites are a first step toward not only servicing the Black gay/lesbian community, but also informing everyone about this important part of the Black community.

## Audre Lorde Project

www.alp.org

This is a center dedicated to carrying out the work of Audre Lorde (1934–1992). She was a writer and activist who helped create a space in African American literature for the gay and lesbian experience to be explored and celebrated. This organization is a community organization with the mission to mobilize, educate, and engage in capacity building.

They define themselves as "an organization seeking social and economic justice for all peoples. ALP is committed to promoting multiracial coalition building, advocacy and community organizing activity among LGBTST people of color, and with allies in struggles for equality and liberation." Their site contains a comprehensive listing of events in the New York area. They also provide political alerts and guidelines for action concerning topical issues like war and peace.

The importance of this activist organization is that it is a good example of how people united around one issue, in this case the interests of the LGBTST communities, and can be a vital part in the overall motion of all people to build unity and work together.

## Black Light

www.blacklightonline.com

This is an online publication with lots of very good information. There are full text articles that cover a variety of issues. One of the strengths is a section that focuses on recent books and gives images of the covers and full text reviews. This is a valuable service as many of these books are not available in the typical bookstore so checking with this site can keep you current with the books being published.

The great asset of this site is an archive that contains articles and documentation on individuals and issues. This archive can be searched by name, topic, and ethnicity. There are about 600 entries to choose from. As of March 2003 there were 36 entries for Audre Lorde, 34 for James Baldwin, and 86 for African Americans.

The site has a section of letters submitted by Black Light readers.

**Notable Gays and Lesbians in African American History**

clem.mscd.edu/~diguardi/aagl.html

Lisa Diguardi created this site of links to biographies of Notable African Americans who were lesbian or gay. The important aspect of this is that they represent the diversity of people who have had their lives shaped by the hidden nature of much of their life. Only in recent times have Black gays and lesbians who achieved public notoriety been open and fully identified with their life style.

The people included on this site are the following: Alvin Ailey, James Baldwin, Benjamin Banneker, Deborah Batts, Jopseph Beam, Carl Bean, Gladys Bently, Keith Boykin, Glen Burke, Countee Cullen, Samuel Delaney, Melvin Dixon, Jewell Gomez, Angelina Emily Weld Grimke, Lorraine Hanberry, Essex Hemphill, Langston Hughes, Alberta Hunter, Bill Jones, Edmonia Lewis, Audre Lorde, Johnny Mathis, Pat Parker, Michelle Parkerson, Gertrude "Ma" Rainey, Toshi Reagon, Marlon Riggs, Bayard Rustin, Assotto Saint, Barbara Smith, Bessie Smith, and Alice Walker.

**Zami**

www.zami.org

This website is about a not for profit collective in Atlanta Georgia for lesbians of African descent founded in 1989. They explain their name on the site: "Zami is a Carriacou word meaning women who work together as friends and lovers. The name Zami also honors the late Audre Lorde, a Black lesbian feminist who was poet laureate for New York State and who wrote the biomythography ZAMI: A New Spelling of My Name." The site provides a map to locate where support groups meet. One of the organization's programs is "Drum Sista: A ZAMI Drum Circle" that is open to all lesbians of color that meets every 2nd and 4th Sunday. The group provides scholarship programs and has a full discussion of the criteria on the website as well as a listing of past award winners. There are awards for both females and males. The site also contains a useful set of links to a variety of topics.

**Zuna Institute**

www.zunainstitute.org

This website is about an organization that seeks to work on the national level. They have national conferences and this website provides information about their activities. They started in 1999, and in addition to using the conference for networking they discuss critical issues facing lesbians: estate planning, health issues, domestic violence, and lots of topics about how to enjoy life and survive.

One of their important initiatives is the "Black Lesbian Elder Speak Project." This project is important because it honors the experiences of people and gives them a safe place to record their stories. Much like the slave narratives, the narratives of older lesbians and gays who are over 55 can help us understand how people survive under conditions of humiliation and silence. It will be a wonderful addition to this site if these narratives are eventually posted here for all to share and learn from.

## General

**Affinity**
www.affinity95.org/affinity/index.htm

**Howard Brown Health Center**
www.howardbrown.org/

**BLSG – Black Lesbian Support Group**
www.blsg.org

**BlackBerri.com**
www.blackberricafe.com

**Women in the Life**
www.womeninthelife.com

**Black Pride NYC, Inc.**
www.blackpridenyc.com/

**Black Stripe**
www.blackstripe.com/

**Arise Magazine**
www.arisemag.com/about.html

**Blakout.net**
www.blakout.net/

**BLK**
www.blk.com/blkhome.htm

**Keith Boykin**
www.keithboykin.com/

**Fo Brothers.com**
www.fobrothas.com/

**Gayhiphop.com**
www.gayhiphop.com/

**Living Down Low**
www.livingdownlow.com/

**Book House Cafe**
www.bookhousecafe.com/

**Femme Noir**
www.femmenoir.net/

**Beta Phi Omega**
www.betaphiomega.net/

**Black LBGT Film Festival**
www.blacklgbtff.org/mainpage.htm

**Gay Men of African Descent – GMAD**
www.gmad.org/

**Sable Magazine**
www.sablemagazine.com

**Venus Magazine**
www.venusmagazine.com

**Black C.A.R.E.** (Black Community AIDS Research and Education)
www.stat.ucla.edu/~cochran/blackcare/blackcare.html

**Sisters in the Life**
www.sistersinthelife.com

## Good books

Boykin, Keith. (1996) *One more river to cross: Black and gay in America.* New York: Anchor/Doubleday.

Boykin, Keith. (1999) *Respecting the soul: daily reflections for Black lesbians and gays.* New York: Avon Books.

Brandt, Eric, ed. (1999) *Dangerous liaisons: Blacks, gays, and the struggle for equality.* New York: New Press.

Carbado, Devon W., McBride, Dwight A., and Weise, Donald, eds. (2002) *Black like us: a century of lesbian, gay, and bisexual African American fiction.* San Francisco: Cleis.

Cohen, Cathy. (1999) *The boundaries of blackness: AIDS and the breakdown of Black politics.* Chicago: University of Chicago Press.

Comstock, Gary David. (2001) *A whosoever church: welcoming lesbians and gay men into African American congregations.* Louisville: Westminster John Knox Press.

Constantine-Simms, Delroy, ed. (2001) *The greatest taboo: homosexuality in Black communities.* Los Angeles: Alyson Books.

Hunter, B. Michael, ed. (1993) *Sojourner: Black gay voices in the age of AIDS.* New York: Other Countries Press.

Lorde, Audre. (1984) *Sister outsider: essays and speeches.* Freedom, Calif.: Crossing Press.

McKinley, Catherine E., and DeLaney, L. Joyce, eds. (1995) *Afrekete: an anthology of Black lesbian writing*. New York: Anchor Books.

Nugent, Richard Bruce. (2002) *Gay rebel of the Harlem Renaissance: selections from the work of Richard Bruce Nugent*. Durham: Duke University Press.

Pettiway, Leon E. (1996) *Honey, honey, miss thang: being Black, gay, and on the streets*. Philadelphia: Temple University Press.

Reid-Pharr, Robert. (2001) *Black gay man: essays*. New York: New York University Press.

Ruff, Shawn Stewart, ed. (1996) *Go the way your blood beats: an anthology of lesbian and gay fiction by African-American writers*. New York: H. Holt.

Smith, Barbara. (1998) *The truth that never hurts: writings on race, gender, and freedom*. New Brunswick, N.J.: Rutgers University Press.

# 28
# Media

The generally accepted role of the media is to serve democracy by educating the public consciousness and thereby contribute to the public sphere debate that is a necessary aspect of a democratic society. The counter thesis is that the media serves to maintain the dominance of ideas that serve the status quo in the interest of a ruling class. In general, the latter argument fits the role of mainstream media, while the former argument has been the role of the Black media. This has been true on the issue directly facing African Americans, but also on broader questions of social policy and international affairs. The actual left press at the grass roots level in the United States is the Black press. Perhaps the best example of this is the Jackson Advocate in Jackson, Mississippi.

The foundation of African American media was in print, mainly newspapers but also including magazines and journals. Black newspapers began in 1827 with the moral mission to build the Abolitionist movement and encourage slave rebellions and runaways. Today there is usually at least one Black newspaper in every major urban area, and some of these newspapers have at various times had national circulation, especially the *Chicago Defender* and *Pittsburgh Courier*.

The 20th century electronic media have been important in establishing a national culture as national programs spread musical trends quickly and eliminated the cultural lag that maintained stark regional differences. Radio programs spread new music from Northern to Southern cities (and vice versa) faster than men who worked on the railroad or people who traveled to visit relatives. Black oriented radio stations and programs can now be heard in every city, including nationally syndicated programs featuring such commentators as Bob Law of New York and the national DJ, the "fly jock" Tom Joiner who started in Chicago. Black people are also featured on television, although the main trend is to have Black sit-coms, comedy, and musical presentations. There are a few exceptions to this including the news programs on the only Black oriented TV channel BET (Black Entertainment Television).

**The Black Press** (PBS)
www.pbs.org/blackpress/
This is one of the excellent websites created by PBS to support one of its films. This site is a companion to a film by the noted African American filmmaker Stanley Nelson, *The Black Press: Soldiers Without Swords*. This website is full of interesting information about the Black press and is strong enough to stand alone for everyone interested in the subject.

There are six key parts of this website:

1. There are 19 transcripts of interviews done for the film of key people associated with the Black press.
2. Biographical sketches are presented of key figures in the history of the Black press, including Frederick Douglass, Ida B. Wells, Robert Abbott, Carl Murphy, Charlotta Bass, T. Thomas Fortune, Ollie Harrington, and John Sengstacke.
3. Individual newspapers are featured in descriptive essays including the *Chicago Defender*, the *California Eagle*, the *Amsterdam News*, the *Atlanta Daily World*, the *Afro-American*, and the *Pittsburgh Courier*.
4. Biographical sketches of current working journalists along with video statements of their views, from people such as Margo Jefferson of the *New York Times*, Susan Taylor of *Essence*, and Brent Staples and Ellis Cose among others.
5. A timeline of major events in the history of the Black press from 1827, the founding year of the first Black newspaper *Freedom's Journal*, to 1975.
6. An extensive list of references including books, articles, and websites.

This is a wonderful site that can be used in any course that focuses on the Black press or for any Black history course as these men and women and newspapers have made important historical contributions all along the way. One example of this is that one needs to consider the contribution of Robert Abbott and the *Chicago Defender* when dealing with the great migrations, or with T. Thomas Fortune when dealing with Black nationalism and the rise of the UNIA and Marcus Garvey.

## National Newspaper Publishers Association

www.nnpa.org/news/default.asp

This organization is 62 years old and has as its members over 200 Black community newspapers. It is the successor to the Associated Negro Press Association and is the main organization of the Black press. The founding leadership was provided by John Sengstacke of the *Chicago Defender*, the nephew of Robert Abbott the newspaper's founder.

This organization appeals to potential advertisers by giving them a way to reach out to the entire Black press or whatever part of it will serve the intended commercial purpose. The website indicates that the readership of the Black press is a viable market: average age 43.9 years, 54% female, 60% college graduates. This is the employed Black middle class.

The organization provides scholarships and arranges internships for prospective journalists. It holds an annual national Black Press Week that takes place every March in Washington D.C. This is a major policy event for networking and developing positions that impact editorial policy for the coming year.

## National Association of Black Journalists

www.nabj.org/

This organization was founded in 1975 and currently has 3,300 members. Its chapters are listed with contact information on the website. The site is rich with press releases and links of interest to people in the media.

The outstanding feature of this site is that it includes the work of about 40 journalists who have regular columns with bylines. These are the Black journalists of record, some of whom are syndicated and appear in the mainstream press. Of these 40, 16 are women. This is a major force in the media as Black voices are just beginning to be heard. When the opinions and values of the Black community diverge from the white mainstream sometimes there is no connection that cuts across the media so that people get a chance to hear Black voices and to understand the reasonableness of Black perspectives.

## Black Entertainment Television

www.bet.com/bethome

This is the main Black presence in mainstream television. Robert L. Johnson created this network in 1980, and it is now a cable option in most of the cities in the USA. This website is a full service media portal to news, sports, and entertainment. It features BET's programs and provides additional information in the style of all of the national TV networks.

BET offers a Black approach to this media and yet it is mainstream all the way. This is one stop shopping for how Black people see things. Just as the main networks have analysts to discuss the topical issues of the day, so BET is where you can find the most consistent discussions of these same issues by many more Black public intellectuals than anywhere else.

## Johnson Publishing Company

www.ebony.com/

This company is the oldest Black magazine and book publishing company in the USA. In the now legendary story, John Johnson and his mother created his magazine *Negro Digest* with a $500 loan. He modeled this magazine on *Reader's Digest*. The rest is history as his magazine *Ebony* became second only to *Crisis*, the NAACP magazine created by W. E. B. DuBois, as must reading for Black people. This website is an introduction to his entire company. Eunice W. Johnson, John Johnson's wife, created the Ebony Fashion Fair, a national touring show that features world class designers and raises money for charities. Now the CEO is his daughter Linda Johnson Rice. This is a rare example of a Black entrepreneur being succeeded by an offspring.

The major intellectual in this media company is Lerone Bennett. He is one of the major Black voices in the historical profession and his books have challenged and provoked the rethinking of African American history for the last 40 years. His work is advertised on this site, but one would love to see an archive of his articles here so that new generations of young people would have ready access to them.

## History

**Black Press USA**
www.blackpressusa.com/

**Robert Sengstacke Abbott**
www.africanpubs.com/Apps/bios/1002AbbottRobert.asp?pic=none

## Organizations

**National Association of Black Owned Broadcasters**
www.nabob.org/

**National Association of Minority Media Executives**
www.namme.org/

## Media

**World Wide Black Radio Stations**
www.radioblack.com/

**Tony Brown**
www.tonybrownsites.com/tonybrown

**Tom Joiner**
www.tomjoiner.com

**Atlanta Tribune**
www.atlantatribune.com/!live/

**The Indianapolis Recorder**
www.indianapolisrecorder.com/

**The Afro-American Newspapers**
www.afro.com/

**The Dallas Post Tribune**
www.dallaspost.com/

**The Philadelphia Tribune**
www.phila-tribune.com/

**The Final Call**
www.finalcall.com/artman/publish/

**The Black Scholar**
www.theblackscholar.org/

**Amsterdam News**
www.amsterdamnews.org/news/default.asp

**The Black Book Review Online**
www.qbr.com/

## Comics

**The Boondocks**
www.ucomics.com/boondocks/

**Jump Start**
www.comics.com/comics/jumpstart/

**Mama's Boyz**
www.mamasboyz.com/index.html

**The Pioneers**
www.clstoons.com/paoc/paocopen.htm

**The Museum of Black Superheroes**
www.blacksuperhero.com

**Tribal Science**
www.geocities.com/~tribalscience/

**Black Anime Network**
www.geocities.com/blackanimenet/

**Jamurai**
www.dreadfullyslick.com/

**Gettosake Entertainment**
www.gettosake.com/

## Social justice

**Elombe Brath: Africa Kaleidoscope** (WBAI, New York)
www.afrikaleidoscope.net

**Walter Turner – Africa Today** (KPFA, Berkeley, California)
www.kpfa.org/1pro_bio/1b_afric.htm

**Black Panther Newspaper Collection**
www.etext.org/Politics/MIM/bpp/index.html

**Independent Media Center**
www.indymedia.org/

**Mabili Ajani, Critical Times** (WMNF Tampa, Florida)
www.wmnf.org/

**Radio Free Georgia** (WRFG Atlanta, Georgia)
www.wrfg.org/home.asp

**Black Liberation Radio**
burn.ucsd.edu/~blr/

## Online portals

**Melanet**
www.melanet.com

**AfroNet**
www.afronet.com

## Good books

Barlow, William. (1999) *Voice over: the making of Black radio*. Philadelphia: Temple University Press.

Bogle, Donald. (2001) *Prime time blues: African Americans on network television*. New York: Farrar, Straus & Giroux.

Cosby, Camille Olivia. (1994) *Television's imageable influences: the self-perceptions of young African-Americans*. Lanham: University Press of America.

Durham, Richard. (1989) *Richard Durham's destination freedom: scripts from radio's Black legacy, 1948–50*. edited by J. Fred Macdonald. New York: Praeger.

Farrar, Hayward. (1998) *The Baltimore Afro-American, 1892–1950*. Westport, Conn.: Greenwood Press.

Gray, Herman. (1995) *Watching race: television and the struggle for "Blackness"*. Minneapolis: University of Minnesota Press.

Jordan, William G. (2001) *Black newspapers and America's war for democracy, 1914–1920*. Chapel Hill: University of North Carolina Press.

Newkirk, Pamela. (2000) *Within the veil: Black journalists, white media*. New York: New York University Press.

Ottley, Roi. (1955) *The lonely warrior: the life and times of Robert S. Abbott*. Chicago, Ill.: H. Regnery Co.

Simmons, Charles A. (1998) *The African American press: a history of news coverage during national crises, with special reference to four Black newspapers, 1827–1965*. Jefferson, N.C.: McFarland & Co.

Thompson, Julius Eric. (1993) *The Black press in Mississippi, 1865–1985*. Gainesville: University Press of Florida.

Ward, Brian. (2001) *Media, culture, and the modern African American freedom struggle*. Gainesville: University Press of Florida.

# 29
# Sports

Every culture includes some form of physical activity that includes games, teams, and competition. Status comes to those who are the fastest, the strongest, the best at every major game. Perhaps more importantly these activities are vital parts of a healthy lifestyle and contribute to the social bonding necessary to productive social life.

African Americans have used sports in these ways, but also as a vehicle to overcome the limits imposed by racism and segregation. Excelling at sports has become a way to go to college, to even try and earn a living. However, many more people get to go to college by playing sports than end up being a professional athlete.

As in all aspects of social life, African Americans have had to struggle for equality and full participation in sports on the college and professional levels. Under segregation there were Black schools and sports leagues, as well as Black professional leagues. The icon for the integration process is Jackie Robinson who joined the Brooklyn Dodgers baseball team in 1947. From a historical point of view the first Black player in mainstream professional baseball was Moses Fleetwood Walker from Toledo, Ohio. Both Robinson and Walker are in the Baseball Hall of Fame. Today, African Americans are a dominant force in professional golf, tennis, boxing, football, baseball, basketball, and many aspects of track and field events.

The Black athlete is a category in every community because of status and the potential of upward social mobility. However, what often gets lost is the universal appeal of sports for health reasons and for the social life of a community.

**Black Coaches Association**
www.bcasports.org/

This is a site about the level of power and control of sports. Black football and basketball coaches joined together in 1988 and created this organization to promote the rise of Black coaches in college and professional sports. They are focused on employment, but also the preparation process so Black coaches can maintain the same level of excellence that is associated with the Black athlete.

The members of this group reflect the diversity of the African American coach: 20% are head coaches on some level, 25% are women, 50% are already at the NCAA Division I level, and 30% are in basketball. The membership comes from 44 states. The group has a journal and has some of the full text articles online.

The role of Black coaches is critical as the Black athlete is often regarded as having natural talent. This is a racist view as it denies the athlete the moral and physical discipline to maintain physical capacity, the intelligence necessary to use strategy and planning, as well as the leadership necessary to organize and coordinate a team. If you have it naturally you don't have to think about it. This can't be said about coaching. The skills to coach are obvious, including general managerial skills involving bureaucratic organization and budget control. The rise of the Black coach in sports is a big blow against racism and this organization is one of the forces that are getting this job done. People in sports can gain a lot by visiting this site.

### Jackie Robinson and Other Baseball Highlights 1860–1960

memory.loc.gov/ammem/jrhtml/jrhome.html

This site is part of the American Memory Project of the Library of Congress. Jackie Robinson is the central figure in this site that takes up the entire sport of baseball. It is divided into five basic sections: Drawing the Color Line (1860–1890s), Negro Leagues (1900–1930s), Breaking the Color Line (1940–1946), Jackie Robinson as a Brooklyn Dodger (1947–1956), and Robinson's Late Career (1956–1972).

The site is mainly text with pictures. The set of pictures on the Negro Leagues is particularly interesting. There is also a 1904 picture of the Harvard baseball team with its one Black player that can be contrasted with a 1900 photo of the all-Black baseball team of Morris Brown College of Atlanta.

There is also an extensive bibliography that covers the entire history of the African American in baseball.

## Center for the Study of Sport in Society
www.sportinsociety.org/
This site is maintained at Northeastern University in Boston, Mass. Richard Lapchick established the Center in 1984 as a forum to help the athlete and the society move sports in the direction of social justice. He has been a fighter against racism in this country and in South Africa during the period of apartheid.

One of the major projects is a report that produces a "Race and Gender Report card" on the professional sports leagues. The report card and an executive summary for 1997, 1998, and 2001 are available on the site, while the full reports are for sale by the Center. It is very interesting to examine this, as it constitutes an unbiased appraisal of what is happening in professional sports without the hype of mass media marketing.

This center is also involved in proactive programs to assist the Black athlete: Athletes in Service to America, Disability in Sports Initiative, Mentors in Violence Prevention, and others.

## African Americans in the Sports Arena
www.liu.edu/cwis/cwp/library/aaitsa.htm
This is an extensive set of texts, short essays that cover a wide range of sports activities. The focus is on the history of the Black athlete in baseball, basketball, boxing, cycling, football, horse racing, and track and field. There are also special essays on a few outstanding individuals: Jackie Robinson, Paul Robeson, Michael Jordan, and Fritz Pollard.

This is a very useful site for the young athlete because in a short essay one can learn the history of those who established a tradition of excellence in the earlier period of the 19th and 20th centuries. Too often young people think they are isolated in history, and either have egos that are too big or believe that nothing can happen because the odds are stacked against them. History can be a wonderful teacher here to help keep things in their proper perspective. Each athlete plays in their time and is judged accordingly, but people are often too quick to call a living athlete the greatest of all time. Knowing the history of the Black athlete might help people be more humble and encourage hard work even when one has a great deal of talent.

## Guide for the College Bound Athlete
www.ncaa.org/eligibility/cbsa/clearinghouse.html
This site is part of the official website of the NCAA, the official organization for collegiate athletics. Every high school athlete and their parents should be familiar with this site as it is the official information for what it will take to get into college and be successful. The odds are against eventually becoming a professional athlete, but they are good for being able to use athletic ability to assist in getting admitted to college with some level of financial support. This is a website to help you do just that.

It presents the specifics on academic eligibility including information on SAT and ACT standardized tests. It covers the rules for recruitment at all levels of college sports, and gives sound advice on what to avoid when in a compromising situation. Ignorance of the rules is no excuse. It is not too early to begin using this site in your first or second year in high school. It takes a lot of planning to select the right school so that you can be a successful athlete and a successful student. The value of a college education is greater job stability and a higher income. Studying this site is a big first step.

# General history

## Black Athlete Sports Network
www.blackathlete.net/main.shtml

## The Changing Status of the Black Athlete in the 20th Century United States
www.johncarlos.com/walters.htm

## The Struggle of the Black Athlete
www.geocities.com/dblimbrick/

**African Americans in the Kentucky Derby**
(Churchill Downs Network)
www.kentuckyderby.com/2002/derby_history/african_americans_in_the_
derby

## College and high school

**Inside Black College Sports**
www.ibcsports.com

**Onnidan Online: HBCU Sports**
www.onnidan.com

**Eddie Robinson Foundation**
www.eddierobinson.com/home.jsp

**SWAC** (Black College Athletic Conference)
www.swacpage.com

## Professional basketball

**Pop Gates**
www.hoophall.com/features/renaissance_man_gates.htm

**Bill Russell**
www.hoophall.com/halloffamers/RussellW.htm

**Earl Monroe**
www.hoophall.com/features/earl_monroe.htm

**Wilt Chamberlain**
www.wiltchamberlain.com

**Michael Jordan**
jordan.sportsline.com/

**Shaquille O'Neal**
www.shaq.com/

**Harlem Globetrotters**
www.harlemglobetrotters.com/index.php

**Notable African American Basketball Players**
www.infoplease.com/spot/bhmpeople8.html

## Professional baseball

**Negro Baseball Leagues**
www.blackbaseball.com

**Satchel Paige: The Official Site**
www.cmgww.com/baseball/paige/index.html

**Notable African American Baseball Players**
www.infoplease.com/spot/bhmpeople7.html

## Professional boxing

**Notable African American Boxers**
www.infoplease.com/spot/bhmpeople9.html

**Joe Louis**
www.cmgww.com/sports/louis/louis.html

**Sugar Ray Robinson**
www.cmgww.com/sports/robinson/

## Professional football

**African Americans in Pro Football**
www.profootballhof.com/history/mainpage.cfm?cont_id=91955

**Notable African American Football Players**
www.infoplease.com/spot/bhmpeople10.html

## Professional golf

**Tiger Woods**
www.tigerwoods.com/splash/splash.sps

**Tiger Woods Foundation**
www.twfound.org/home/default.sps?sid=941&lid=1&atpval=0

**Afro-Golf**
www.afrogolf.com/indexMain2002.html

## Professional tennis

**Venus and Serena Williams**
www.venusserenafans.com/index2.htm

**Arthur Ashe**
www.cmgww.com/sports/ashe/

## Professional track

**Florence Griffith Joyner**
www.florencegriffithjoyner.com/

**Jesse Owens**
www.jesseowens.com/

**Jesse Owens Foundation**
www.jesse-owens.org/jof.html

**Wilma Rudolph**
www.gale.com/free_resources/bhm/bio/rudolph_w.htm

**Notable African American Track and Field Athletes**
www.infoplease.com/spot/bhmpeople11.html

## Organizations

**National Brotherhood of Skiers**
www.nbs.org/

**The National Bowling Association**
www.tnbainc.org/

**Black Sports Agents Association**
www.blacksportsagents.com/

**National Association of Black Scuba Divers**
www.nabsdivers.org/

## Statistics

**Statistics in Sports**
www.amstat.org/sections/sis

## Good books

Aaseng, Nathan. (2003) *African American athletes*. New York: Facts on File.

Ashe, Arthur. (1993) *A hard road to glory*. New York: Amistad.

Bass, Amy. (2002) *Not the triumph but the struggle: the 1968 Olympics and the making of the Black athlete*. Minneapolis: University of Minnesota Press.

Dawkins, Marvin P., and Kinloch, Graham C. (2000) *African American golfers during the Jim Crow era*. Westport, Conn.: Praeger.

Edwards, Harry. (1970) *The revolt of the Black athlete*. New York: Free Press.

Entine, Jon. (2000) *Taboo: why Black athletes dominate sports, and why we're afraid to talk about it*. New York: PublicAffairs.

Hauser, Thomas. (1992) *Muhammad Ali: his life and times*. New York: Simon & Schuster.

Hoberman, John Milton. (1997) *Darwin's athletes: how sport has damaged Black America and preserved the myth of race*. Boston: Houghton Mifflin.

Hotaling, Edward. (1999) *The great Black jockeys: the lives and times of the men who dominated America's first national sport*. Rocklin, Calif.: Forum.

McDaniel, Pete. (2000) *Uneven lies: the heroic story of African-Americans in golf*. Greenwich, Conn.: American Golfer.

Nuwer, Hank. (1998) *Legend of Jesse Owen*. New York: Franklin Watts.

Peterson, Robert. (1999) *Only the ball was white: a history of legendary Black players and all-Black professional teams*. New York: Gramercy Books.

Ribowsky, Mark. (2002) *A complete history of the Negro leagues, 1844 to 1955*. New York: Citadel Press.

Ross, Charles Kenyatta. (1999) *Outside the lines: African Americans and the integration of the National Football League*. New York: New York University Press.

Thomas, Ron. (2002) *They cleared the lane: the NBA's Black pioneers*. Lincoln: University of Nebraska Press.

Wiggins, David, and Miller, Patrick, eds. (2003) *The unlevel playing field: a documentary history of the African American experience in sport*. Champaign: University of Illinois Press.

# 30
# Internet Communications

This entire book has been about the African American experience being recreated in cyberspace. This last chapter is about you the reader going out into cyberspace for an interactive experience with others. The main focus is on discussion, using email to connect with other people. This is the most common way that people go into cyberspace. Email is usually something people can get for free, either from school, a job, or some of the commercial or community institutions that will set you up. The deal is you use their name and it's a form of free advertisement every time you give someone your email and they use it.

Most people have heard of email or are already using it in some form. Some people are hooked on it and are obsessed to almost check it every hour. People have it on their "smart" cell phones and send text messages. The main thing is that it is asynchronous in that you can send a message and the person can read it whenever they like. On the other hand, one can email in real time with a form of "instant messaging." There are many ways to be in cyberspace.

The key thing is that joining in a group is a personal choice that one has to experiment with and feel free to leave whenever it stops meeting your needs or is no longer comfortable for you. Parents should guide their children in this process, but trust them to make good decisions based on the moral teachings of family life and their education in school. Most people are not fools, including children.

Once you know that there is great information out there in cyberspace about the Black experience it's time for your experience to hit the cyber-road. Hopefully this book will help you get there.

**Africana.com**
www.africana.com/news-home/index.htm

This website is a full service portal to the many aspects that a corporate website can provide. The site was originally set up by Harvard Black Studies Professors and sold to major corporate interests. It provides email and chat room discussion opportunities, as well as a full set of information outlets. When you join this site you enter into a relationship with a full set of corporations, including Netscape, AOL, CNN, and Time.

There are areas on the site called channels (using a TV analogy for cyberspace): Blackworld, lifestyle, movies and TV, music, books, people, arts, and health and beauty. The site hires a staff of writers to provide articles and short essays for topics within each of these channels. It also provides a box office offering tickets to national events, including professional sports. There is also a politically oriented bulletin board to which various groups post announcements.

This site is like the other corporate websites that provide a major entertainment portal with an African American focus. The key is that it is corporate, and designed for people who shop in large department stores and in malls. This is the fast food approach to cyberspace. There is little connection with the historical motion on the ground in Black communities throughout the USA. For this you have to go to sites that are created by African Americans and continue to be updated from there.

**The Black World Today**
www.tbwt.com
The Black World Today is the premiere site for keeping in touch with Black currents of ideological and political thinking. They publish the most op-ed pieces of any site on the web as well as a consistently high level of critical journalism by one of their national editors Herb Boyd. Don Rojas founded it in 1996, after having served in many key positions including being Press Secretary to Maurice Bishop, assassinated leader of Granada.

The following are regular contributors: Conrad Worrill (National Black United Front), Ron Daniels (Center for Constitutional Rights), Ron Walters (University of Maryland), Bill Fletcher (TransAfrica), Hugh Price (National Urban League). Manning Marable (Columbia University), and Kevin Powell (Cultural activist), and many others.

Otherwise this is also modeled on a corporate site to provide one stop shopping for information needs, including ecommerce.

**Black Planet**

www.blackplanet.com/

This is perhaps the most popular site for online participation in chat rooms. It's a free membership site that is for virtual recreation. There are online bulletin boards (forums) to post messages to as well as a large number of diverse "rooms" for real time chat. Also, one can find games, clubs, news, and a job market.

It also provides one of the most popular places to network for the love game. Members can post information and take their chances on being just the person someone is looking for. The site keeps track of its members online and it is not unusual to find that 25,000 or more are online at peak time. This may be the way that the Black community begins to get virtual. This has taken over from talk radio as the conversation center for public discourse.

**Information Competence for the Discipline of Black Studies**

www.csulb.edu/~ttravis/BlackStudies

Three librarians at California State University at Long Beach put this site together: Susan Levano (Ethnic, Women's & Multicultural Studies Librarian), Tiffini Travis (Psychology & Communications Librarian), Eileen Wakiji (Nursing & Allied Health Librarian). It is a professional resource that could be used by every Black Studies program at the high school and college level. The need for this kind of information is universal as many programs are behind the learning curve and there is an urgent need to incorporate these new technological tools into everyday teaching and research. This is a handbook for eBlack Studies.

The site is broken down into three aspects of the use of information technology in Black Studies: finding information, evaluating information, and applying information. Within each of these are useful links to books and articles and web resources, as well as suggested class assignments and projects for community service. This is a site for students and faculty.

There is an online test to use in evaluating your grasp of information in the field. The site has a section on "Where do we go from here?" that should be discussed and implemented by Black Studies organizations.

**Black Caucus of the American Library Association**
www.bcala.org/
This is the national networking center for Black librarians in the USA. The Black Caucus was officially set up in 1970, but had its early representation in the small meetings that took place by Black librarians who attended ALA meetings from as early as the 1930s and 1940s. The leading figure in forming this organization was E. J. Josey, Professor Emeritus Department of Library and Information Science, University of Pittsburgh.

This site is a service to Black librarians and the library community in general. They have engaged in active discussion of policies taken up by the ALA. This site includes information about the ALA, especially the Black Caucus. There is information about the conferences of the Black Causus, including some proceedings. It has an excellent compilation of announcements for conferences, grants, jobs, awards, calls for papers, and publication opportunities.

## Links to online communications

**Black Voices**
new.blackvoices.com

**Cyndi's Mailings, Newsgroups, and Chat**
www.cyndislist.com/african.htm#Mailing

**Boston Blacks Online**
www.innercity.com/bbo/

**Black Cyberspace**
www.blackcyberspace.com/

**Everything Black**
www.everythingblack.com/cgibin/search/hyperseek.cgi?

**African American Listservs and Chat Rooms**
www.inform.umd.edu/EdRes/Topic/Diversity/Specific/Race/Specific/African_American_Resources/Listserv

# Index